Reason and Relativism

Reason and Relativism

A Sartrean Investigation

Steve Hendley

State University of New York Press

Published by
State University of New York Press, Albany

© 1991 State University of New York

For information, address State University of New York
Press, State University Plaza, Albany, N.Y., 12246

Production by E. Moore
Marketing by Dana E. Yanulavich

Library of Congress Cataloging-in-Publication Data

Hendley, Steve, 1956–
    Reason and relativism : a Sartrean investigation / Steve Hendley.
        p. cm.
    Includes bibliographical references and index.
    ISBN 0–7914–0723–3 (alk. paper). — ISBN 0–7914–0724–1   (pbk. :
alk. paper)
        1. Sartre, Jean Paul, 1905–80   Critique de la raison dialectique.
    2. Existentialism.   3. Dialectical materialism.   4. Reason.
    5. Relativism.   I. Title.
    B2430.S33C774   1991
    142'.78—dc20   90-44726
                                                                              CIP

10 9 8 7 6 5 4 3 2 1

to Mar'

Dialectical Reason . . . is Reason constituting itself in and through the world, dissolving in itself all constituted Reasons in order to constitute new ones which it transcends and dissolves in turn.

Jean-Paul Sartre, *Critique of Dialectical Reason*

La véritable éthique fond et dissont les morales aliénées, en ce qu'elle est le sens de l'histoire: c'est-à-dire le refus de toute répétition au nom de la possibilitié inconditionnée de FAIRE L'HOMME.

Jean-Paul Sartre,
"Notes sur les rapports entre le morale et l'histoire"

Contents

Preface

The question of relativism usually commands the attention of only a very limited number of philosophers and philosophically disposed students of the humanities and social sciences. For a few months in 1987, however, this audience was enlarged considerably as Allan Bloom's *The Closing of the American Mind* began to dominate nonfiction book sales throughout the country. Though ostensibly a book about higher education, Bloom wastes no time in getting to his deeper concern—the prevalence of relativism in contemporary culture. He begins his introduction by writing,

> There is one thing a professor can be absolutely certain of: almost every student entering the university believes, or says he believes, that truth is relative. . . . The relativity of truth is not a theoretical insight but a moral postulate, the condition of a free society, or so they see it. They have all been equipped with this framework early on, and it is the modern replacement for the inalienable natural rights that used to be the traditional grounds for a free society.[1]

Bloom goes on in his book to chronicle the damage he believes this has caused, from the breakdown of the family to the impoverishment of our sense of self. Having lost our faith in the traditions which formed us, we have lost that historical inheritance which allows us to coherently evaluate and make sense of our present predicament. We can no longer take for granted who we are, for we know ourselves as historical accidents. And lacking good reasons for what we do, our lives become a shifting series of subjective preferences and groundless decisions. We are given the worst of both worlds in that our rationalist heritage demands we justify our form of life, while our new-found relativism prevents us from doing so. Cultural relativism, Bloom writes,

> succeeds in destroying the West's universal or intel-
> lectually imperialistic claims, leaving it to be just an-
> other culture. So there is equality in the republic of
> cultures. Unfortunately the West is defined by its
> need for justification of its ways or values, by its need
> for discovery of nature, by its need for philosophy
> and science. This is its cultural imperative. Deprived
> of that it will collapse.[2]

The end of Western Civilization as we know it? This surely depends on what one *means* by "Western Civilization."
And this is as much a matter of politics, as anything else.
When Bloom speaks defensively of the "dominant majority"
which "gave" America its culture, one cannot help but won-
der precisely *whose* civilization is in danger. A civilization in
which minorities and "outsiders" are expected to conform to
the standards and tastes of the majority or "be doomed to an
existence on the fringe"[3] may be in danger of collapse because it deserves to.

There is, however, more at stake here than merely the
chauvinistic defense of a *particular* culture, founded on particular values. For it is the aspiration to *universality* that animates this culture that is in danger. Western Civilization may
be the product of particular circumstances, but it has fash-
ioned for itself the idea of a universal "vocation," which
Edmund Husserl described in his essay, "Philosophy and the
Crisis of European Man," as that of "a humanity that from
now on will and can live only in the free fashioning of its
being and its historical life out of rational ideas. . . ."[4] The
sense of Western Culture in crisis that Bloom evokes—a
sense of crisis that, judging from the success of his book, has
apparently struck a popular chord—is, in the final analysis,
a crisis in the coherence and credibility of that vocation: a
crisis in the vocation of reason itself.

The image of a "crisis" may be somewhat misleading,
though, insofar as it tempts one to imagine one's own time
and place as somehow privileged—at a decisive breaking

point in history.[5] Our historical situation may certainly be distinguished by its own unique problems and concerns with the idea of reason, but it is not as if those problems and concerns are without precedent. Relativism, and the problems it poses, was as much an issue for Plato[6] as it is for us. If there is a "crisis of reason," then, it is best to think of it as a structural crisis: a crisis that is not unique to our own time and place, but inherent in the "adventure" of reason itself in Western Culture. We would do well to remember Nietzsche's insight that it is the will to truth itself which harbors the seeds of its own undoing.[7]

It is pointless, therefore, to complain of our predicament and become nostalgic for "better" days, for there never were any "better" days. The vocation of reason is interminably problematic. Indeed, that may be what is most definitive of it as a cultural project that demands its own critical justification, a discursive arena that must put itself up for question. Perhaps, unlike Bloom, we should welcome the crisis of reason as a moment in the vocation of reason itself when it is forced to take stock of itself in the light of contradictions that can only emerge in terms of the particulars of any given social-historical situation; as that moment in which a culture that aspires to "live only in the free fashioning of its being" may begin to do just that as it engages in a critique of its own forms of life and thought.

My own investigations here are meant as a very minor contribution to that critique. Specifically, I want to consider the issue of cognitive or epistemic relativism as it emerges in an important, but rather overlooked, contribution to contemporary social theory and epistemology—Jean-Paul Sartre's *Critique of Dialectical Reason*. Though that work is framed by Sartre as an attempt to answer an epistemological question concerning the conditions of the possibility of historical knowledge,[8] the account of knowledge he sketches there has, for the most part,[9] gone without the attention it deserves. This is especially unfortunate as it constitutes an ambitious attempt to articulate an account of knowledge and rationality that can embrace both its own inextricable historicity as well as its irreducibility to the contingencies of the history in which it is embedded—precisely the sort of epistemology that is needed to come to terms with the increasingly unavoidable recognition that though we must rely on a sense of rationality that can ground, in some sense, our claims to know the world, there is no sense of rationality that can claim to absolutely transcend the social and historical conditions which engender it. Motivated by a desire to avoid the sort of historical relativism to which dialectical thought has been traditionally drawn, Sartre's work, nevertheless, remains firmly committed to a historically situated sense of rationality that comes to terms with the problem of relativism by attempting to rethink the character of the problems which give rise to it. Knowledge is, after all, a product of historically contingent social practices. It is, then, the nature of these connections between history, knowledge and practice that must be rethought if we are to do justice to both the historicity as well as the rationality of our epistemic practices.

The care with which Sartre maintains this balance between history and reason provides an instructive path through the extremes to which more recent thought is sometimes drawn. Cast in terms of an exclusive option between uncovering, as Descartes desired, the one method for rightly conducting one's reason or recognizing one's commitment to rationality as nothing more than an ethnocentric commitment to one's own historical tradition,[10] we are set up for the equally bleak prospects of transcending or remaining uncritically immersed in our own time. It is for this reason that I will consider Sartre's work in the context of some of the more recent developments in social theory and epistemology. In particular, the work of Michel Foucault, Richard Rorty, Paul Feyerabend, Jean-François Lyotard, and Jürgen Habermas have all, in different contexts, raised the question of the historicity of reason in ways that pose radical challenges to Sartre's project. Considering Sartre's efforts in the light of their work will provide both a medium for critically articulating his largely implicit epistemological positions, as well as a way of arguing for the contemporary relevance and value of that work. As such, my own endeavors will constitute less an investigation into Sartre's approach to the issues of reason and relativism for its own sake, than a Sartrean investigation of those issues. Or, at least, that is my intention.

There are many people who have, in one way or another, aided me in completing this work. I would like to thank, in particular, John Scanlon, Bob Madden, and Hazel Barnes for their comments and support; my colleagues, Jim Goland and Dave Ullrich, whose conversations helped me clarify my ideas about "reciprocity and negotiation"; and special thanks to Tom Flynn, without whose comments and encouragement this work would never have seen the light of day. Thanks are also due to Birmingham–Southern College, and in particular Irvin Penfield, for granting me time off to complete the project; Martinus Nijhoff, The Hague, for permission to draw on my paper, "Power, Knowledge, and Praxis: A Sartrean Approach to a Foucaultian Problem," in *Man and World* 21 (1988): 171–89, which was taken from chapters 3 and 4; and finally, NLB, Verso Press and Random House, Vintage Books, for their permission to reprint passages from, respectively, Jean-Paul Sartre's *Critique of Dialectical Reason*, translated by Alan Sheridan Smith (London: NLB, 1976) and Jean-Paul Sartre's *Search for a Method*, translated by Hazel E. Barnes (New York: Vintage Books, 1963).

Part I

Sartre and Relativism

Chapter 1

Sartre's Critique of Empiricism

The issue of relativism emerges in a twofold way in Sartre's later philosophy—as a problem that appears to infect his own approach to the relations between history, knowledge and praxis as well as a concern that motivates that very project. By way of beginning, I will examine his own concerns with the problem of relativism and attempt to discern the basis and significance of those concerns. For in seeing clearly what Sartre was trying to avoid, it should be easier to discern the character of the position he came to embrace as a result.

Near the beginning of the *Critique of Dialectical Reason*, Sartre writes,

> The totalising thought of historical materialism has established everything but its own existence. . . . contaminated by the historical relativism it has always opposed, it has not exhibited the truth of History as it defines itself. . . . In other words, we do not know what it means for a Marxist historian to *speak the truth*. Not that his statements are false—far from it; but he does not have the concept of *Truth* at his disposal.[1]

As is apparent from the above passage, Sartre's own concerns with the problem of relativism emerge in connection with the failure of historical materialism to adequately establish its own epistemological basis as a theory of history. By failing to adequately understand itself, it has been "contaminated" with a form of relativism which makes nonsense of its

3

own claims to truth. This, in turn, places the problem of relativism at the very heart of the *Critique*. For Sartre attempts there to rethink the philosophical foundations of that theoretical tradition in the light of this shortcoming. In fundamental agreement with the Marxist critique of capitalism and the materialist conception of history, he takes issue only with the inability of the tradition to account for its own existence—to account for its own existence as a *theoretical knowledge* of history. As is evident from the title, Sartre's *Critique* bears more than a mere passing resemblance to Kant's own *Critique of Pure Reason*. Beginning with a specific theoretical tradition, in the one case, that of mathematics and a newly emerging natural science, in the other that of a Marxist approach to history, they both attempt to establish the conditions of the possibility of their validity. What Kant attempted to do for the natural sciences, Sartre attempts for one approach within the Human Sciences—to establish "on what conditions . . . the knowledge of a History is possible."[2]

The External Dialectic

Sartre is not, of course, the first to have engaged in a philosophical reflection on the epistemic status of historical materialism. Marxism has its own history of dealing with this issue. This, indeed, constitutes much of the problem. For its own understanding of itself has been fundamentally flawed, "contaminated," as Sartre has it, "with the historical relativism it has always opposed." Consequently, the tradition has not only failed to account for itself (resulting, at worst, in only a naivety as regards the epistemological status of its own claims) but has instituted an account which has denied it access to the very concept of truth.

The major example of this is, of course, Engels's concept of a 'dialectic of nature'. Characterized by an understanding of the historical dialectic of human action and thought as an effect of a more encompassing dialectic of nature itself, Engels's approach came to dominate Marxist philosophical reflection among the "orthodox" of the Second International.[3]

And, for Sartre, it has served as the paradigmatic instance of Marxism's own misconception of itself since his first detailed criticisms of it in the 1949 essay, "Materialism and Revolution." Taking it to task on various fronts in both that essay and the *Critique*, the charge that the position undermines its own epistemic status stands out, on the front end, as Sartre's most telling criticism.

> How could a captive reason, governed from without and manoeuvered by a series of blind causes, still be a reason? How could I believe in the principles of my deductions if it were only the external event which has set them down within me and if, as Hegel says, "reason is a bone"?[4]

If the dialectical processes which account for human history have the status of natural laws, controlling human action and thought as passive effects of a natural process external to them, then what becomes of our ability *to know all this*? What becomes of the dialectical rationality that is responsible for uncovering that truth? All knowledge and every reasoned inference, whether dialectical or not, are without exception reduced to the status of effects of a natural process which, in and of itself, is neither true nor false, reasonable nor unreasonable. Contrasting claims ultimately possess the same 'validity'. They are all necessary in the way that every effect is necessary in relation to its cause. The most that could be said for the dialectical rationality which Marxism embodies is that it has "a practical advantage over contemporary ideologies in that it is the ideology of the rising class."[5] But this sort of subjectivism goes nowhere in restoring anything like "truth" to the historical materialist's claims. As a blind weapon or expression of the class struggle, the claim that Marxism is the ideology of the *rising* class would itself be undercut. For how could one *know* such a thing?

Sartre's arguments here are of a recognizable form. They accuse Engels's own assertions of undermining their implicit claim to validity. If what Engels says is true, then no sense can be made of them "being true." This form of argument, in a variety of manifestations, is the most historically pervasive kind of criticism leveled against relativistic epistemological positions. What they implicitly assert on the one hand (a claim to truth), they make impossible with the other. The argument with Engels is a bit more involved, though, because his position is not explicitly relativistic. As Sartre notes, conceiving the dialectic uncovered by historical materialism as a law of nature does not take a position on the problem of knowledge so much as it "avoids" it.[6] But as the position it implicitly takes affords no autonomous status to knowledge as a process irreducible to the nonepistemic developments of nature, it makes knowledge itself completely relative to the natural forces which produce it. And this undermines its potential truth, inasmuch as no place can be found for "truth" in the account of nature given there—only an infinite series of natural events, external to one another, combined according to the 'logic' of a dialectic that produces beliefs in the same way as it produces chemical reactions.

For this reason, Sartre notes, it is also implicitly an absolute idealism. In offering a knowing account of a world where knowledge cannot be found in its own right, Engels places himself in an impossible position outside the world, knowledgeable of it, but for this very reason no longer a part of it. Dialectical materialism becomes, thus, a "transcendental" or "external" materialism, for it "allow(s) the world to unfold itself by itself . . . to *no one*."[7] Knowledge, consequently, finds itself in the position of this "no one," in absolute, contemplative transcendence of the world. "We are offered two thoughts," Sartre writes,

> neither of which is able to think *us*, or for that matter, *itself*: the thought which is passive, is really only the delayed effect of external causes, while the thought which is active, synthetic and desituated, knows nothing of itself and, completely immobile, contemplates a world without thought.[8]

As a relativistic account of thought as a product of nature, the external dialectic ends in scepticism, unable to account for the rationality of its own position. As contemplative idealism, it offers an account of everything but itself. Either way it fails to give an account of knowledge which could justify the sort of validity to which it must itself lay claim.

The Dialectic as a Matter of Fact

The external dialectic is, therefore, untenable because of its sceptical consequences. And yet, to say this much is only to tell half the story. We know *that* Engels's position undermines itself by making it impossible for us to understand how and in what sense it could be true. But we do not know precisely *why* this is so. Certainly, the reduction of human subjectivity to an object of nature alongside other objects of nature—Engels's crude materialism—may be faulted. For Sartre especially, it is the transcendence of our status as objects that is the necessary condition of there being objects *for anyone*. And so to cite Engels's reductivist materialism as the source of his epistemological difficulties is not incorrect. But, in this context, there is more to be said. For, in addition to offering an impoverished picture of *what* the dialectic is, Engels commits a more general mistake in *how* he attempts to uncover it. "Engels' mistake," Sartre writes, "was to think that he could extract his dialectical laws from Nature by non-dialectical procedures—comparison, analogy, abstraction and induction. In fact, dialectical Reason is a whole and must ground itself by itself, or dialectically."[9] In order to fully understand Sartre's criticism of the external dialectic it is necessary, therefore, to understand this more general criticism of the attempt to ground dialectical reason nondialectically.

Engels attempts to ground the laws of the dialectic by induction from nature. On the basis of a set of particular empirical regularities which, purportedly, express or embody a kind of dialectical logic, Engels wants to abstract a set of laws that hold universally. Granting that such generalizations might, in principle, attain a very high level of probability, rendering them all but certain, Sartre, nevertheless, goes on to ask where this sort of move would lead to. Clearly, he answers, "To a discovery of the laws of Reason in the universe, like Newton's discovery of gravitation."[10] The laws of dialectic would have the same status in nature as does the law of gravity: a de facto principle of empirical regularities, for which it makes no sense to ask *why*. As a matter of fact, we happen to find nature behaving in a way consistent with the laws of gravity and of the dialectic. It just so happens. Things fall down and opposites interpenetrate. Engels himself finds three general dialectical laws. And it is just as irrelevant to ask, Why these three and not more, or perhaps others?[11] as it is to ask why the law of gravity, as opposed to something else, holds throughout nature. In the context of analytically deriving the laws of the dialectic, the dialectic itself necessarily assumes the contingent status of an empirical matter of fact.[12]

This line of thought, as I have noted, is more general than that which limits itself to Engels's reductivist materialism. For one need not embrace an ontology such as Engels's to regard the dialectic as something to be empirically discovered as a de facto principle of human history. Take, for instance, the case of Gurvitch's "dialectical hyper-empiricism." As Sartre reads it, this approach does not attempt to limit itself to either analytical or dialectical modes of thought exclusively, but is ready to employ both when appropriate. "The object itself dictates the method, the manner of approach. . . . His [Gurvitch's] dialecticism is thus itself an empirical conclusion."[13] Here there are no obvious ontological commitments, whether materialist or otherwise. And yet, the same insistence on the dialectic as an empirical discovery is maintained. The dialectic emerges once again as a de facto principle of the way things just happen to be, with the exception that with Gurvitch it need not hold everywhere but only here and there, as the case may be.

Sartre's rejection of Gurvitch's "hyper-empiricism" should not, therefore, be sharply distinguished from his rejection of Engels's external dialectic inasmuch as they both involve an attempt to ground dialectical reason analytically; an attempt which leads to an empirical understanding of the dialectic itself. The dialectic becomes a de facto principle of nature as a whole (with Engels) or of specific aspects of human history (with Gurvitch) depending on how the facts present themselves. Such an empiricism is, moreover, no accident within the Marxist tradition. Engels's and Gurvitch's approaches are both symptomatic of a general tendency toward empiricism inherent within the tradition, arising from difficulties with the equivocal status of the dialectic as "both a method *and* a movement in the object."[14] For 'the dialectic' is both a form of knowledge, a specific style of reasoning, *and* an objective process animating and controlling human history—the object known in its historical development as well as the knowledge of this object. Before the materialist turn is made with Marx, this 'doubling' does not constitute a major problem. With Hegelian idealism, the object of thought is, after all, only an alienated objectification of thought itself. Knowledge of the dialectic is ultimately a matter of self-consciousness, and "consciousness can see the strict necessity of the sequence and of the moments which gradually constitute the world as a concrete totality, because it is consciousness itself which constitutes itself for itself as absolute knowledge. . . ."[15] When thought and its object are identified in this idealist fashion, the necessity of the developmental sequence of the object is intelligible to thought as the necessity of its own rational development. Our understanding of the object known is only a disguised understanding of ourselves and so the doubling of the dialectic is merely apparent. In fact, there is only the unfolding of Reason itself. Both the object and subject of the dialectic are, therefore, intelligible as rationally necessary processes.

For Marxists, however, this doubling results in an antinomy which Sartre refers to as a "contradiction between the knowledge of Being and the being of knowledge."[16] Through its rejection of idealism and consequent affirmation of the irreducibility of material existence to thought, our knowledge of the dialectic ceases to be an adventure of self-consciousness for Marxism, and becomes only a partial aspect of the material dialectic to which it belongs. Knowledge of the dialectic becomes "subject to the dialectic as its law,"[17] insofar as it is a material being or material praxis embedded within a historical dialectic that outruns it on all sides. And insofar as the historical dialectic is no longer reducible to reason, working itself out within history, our knowledge of the dialectic comes to lose sight of its own unique status as a *rational* process. Its rational necessity is subordinated to its material contingency as a product of the historical dialectic. "If," as Sartre observes,

> thought were no longer the whole (as with Hegelian idealism), it would see its own development as if it were an empirical succession of moments, and this lived experience (le vécu) would appear as contingency and not as necessity. If thought were to understand itself as a dialectical process, it could not formulate its discovery except as a simple fact.[18]

Two Senses of Rational Necessity—Husserl and Sellars

The key to Sartre's concern here is with reason's loss of necessity. Within an empirical framework, dialectical reason becomes a de facto series of givens. Principles of inference become more-or-less general formulas for observed empirical regularities. Now, it is impossible at this point to specify fully what Sartre means by "necessity" in this context. Sartre's own understanding of necessity, consistent with his philosophy of practical freedom situated within the constraints of a social, historical and material world, will take some time to flesh out. But, by following through on some initial clues in the first chapter of the *Critique*, its broad outlines can begin to be seen. For clearly, Sartre is concerned with the kind of *rational* necessity which goes with the drawing of inferences and the giving of reasons. He writes, "we must stress this crucial fact: Reason is neither a bone nor an accident. In other words, if dialectical reason is to be a rationality, it must provide Reason with its own reasons."[19] Reason demands its own reasons—it must be justifiable as a valid form of thought. And this implies a critique, in Sartre's and Kant's sense of the term as a critical justification of the limits and extent of the *validity* of reason. Dialectical reason, if it is to be a form of rationality, must be capable of giving a *rational* account of itself—one consistent with its status as a practice of drawing valid inferences and producing true assertions. If all that can be said of the utterances of Marx and Engels is that they are one de facto series of utterances in a discursive field of other equally contingent series, then all are equally unjustifiable with respect to each other. Within such an account it makes no sense to even speak of reasoning as valid or invalid. But as a form of reason, the dialectic must have these concepts at its disposal. It, therefore, demands an account of itself which preserves for itself at least as much necessity as goes with the giving of reasons that are justified, and because of that, rationally compelling.

At this point two rather different parallels suggest themselves: one to Edmund Husserl's refutation of psychologism, and another to Wilfred Sellars's argument against "the myth of the given." Beginning with Sellars, one finds, as with Sartre, an emphasis on the impossibility of capturing in any empirical account of knowledge that which is crucial to it *as* knowledge. In his essay, "Empiricism and the Philosophy of Mind," he writes, "The essential point is that in characterizing an episode or a state as that of *knowing*, we are not giving an empirical description of that episode or state; we are placing it in the logical space of reasons, of justifying and being able to justify what one says."[20] Sellars makes this point in arguing against the epistemological idea of "the given": the idea that claims to knowledge may be authorized or justified by a simple appeal to immediate observational states of mind or, as he puts it, "self-authenticating non-verbal episodes."[21] Like Sartre, Sellars argues that knowledge cannot be adequately treated as a matter of fact. The perceptually given, for Sellars, cannot count by itself as knowledge because, as a de facto state of affairs, it is understood as occurring apart from a context of having reasons for holding it as authoritative in relation to any epistemic claims. And this indispensable context is not one of simply having more facts at one's disposal, but of having one's facts ordered in relation to each other in a normative way. One must know that this perceptual state of affairs is the right sort of thing *to count* as a certain type of knowledge. The point is that knowledge has a dimension of authority that cannot be captured in any empirical account. The perceptually given only counts as knowledge when it is recognized as appropriate to authorize a particular assertion, carrying with it an epistemic commitment of some kind. If I do not know anything about when it is appropriate to utter an assertion about some state of affairs, my simple "presence" to that state of affairs can hardly count as knowledge of it. Knowledge always presupposes this prior level of epistemic norms—this "logical space of reasons"—which constitutes the authority of our epistemic claims to justify and be justified by other claims or appropriate states of affairs.

Rational necessity is, therefore, at least in part a matter of *normative* necessity, as when one says that someone's argument is valid and so *ought* to be accepted. Not that it will *in fact* persuade everyone or anyone, but given its validity, it ought to. It constrains one not in the way a cause constrains its effect, or a locked room constrains one's movements, but in the way an imperative constrains one's actions. The rational necessity of assenting to Q on the basis of "If P, then Q and P" is a matter of doing the *right* thing; of constraining one's actions to a norm. Sartre himself hints at this point in a passage concerning the failure of Marxism to critically account for itself where he mentions the need to "distinguish it [Marxism] from conservative ideologies which are mere *products* of the universal dialectic . . . [so that] thought as the vehicle of truth can recover what it has lost ontologically since the collapse of idealism, and become a Norm of knowledge."[22] Dialectical reason, in other words, must be more than a de facto product of the historical dialectic, discovered by empirical methods of observation. It must present itself as a Norm, according to which our assertions must be constrained if they are to count as knowledge—if they are to be a "vehicle of truth." If dialectical reason is interpreted empirically, the account undermines its normative character and so strips it of its rational necessity. And, as Sartre says following Hegel, "Reason once more becomes a bone, since it is merely a fact and has no knowable necessity."[23]

Husserl's refutation of psychologism in the *Logical Investigations* is also useful to consider here. His arguments against construing the laws of logic as laws of mental activity, properly studied by psychology, involve showing this position as a relativistic and ultimately sceptical theory that "goes against *the self-evident conditions for the possibility of a theory in general*."[24] Like the positions of Engels and Gurvitch examined by Sartre, psychologism treats the laws of reason as empirically given matters of fact. And it is precisely here, in its empiricism, that it goes astray. Indeed, Husserl goes so far as to extend his critique to the position of relativism in general, taking it, as he says, in "the widest sense of the word, as a doctrine which somehow derives the pure principles of logic from facts."[25] For such a move amounts to undermining the necessity that belongs to the laws of logic essentially. As with dialectical reason for Sartre, the laws of logic for Husserl, cannot be founded on matters of fact without sceptical consequences which are self-defeating for it as a theoretical position.

Husserl's arguments do not, however, turn on the normative status of reason. Normativity, he claims, is no part of the essence or "thought-content" of the laws of logic. Certainly, these laws have normative application. We can admonish someone for not reasoning as they should when they violate, say, the law of noncontradiction. But, the law itself is a purely theoretical proposition. The normative rule, which is its application, is just "the obvious, apodictic consequence of the law."[26] Husserl grants that "the psychologistic logicians ignore the fundamental, essential, never-to-be-bridged gulf between . . . normative and causal regulation. . . ." But, he understands this gulf as secondary to that between "real and ideal laws."[27] The laws of logic are ideal laws which concern eidetic relations among the concepts which form the objective conditions of the sense of truth itself. And "Truth . . . is 'eternal', or better put, it is an Idea, and so beyond time. . . . Each truth . . . is a case of validity in the timeless realm of Ideas."[28] For Husserl, therefore, logical laws intrinsically possess the necessity of timeless eidetic relations.

There are, then, at least[29] two senses of necessity which elude an empiricist conception of reason:[30] a normative and an eidetic sense. When Sartre speaks of empiricist accounts of dialectical reason failing to capture the necessity that is proper to it as reason, we cannot be sure, on the front end, how he means it. Surely, he must *at least* intend the sort of normative necessity which Sellars emphasizes as crucial to "justifying and being able to justify what one says." He may, however, intend the sort of eidetic necessity that Husserl elaborates as well. Something like this is suggested in the very way he formulates his project as an attempt "to establish the dialectic as the universal method and universal law of anthropology."[31] The phrase *universal law* seems to imply that the normative force of dialectical reason is grounded in an eidetic intuition that holds independently of any social-historical boundaries. In this way, Sartre's *Critique* would have the status of what Husserl calls a "regional ontology" or "regional eidetic science," analyzing the eidetic unity of the region of empirical studies that go to form the human sciences.

And yet, one also finds statements that seem to radically undermine this possibility, such as: "the universals of the dialectic—principles and laws of intelligibility—are individualised universals; attempts at abstraction and universalization can only result in schemata which are continually valid *for that process.*"[32] If the above statement is taken at face value, the timeless, eidetic necessity for which Husserl argues would be impossible for dialectical reason. The necessity of reason, its normative force, could not be grounded in an intuition of timeless ideal relations, but would exist only as a function of the historical process in which it is produced.[33]

This question of interpretation is clearly crucial to my concerns in this essay. The question of epistemic relativism in Sartre's later philosophy hinges on how it is decided. The Husserlian option would effectively exorcise any specter of relativism. The other would apparently introduce *some* form of relativism, whether defensible or not, into the very heart of Sartre's epistemology. I will need, therefore, to return to this question as it forms the broadest parameters of the investigation.[34]

For now, however, we may conclude by stressing the reducibility of the problem of relativism, for Sartre, to that of empiricism. The issue of relativism as it is raised explicitly in his work, under the rubric of the historical relativism that has "contaminated" Marxism, is, at bottom, the issue of the empirical treatment of reason as a contingent matter of fact. Engels's external dialectic undermines its own epistemological foundation as a result of its empiricist approach to knowledge. It is relativistic in the general sense that Husserl gives to it as "a doctrine which somehow derives the pure principles of logic from facts." Sartre's rejection of historical relativism is, thus, the rejection of empiricism as an inadequate theory of knowledge. It is not, in and of itself, an acceptance of a conception of knowledge as independent of all social-historical determination. Knowledge, for Sartre, could still be a matter relative to specific social-historical contexts, as long as these contexts could be understood in a nonempirical manner. His own account of knowledge must, then, attempt to rethink the traditional Marxist question of the relation of knowledge and historical praxis in a way that avoids the pitfalls of empiricism. The question of relativism will hinge on just how this is accomplished and what sense of rational necessity can be preserved for dialectical reason within that account.

Chapter 2

The Knowledge of Being
and the Being of Knowledge

The relativism implicit in any empirical account of knowledge is unacceptable inasmuch as it robs knowledge of its
rational necessity, leaving a "flat" picture of diverse and contesting claims to truth, all equally contingent in relation to
each other. We may understand their empirical genesis but
not their claims to be rational or true. To the extent that
Marxism has tended toward this conception of knowledge, it
needs to be rethought. Sartre's own efforts to this end in the
Critique remain, however, firmly entrenched in historical materialism. They constitute, in his own eyes at least, a deviation within and not beyond it. The *Critique* stems, as he puts
it, from a "fundamental agreement with historical materialism"[1] concerning a rejection of idealism and an acceptance
of a material dialectic. To this extent, Sartre's thought remains within and attempts to resolve, but not reject, the
fundamental epistemological problem at the heart of
Marxism—the "contradiction between the knowledge of
Being and the being of knowledge."

As noted, this antinomy stems from Marx's rejection of
Hegel's idealist identification of being and knowledge. Sartre
assumes with Marx that "material existence [is] irreducible to
knowledge, that *praxis* outstrips Knowledge in its real
efficacy." But, as Sartre continues,

> this position gives rise to new difficulties; how can we
> establish that one and the same movement animates
> these different processes? In particular, thought is
> both Being and knowledge of Being. It is the *praxis* of

17

an individual or group, in particular conditions, at a definite moment of History. As such, thought is subject to the dialectic as its law, just like the historical process. . . . But it is also knowledge of the dialectic as Reason, that is, as the law of Being. But this presupposes an explanatory separation from dialectical objects allowing us to unveil their movement.[2]

An empiricist conception of the dialectic plays on this contradiction without resolving it. It accounts for the being of knowledge (its historical conditioning) while suppressing the knowledge of being (the question of the validity of its own theoretical claims), which it then implicitly presupposes in its own theoretical posture, though without accounting for the being of the very knowledge it presupposes. The task Sartre sets for himself is to somehow do justice to both sides of the contradiction; to account for the dialectic as knowledge, subject to the necessity of reason, while also recognizing that very knowledge as a definite historical praxis, subject in its being to the historical dialectic as a whole.

This, of course, has the ring of an *unresolvable* contradiction. If thought is subject to rational necessity, developing according to its own epistemic norms, how can it also be subject to the nonepistemic constraints of the historical dialectic as a whole? An adequate resolution must show, as Sartre has it, "how one and the same movement animates these different processes" without reducing either process to the other. But in the attempt to hold on to both sides of the contradiction, there emerge in Sartre's work two very different and *seemingly* conflicting ways of talking about knowledge. On the one hand, there is a clear insistence on knowledge as a moment of historical praxis, and on the other, his emphasis on the a priori necessity of dialectical reason in the human sciences. The first way of talking seems to commit Sartre to the sort of historical relativism he rejects in the empiricist tendency within Marxism, while the second seems to free knowledge of any social-historical boundaries, returning to thought an apodictic necessity which the first would disallow.

The Being of Knowledge—Praxis

I have already referred, for example, to the text where Sartre apparently limits the validity of our claims-to-know to the historical process in which they arise. Commenting on his earlier work in *The Transcendence of the Ego* and *Being and Nothingness*, he notes that just as reflection cannot be separated from the consciousness reflected on, but must be regarded as a "distinctive structure" of that consciousness, so neither can any critical reflection be separated from the historical totalization[3] to which it belongs and seeks to articulate. Generalizing from this, he writes of all conceptual knowledge,

> If a totalisation is developing in a given region of reality, it must be a unique process occurring in unique conditions and, from the epistemological point of view, it will produce the universals which explain it and individualise them by interiorising them. (Indeed, all the concepts forged by history, including that of man, are similarly individualised universals and have no meaning apart from *this* individual process.) . . . attempts at abstraction and universalisation can only result in schemata which are continuously valid for that process.[4]

Historical totalizations appear here to produce their own epistemic regimes[5] whose meaning and validity are strictly limited to those specific totalizations. Taken simply on its own, this passage seems to assert a form of radical incommensurability for both the validity of different epistemic regimes and the very sense of the concepts deployed there. Such a claim would find good company with Michel Foucault's account of historically discontinuous "epistemes,"[6] and Paul Feyerabend's arguments against the idea of a universal form of reason that could arbitrate the competing claims of different periods in the history of science.[7] If every historical period has its own set of individualized universals that explain that period to itself, and whose sense and validity are somehow grounded in the specificity of the historical totalization of that moment, how can one avoid concluding that knowledge and what gets to count as "true" are historically relative matters, assessable only in terms of the differing epistemic regimes we may choose to investigate?

The status and interpretation of the above passage is, of course, subject to question. Taken in isolation it is difficult to know quite what to make of it. Its suggestion of a radically historicist epistemology, however, is no mere aberration in Sartre's later work. This general tendency, in some form or other, is implied throughout his insistence that knowledge and subjectivity are moments of an objective, material praxis. In *Search for a Method*, for instance, after dismissing both the idealist strain in Marx's account of his theory as a "conception of nature as it is without foreign addition," and the empiricist strain in Lenin's reduction of knowledge to "an approximately accurate reflection of being," he writes,

> There are two ways to fall into idealism: the one consists of dissolving the real in subjectivity; the other in denying all real subjectivity in the interests of objectivity. The truth is that subjectivity is neither everything or nothing; it represents a moment in the objective process (that in which externality is internalised), and this moment is perpetually eliminated only to be perpetually reborn.[8]

Here again one finds Sartre attempting to balance both sides of the contradiction of the knowledge of being and the being of knowledge. Subjectivity cannot disappear from our account of history. But neither can it transcend that history. It is a moment of the material totalizations which go to form history. Praxis, as material labor, produces and reproduces its historical situation, and our knowledge of that situation is only a "clarification" which that praxis produces itself "in the course of its accomplishment."[9]

Knowledge is inescapably practical for Sartre. Drawing a lesson from modern physics, he writes, "The only theory of knowledge which can be valid today is the one which is founded on that truth of microphysics: the experimenter is part of the experimental system . . . the *revelation* of a situation is effected in and through the *praxis* which changes it."[10] There can be, therefore, no knowledge of a situation independent of the historical praxis that is productively engaged to it. With such an intimate link to praxis, how could knowledge ever hope to aspire to a truth that would transcend its historical specificity? As a "clarification" of praxis, or "revelation" of the situation in terms of a specific practical orientation, knowledge only seems capable of more-or-less historically generalizable conclusions, depending on the relevant similarities of the practical situations under consideration. As a moment of praxis, the essential historicity of our knowledge apparently forecloses all historically transcendent claims to objectivity and, as such, must entail some form of relativism.

The Knowledge of Being—Vision

If, however, Sartre appears to be a relativist on the basis of passages such as these, he could just as well be accused of a kind of transcendentalism on the basis of the way his fundamental project in the *Critique* is formulated. In the first section of the *Critique*, he conceives his task in terms of being "confronted once again with the need to establish the dialectic as the universal method and universal law of anthropology. And this amounts to requiring Marxists to establish their method a priori."[11] True, "the '*a priori*' here, has nothing to do with any sort of constitutive principles which are prior to experience."[12] Sartre's sense of *a priori* is not Kant's. It has more to do with his rejection of the empiricist attempt to establish the dialectic a posteriori, than with any attraction to ahistorical constitutive principles. Still, the intent is clearly one of showing how dialectical reason is the necessary form of intelligibility for all experience. Apodictic certainty, moreover, is promised and even demanded of the critical investigation itself. Again, matters are complicated by Sartre's insistence that "for us, it is necessary to find our apodictic experience in the concrete world of History." Sartre's apodictic experience will not be found "on the level of pure, formal consciousness apprehending itself in its formality,"[13] as with

Husserl. But the very idea of apodictic certainty, connected as it is with the Cartesian/Husserlian tradition of understanding knowledge as a pure intuition of timeless essences, and consciousness as an immanent sphere of indubitable extramundane investigation—the very idea of apodictic certainty coupled with the demand for an a priori foundation for dialectical reason seems to presuppose a radical transcendence of the historical situation on the part of knowledge. Far from being a moment of praxis, knowledge, on this score, looks more like a form of transcendental consciousness standing apart from and actively constituting the empirical varieties of historical praxis. In its being, knowledge is a product of historical praxis. But, as reason, it distances itself from that praxis and assumes the role of a constitutive ground for it.

This apparent conflict has also been noticed, in a somewhat different context, by Thomas Flynn. In his article, "Praxis and Vision: Elements of a Sartrean Epistemology,"[14] Flynn argues for the presence of two distinct epistemologies in Sartre's work. The first, a product of his earlier philosophical work, is an epistemology of "vision," consisting in a traditional phenomenological understanding of knowledge as intuition. In fundamental agreement with Husserl, Sartre argues in *Being and Nothingness* that "There is only intuitive knowledge. Deduction and discursive argument, incorrectly called examples of knowing, are only instruments which lead to intuition. When intuition is reached, methods utilized to attain it are effaced before it." And intuition is just "the presence of the thing (Sache) 'in person' to consciousness. Knowledge, therefore, is of the type of being which we described . . . under the title of 'presence to _____'."[15] As such, knowledge is a mode of being of the for-itself or consciousness, which Sartre understands as a complete and transparent (though nonthetic) presence (to) self. Subtracting (in the sense of the phenomenological reduction) all reference to transcendent reality, such knowledge must possess indubitable certainty. Indeed, as early as his *Psychology of the Imagination*, Sartre reiterated the point "known since Descartes . . . that a reflective consciousness gives us knowledge of absolute certainty."[16] The distinction in the table of contents between that part of the essay dealing with "the certain" and that part dealing with "the probable" attests to how thoroughly Sartre embraced the idea that one could clearly and distinctly divide knowledge as apodictic intuition from its merely probabalistic counterpart. Caught up in this phenomenological approach to putting philosophy back on solid cognitive foundations, knowledge, in its ideal sense, is equated with an absolutely indubitable vision of things "in person"—the clear and distinct intuition of evidence which gives itself without reservation as to its certainty.

Sartre's second epistemology, emerging in the later works, is centered on the notion of *praxis*. Based on the idea that knowledge is a moment of praxis, it introduces an historical dimension to knowledge not found in the paradigm of vision, and so comes to reconceptualize Sartre's theories of evidence, truth and rationality.[17] But, as Flynn observes, this later epistemology was intended by Sartre to conserve rather than simply negate the moment of vision. In his 1947 address to the French Philosophical Society, Sartre's emerging epistemological direction is clearly indicated in his programmatic call for "a synthesis of Husserl's contemplative and non-dialectical consciousness . . . with the activity of the dialectical but non-conscious and consequently unfounded project found in Heidegger's thought."[18] Even in *Being and Nothingness*, where the phenomenological understanding of knowledge as intuition is most developed, this attempt at synthesis is prefigured in his reinterpretation of Husserl's notion of consciousness as ek-static temporalizing transcendence. It is through this search for a synthesis of these two positions that there finally comes to fruition in Sartre's work a hybrid epistemological discourse winding its way through a diverse conceptual field, bounded on the one side by apodictic certainty, and on the other by the material totalizations of a history which perpetually outrun our knowledge of it.

The coherence of these distinct epistemological tendencies is, at best, questionable.[19] As I have attempted to show, they embody diverging orientations toward the problem of knowledge and very different prima facie implications regarding the issue of epistemic relativism. But for all this, I do not intend to foreclose the possibility of their synthesis, but only to underscore the difficulty of the project. At bottom, it is the difficulty of working through and resolving the contradiction of the knowledge of being and the being of knowledge, and so is at the heart of Sartre's project in the *Critique* as a whole.

Committed to a properly dialectical resolution of this Marxist antimony, recognizing that "subjectivity is neither everything nor nothing," Sartre's epistemology is born of a dual concern for both certainty and history; for the preservation of a sense of certainty compatible with the historicity of knowledge and the elaboration of a notion of historicity expansive enough to allow for that measure of certainty indispensable to our epistemic practices. These concerns reflect, in turn, dual philosophical commitments *against* empiricism, as an epistemology which undermines all claims to certainty and resolves itself in scepticism, and *for* a "realist materialism" which would articulate "the thought of an individual, who is *situated* in the world, penetrated by every cosmic force, and treating the material universe as something which gradually reveals itself through a 'situated' *praxis*.'[20] Framing an answer to the web of questions that have so far been raised requires a detailed investigation of this "realist materialism" and the relations of knowledge and praxis it sketches. Only through understanding precisely how and to what extent knowledge is embedded within history can we adequately determine the status of dialectical reason, and the sense of certainty and necessity compatible with it. We are, therefore, confronted with two general questions: that of knowledge as a moment of praxis, and dialectical reason as a form of thought or "method" which is a priori necessary for the intelligibility of that praxis.

Two Questions

The first question, concerning knowledge and praxis, involves articulating the relations between the epistemic and nonepistemic moments of praxis in Sartre's thought. This problem dates back, for Marxism in general, to Marx's claim that "It is not the consciousness of men that determines their being, but, on the contrary, their social being that determines their consciousness."[21] In this passage from the *Preface to a Critique of Political Economy*, Marx draws his fundamental distinction between infrastructure and superstructure. The economic infrastructure, consisting of the mode and relations of production, constitutes "the real foundation, on which rises a legal and political superstructure and to which correspond definite forms of social consciousness. The mode of production of material life conditions the social, political and intellectual life process in general."[22] Just how this conditioning takes place was never precisely spelled out by either Marx or Engels and has been the source of much controversy in the history of Marxist thought. But its centrality in discussions of Marxist epistemology is incontestable. For whether one completely identifies social being with the economic base[23] or understands economic production as the primary determinant of the social totality, in some form or another the thesis asserts the dependence of knowledge (as an aspect of the superstructure) on nonepistemic social factors, raising serious questions as to the possibility of objective knowledge.

The problem as Sartre formulates it—the contradiction between the knowledge of being and the being of knowledge—is a legacy of this tradition, raising the same range of epistemological questions. Yet, for all their shared conceptual and historical heritage, it may be more useful to look forward historically to the thought of Michel Foucault in considering this problem. For, though the base-superstructure problem is of crucial importance for anyone concerned with the social constitution of knowledge, the epistemological problems it raises seem tame in relation to those posed by Foucault's thesis concerning the relation of power and knowledge. Raising the same problem of the determination of knowledge by nonepistemic social conditions, Foucault's notion of power/knowledge goes beyond Engels's concept of the determination of knowledge "in the last instance"[24] to an apparently complete and unqualified envelopment of knowledge by power. In *Discipline and Punish*, Foucault writes,

> We should abandon a whole tradition that allows us to imagine that knowledge can exist only where the power relations are suspended and that knowledge can develop only outside its injunctions, its demands and its interests. . . . We should admit rather that power produces knowledge (and not simply by encouraging it because it serves power or by applying it because it is useful); that power and knowledge directly imply one another; that there is no power relation without the correlative constitution of a field of knowledge, nor any knowledge that does not presuppose and constitute at the same time power relations.[25]

Foucault's thesis is more radical than the base-superstructure problem because it raises the question of the direct determination of knowledge by power, with no place for any 'relative autonomy'. Knowledge is 'directly implied' by power (and vice versa). The two are inextricably connected, with power conceived as both condition and effect of the deployment of knowledge.

In Foucault's account, although he would doubtless never have put it quite this way, knowledge is a *moment* in the deployment of power relations. As such, his account bears a structural similarity to the traditional Marxist problematic in terms of which Sartre's reflections occur while also posing a set of even more radical questions. It merits consideration, therefore, as a touchstone for Sartre's understanding of the relations between knowledge and praxis. Taking up the issues raised by Foucault in a Sartrean context will make it possible to better articulate Sartre's conception of knowledge as a moment of praxis, as well as to judge the success of that conception by its ability to handle the epistemological problems raised by Foucault's discussions of power and knowledge. My treatment of these issues will constitute the second part of this work.

Part 3 will deal with the second question, that of the status of dialectical reason and Sartre's attempt to account for it a priori as the universal method of the human sciences. Only after an examination of the relations between knowledge and praxis can our ability to discern anything like a universally valid rationality for human history be adequately determined. The question of the coherence of the two epistemological tendencies in Sartre's work, that of 'vision' and of 'praxis', will come to the fore here. What sense can Sartre preserve for terms like *apodicticity* and *a priori* within his account? And, most significantly, what sense of necessity can be maintained for a conception of reason which is situated inextricably within history? In short, after having examined the problem of the being of knowledge in part 2, it will be necessary to take up the question of the knowledge of being in part 3, and so come to some conclusions about the success of Sartre's overall epistemological project in the *Critique*; the resolution of the contradiction of the knowledge of being and the being of knowledge.

In the course of dealing with these questions, it will again be useful to go outside Sartre's own work to examine some contemporary positions on the problem of reason. By way of setting up the problem, we will examine the recent work of Richard Rorty and Paul Feyerabend. Rorty's neo-pragmatism and Feyerabend's anarchist philosophy of science pose profound challenges to Sartre's project. They put in question the very idea of a priori constraints on our epistemic practices, and so attempt to pull the ground out from under reason's purported ability to mandate a unique method for any domain of inquiry. Alluding to the pragmatist heritage from which he draws so heavily, Rorty states the broad outlines of this challenge in the introduction to his major work, *Philosophy and the Mirror of Nature*, where he writes

If we have a Deweyan conception of knowledge, as what we are justified in believing, then we will not imagine that there are enduring constraints on what can count as knowledge, since we will see "justification" as a social phenomenon rather than a transaction between "the knowing subject" and "reality."[26]

Attacking the idea that either nature or human beings have an essential reality, calling forth a unique description that would more adequately mirror it than some other, Rorty argues that epistemic discourse can only be assessed in its pragmatic context as more-or-less appropriate to the purposes for which it is deployed. The idea of a unique methodology especially suited to the human sciences is, in this context, merely the hypostatization of *one* of our practical objectives. Rorty argues, therefore, that we give up the attempt to philosophically ground or legislate methodological constraints on inquiry and allow different vocabularies to flourish and die on their own, relative to their pragmatic value. "Why not," he writes, "just say that there are lots of things you can do with people—for instance, dwelling with them, loving them, and using them—and that you should employ different vocabularies depending upon what you want."[27]

Jürgen Habermas's recent attempts to construct an account of a universally valid form of rationality, latent in the formal-pragmatic structure of speech, and Jean-François Lyotard's critical challenge to that project, will also be of relevance here. For Habermas's account of communicative reason is arguably the most ambitious and sophisticated recent attempt to revitalize the idea of a universally valid form of rationality. His work, and the debate it has generated, place in unusually clear relief the precise stakes at issue in an investigation, such as our own, that concerns the status and scope of rationality. By situating Sartre's approach to that project in the light of the "debate" between Habermas and Lyotard it will be possible to provide not only some perspective on the plausibility of Sartre's claims to universality for his account of dialectical reason, but to gain clarity as well concerning the very idea of universality, at the heart of what Lyotard has described as the "heterogeneity of language games."[28] For the issues raised by Rorty, Feyerabend, Habermas, Lyotard, and indeed by much of what is discussed these days under the rubric of the "crisis of reason," principally concern how to come to terms with our aspirations to universality in the context of an increasing appreciation of the singularity of every social and historical frame of reference—an issue, as we have seen, Sartre was concerned with as well.

Part II

Power and Knowledge

Chapter 3

Foucault's
Political Economy of Truth

Sartre's discussion of the knowledge of being and the being of knowledge raises the question of the social-historical determination of knowledge. Taken at the level of its materiality, the practice of knowledge shows itself as a historical enterprise deployed within a complex field of social-historical conditions, with which it sustains a variety of relations. In bringing to light the specific connection between power and knowledge, Michel Foucault has managed to underscore one of the more epistemologically troubling of these relations. The deployment of knowledge, Foucault has argued, is inextricably connected to the deployment of power—inegalitarian relations of force, subjection, and exclusion. The dark underside of knowledge, power cuts across and runs through our epistemic practices, forming a nonepistemic dimension with which they are inextricably bound. Knowledge, on this score, is close to becoming a smoke screen, dissembling the real operation of power at its basis. Or such, anyway, is the sceptical threat Foucault's work poses—a threat which merits close attention if we are to understand how knowledge may be a material product of history and still claim to know that history within which it is produced.

Foucault's Account of Power

Before proceeding with Foucault's analysis of the connections between power and knowledge, it is important to be clear about his conception of *power*. For one of Foucault's most theoretically innovative moves has been his critique of traditional conceptions of power. Understood as a right or prerogative vis-à-vis another, as a matter of sovereignty, our received concept of power has been based on a juridical model of power as the exercise of law. The State has power over its citizens by virtue of its legal status, however this is thought to be derived. Power as legal sovereignty is a right that the sovereign possesses. Fundamentally negative in its functioning, power is a capacity to prohibit, to repress, to seize property and take life. Stemming historically from theories designed to justify or curb the rule of the Monarch, power is customarily thought of as a capacity to limit freedom, invested in the State and its organs, taking the form of legal prescriptions from which we need to be liberated or to which we need to submit, depending on how one sees things.

Foucault's analysis seeks to reverse, at every point, this juridical model of power. Not a right, but a relation of force; not a possession, but a shifting network of social relations; not a limit set on freedom, but a productive force which makes us who we are—power demands a completely different analytic than that which is modeled on the rule of law. In volume 1 of *The History of Sexuality,*, Foucault provisionally advances his reconceptualization of power centered around the idea that it is a "multiplicity of force relations immanent in the sphere in which they operate. . . ."[1] That is, power is not like the rule of law imposed by someone on someone else. It is a diverse and shifting set of forces operating where they are produced. The power, for instance, which is operative in the hospital to command certain forms of discourse, produce and exclude certain options for patients, and distribute individual bodies in a highly articulated analytical space of observation and manipulation—this power does not come from somewhere else as a quasi-legal right. It is, rather, immanent in the very operation of medical practice in the hospital and coextensive with the way individuals are related there to one another in terms of who may or may not make certain decisions, claim a particular knowledge or record specific information.

Power is, thus, a function of the various practical relations which bind individuals together in a social milieu. As such, it cannot be possessed but exists only in the practices which instantiate these relations. "Power is neither given, nor exchanged, or recovered, but rather exercised, and . . . only exists in action."[2] Foucault's analysis of power centers, therefore, not on who does or does not possess it, but on how particular social practices put various power relations into operation. In this way, power cuts across other aspects of the social field formed, for instance, through linguistic or economic relations. It sets into motion relations of force, exclusion, and subjection in and through the respective operation of these practical domains and so could be said to utilize them. "Relations of power are not in a position of exteriority with respect to other types of relationships . . . but are immanent in [them]. . . ."[3] The exercise of power can, therefore, be found everywhere social practices position individuals in relation to each other in ways that give one or the other the upper hand in those relations. It exists in the local practices through which it is deployed and is exercised from a multiplicity of points which permeate the social body as a whole.

Foucault's characteristic 'post-structuralism' is evident here in both his rejection of a structuralist analysis of power as well as his emphasis on its nonsubjective anonymity. As with Derrida, the notion of structure has been de-centered and de-totalized.[4] What we have left is a moving set of differential relations that form "a complex strategical situation in a particular society."[5] And, needless to say, this complex situation is never the product of the constitutive activity of a subject. Quite the contrary, power is itself productive of subjects, for Foucault. The intelligibility of power is not, however, to be found merely through an analysis of the differential relations through which power is deployed and exercised, but through an account of the *strategies* they concatenate to form. Although power is not analyzed on the basis of a binary opposition between ruler and ruled, powerful and powerless, it is still crucial to detect *for whom and what* power works. The intelligibility of power is based on its intentions and aims, despite the fact that these intentions are never usually formulated by anyone. As he says most straightforwardly *and* paradoxically,

> Power relations are both intentional and non-subjective. If in fact they are intelligible, this is not because they are the effect of another instance that "explains" them, but rather because they are imbued, through and through, with calculation: there is no power that is exercised without a series of aims and objectives. But this does not mean that it results from the choice or decision of an individual subject. . . . the logic is perfectly clear, the aims decipherable, and yet it is often the case that no one is there to have invented them, and few who can be said to have formulated them. . . ."[6]

This idea of aims and objectives without anyone to have formulated them, of intentions without subjects, is certainly not without its share of conceptual difficulties.[7] But its descriptive plausibility can be glimpsed in the sorts of historical phenomena Foucault's studies have focused on: the concatenation of a number of punitive practices, organizational methods and observational techniques in the emergence of the modern prison as an institution oriented toward the *production* of a particularly manageable form of illegality;[8] the growth of a "liberating" discourse about sexuality that, in its very attempt to "free" sex, constrains it all the more in terms of medical and psychiatric notions of normal or healthy sexuality.[9] To these might be added Marx's original articulation of a logic of capital which aims at the systematic exploitation of the working class without this objective originating in any morally reprehensible aims of individual capitalists. In such phenomena as these one can decipher the systematic emergence of strategies and aims that were never the product of an individual will or group consensus. Insidiously impersonal mechanisms develop on the basis of the unforeseen combinations of diverse actions, all tending objectively toward the achievement of an end or set of ends unintended by any of them. As Foucault put it himself, "People know what they do, they frequently know why they do what they do; but what they don't know is what what they do does."[10]

Foucault captures the most crucial features of his concept of power by characterizing it as a form of "government." De-emphasizing its combative dimension, he writes,

> Basically power is less a confrontation between two adversaries or the linking of one to the other than a question of government. This word must be allowed the very broad meaning which it had in the sixteenth century. "Government" did not refer only to political structures or to the management of states; rather it designated the way in which the conduct of individuals or of groups might be directed: the government of children, of souls, of communities, of families, of the sick. . . . To govern, in this sense, is to structure the possible field of action of others.[11]

Power governs. Through the way in which various social practices intersect and combine, the individual's field of possible action is structured, limited and focused. Through the way power is articulated in the practices of various domains (such as the prison, hospital, or school), individuals are produced as particular kinds of subjects with specific possibilities. Careers are sketched in advance, for delinquents and perverts as much as public accountants.[12] Power governs through its production of particular modes of individuation and types of subjectivity. Indeed, Foucault has gone so far as to characterize his entire career as a study of the "history of the different modes by which, in our culture, human beings are made subjects."[13]

Power and the Human Sciences

The object of power, then, is always, in some form or other, the government of human beings; their management and control. This constitutes the hingepin in Foucault's reconceptualization of power. Prohibition and repression are not the essence of power, but only particular tactics which may or may not be utilized in the production of a particular form of life. With this in mind it is readily apparent how the sciences of "man" come to be particularly enmeshed in the deployment of power. For the power to be gained over human beings is not blind, but implies a form of knowledge appropriate to its government. And so, the lion's share of Foucault's latter work has attempted to document the development of the human sciences in the context of newly emerging techniques for the management of life—what he calls "bio-power."

Foucault's thesis is essentially historical. Prior to the seventeenth century, power was largely invested in the sovereign's power over his subjects—a "right to *take* life or *let* live"[14] illustrated, in the extreme, in the spectacle of the public execution whose ritual displayed for all to see the sovereign's "invincible force,"[15] and in more moderate ways in such levies as taxation. It was on this basis that the various juridical models of power arose that framed their discourse in terms of the question of the legitimate limits that power could set on the individual's freedom, and from where, of course, this authority was derived (God, the social contract . . .). On the periphery of this ancient form of power, however, more sophisticated technologies for the control and administration of life slowly began to emerge. Distinct from the limiting, prohibitive nature of sovereignty, their aim was to establish a more productive hold over life. Hence, Foucault's reference to "bio-power," a power over life itself having two general poles. "The first to be formed," Foucault writes,

> centered on the body as a machine: its disciplining, the optimization of its capabilities . . . its integration into systems of efficient and economic controls, all this was ensured by the procedures of power that characterized the *disciplines: an anatomo-politics of the human body.* The second, formed somewhat later, focused on the species body, the body imbued with the mechanisms of life and serving as the basis of biological propagation. . . . Their supervision was

effected through an entire series of interventions and *regulatory controls: a bio-politics of the population.*[16]

The disciplines, to begin with, were a response to the inefficiency of the older punitive techniques of the sovereign. The various humanitarian movements which sought to reform the excesses of that older system of punishment began to bring about a reformulation of the nature of punishment. Its aims shifted from the triumph of the will of the sovereign to the reform of the individual. Complimenting and answering this aim, prisons began to be designed in such a way as to allow for a more precise control over the everyday life of their individual inhabitants. Foucault notes that these methods of control were not especially new. They had existed previously in monasteries, armies and workshops. But around the beginning of the eighteenth century, they began to function as "general formulas of domination"[17] involving a distribution of individuals and their actions in analytically demarcated spaces which were easily supervised and controlled by a minimal staff. The distribution of workers in a workshop, patients in a hospital, pupils in a classroom and prisoners in their cells were all performed according to this disciplinary rule which made possible a maximum of efficiency and control.

The English word *discipline* is a translation of the French *surveiller*. And though serviceable, it is inadequate in bringing out the notion of surveillance that is at the heart of Foucault's account of disciplinary power. Detailed surveillance is crucial to the kind of analysis that the body and its environment undergoes in discipline. Indeed, it is through such surveillance that discipline works. "The exercise of discipline," Foucault observes,

> presupposes a mechanism that coerces by means of observation; an apparatus in which the techniques that make it possible to see induce effects of power, and in which, conversely, the means of coercion make those on whom they are applied clearly visible.[18]

As such, a specific sort of architecture is implied in the exercise of discipline—one that makes its inhabitants both visible and controllable, such as Jeremy Bentham's human observatory, the Panopticon.[19] At the center of his Panopticon, Bentham placed a tower with windows that open out onto a peripheral building encircling it, divided into cells. The inhabitants of the cells are visible to the tower, but not viceversa. The cells, moreover, prevent the inhabitants from mingling together in potentially unmanageable ways and render each individual easily identifiable to his or her observers. The Panopticon, therefore, embodies in an ideal form the sort of analytical visibility that is aspired to in every hospital, classroom, or prison: the serial arrangement and distribution of a population, allowing for the easy individualized supervision of all.

This form of observation culminates in the examination. The systematic examination of individuals in the schools, for instance, is at once a hierarchical ranking and normalizing (according to its own particular criteria) judgement of students that establishes them firmly in an authoritarian relationship to which they must submit or fail. All discipline, as an analytical supervision of individuals, follows this model of examination—ranking, ordering, and judging the individual's performance with a precision that permits unlimited refinement. Foucault notes three general characteristics of this sort of examination that are essential to the exercise of discipline.[20] One, it turns the subject's visibility into an immediate exercise of power. The submission of the subject to the examiner and his or her criteria of excellence are essential components of any examination. Two, it makes possible the documentation of the individual qua individual. "The examination that places individuals in a field of surveillance also situates them in a network of writing; it engages them in a whole mass of documents that capture and fix them."[21] And, finally, this documentation turns each individual into a case. Foucault notes that the chronicle of an individual life was once reserved for nobility—for those whose epoch biographies merited telling and retelling. The examination makes possible the telling of everyone's "story" as a "case which at one and the same time constitutes an object for a branch of knowledge and a hold for a branch of power."[22]

Through its arrangement of an analytical space in which individuals can be managed and supervised, the material practice of the disciplines and their spread to more and more social contexts made possible, for the first time, a science of individuals. "One is no doubt right," Foucault writes,

> to pose the Aristotelian problem: is a science of the individual possible and legitimate? A great problem needs great solutions perhaps. But there is the small historical problem of the emergence, towards the end of the eighteenth century, of what might generally be termed the "clinical" sciences; the problem of the entry of the individual (and no longer the species) into the field of knowledge. . . . To this simple question of fact, one must no doubt give an answer lacking in "nobility": one should look into the mechanisms of examination, into the formation of the mechanisms of discipline, and of a new type of power over bodies. Is this the birth of the sciences of man?[23]

Our knowledge of the individual in his or her individuality is made possible, Foucault argues, by disciplinary forms of power. It emerged in the strict and controlled environment of surveillance, examination and documentation. The relations of subjection and control that characterize discipline produced the individual[24] simultaneously as an object of knowledge and of power; as a target of clinical documentation and management. And, conversely, the development of ever more refined techniques of clinical knowledge furthered the development of the disciplinary mechanisms within which they arose. Here one need only reflect on the increasingly important role of the "behavioral sciences" in such institutions as schools, workplaces and prisons—in short, in every institution whose function is premised on the management and control of its inhabitants. It is no accident, Foucault would argue, that such knowledge finds a warm reception in these disciplinary environments. For the behavioral knowledge of an individual *is* a disciplinary knowledge—an account designed to enhance the management and control of the individual.

The disciplines gave rise to the objectifying human sciences. It is here that the individual as an object of clinical management and control emerged. The second pole of this newly emerging government of individuals—the "biopolitics of the population"—is responsible for that other great tendency in the human sciences, the focus on the individual as a *subject* of desire. In *The History of Sexuality*, Volume I, Foucault begins his genealogy of the "subjectifying" human sciences[25] by reinterpreting Victorian society's repressive silence on the subject of sex. Sex, for the Victorians, was indeed a "touchy" subject, but as Foucault underscores in some detail, not for all that a mute one. To the contrary, around the end of the eighteenth century a diverse and complicated discourse on sexuality began to circulate in terms of pedagogy, medicine, and economics whose aims encompassed the regulation of sexual life itself.[26] Sex became a matter of an articulate and authoritative speaking. It became a secret of the individual to be unlocked, to be told, and in the twentieth century, to be liberated. Foucault speaks in this regard of an "incitement to discourse" operative in a variety of arenas, all aiming at the proper administration of the sexual life of the population.

Of crucial importance to this administration was and is the confession of desire. Stemming from the Christian practice of confession, where the articulation of one's inner desires and temptations was a matter of utmost significance for one's relation to the Church, the procedures of confession began to be slowly detached from their pastoral roots and installed in more secular surroundings. "A great archive of the pleasures of sex was gradually constituted. For a long time this archive disappeared without a trace (thus suiting the purposes of the Christian pastoral) until medicine, psychiatry and pedagogy began to solidify it."[27] And with the accumulation of this archive of pleasures in such authoritative contexts, desire and the telling of it became a matter of theoretical concern. Through a number of procedures in which the incitement to confess was clinically codified, the experience of the individual (as this was spoken of in confession) became an object of knowledge. "Combining confession with examination, the personal history with the deployment of a set of decipherable signs and symptoms . . . all were ways of reinscribing confession in a field of scientifically acceptable observations."[28]

Through these developments, the individuals's most immediate relation to his or her self became inserted in a network of power relations where getting to the truth about one's self is a process strictly controlled and regulated by appropriate medical authorities. Still linked in various ways[29] to the normative project of the administration of sexual life, psychiatry and all the various *psy* offshoots form systems of constraint for what constitutes healthy or abnormal desire. These sciences of the individual as subject deploy a modern technology of the self that guides the individual's constitution of his or her own inner life along acceptable or appropriate channels. They form, therefore, another authoritative (i.e., they establish individuals in authoritarian relations such as patient to doctor, client to therapist, etc.) conduit in the modern government of individuals.

Toward a General Politics of Truth

These limited examples underscore the point that the practice of knowledge cannot be isolated from its social and historical context. The sciences of the individual are, quite naturally, made possible by our society's techniques of individuation and themselves go to enhance and form a part of that practice of individuation. They therefore play a special role in the development of modern techniques for the administration and control of life. But every form of knowledge, as a social practice, is caught up in its own specific set of power relations insofar as it distributes individuals and groups in a network that determines who may legitimately say what sorts of things under what sorts of circumstances. This sense of government, intrinsic to the practice of knowledge, constitutes what Foucault refers to as "an internal regime of power." "It is a question," he writes,

of what *governs* statements, and the way in which
they *govern* each other so as to constitute a set of
propositions which are scientifically acceptable, and
hence capable of being verified or falsified by scientific procedures. In short, there is a problem of the
regime, the politics of the scientific statement. At this
level it's not so much a matter of knowing what external power imposes itself on scientific statements, as
what constitutes, as it were, their internal regime of
power.[30]

This notion of a regime of power internal to knowledge,
governing the epistemic relations between statements,
makes it clear that Foucault does not intend to limit his
claims concerning power and knowledge to the human sciences alone. The specific entanglements of the human sciences in the deployment of bio-power exemplify the inter-
penetration of power and knowledge without exhausting it.
Foucault's earlier work can here be reread in such a way as to
illuminate this more general idea. For, immediately following the passage cited above, Foucault goes on to say that it
was just this idea of a regime of power that he was trying to
describe in *The Order of Things*, but had confused too much
with "systamaticity, theoretical form, or something like a
paradigm."[31] In the foreward to the English edition of that
work, he describes his project as an attempt "to reveal a
positive unconscious of knowledge: a level that eludes the consciousness of the scientist and yet is part of scientific
discourse"[32]—a level he would go on to characterize in the
set of methodological reflections that immediately followed
that work, *The Archeology of Knowledge*, as the rules of formation that organize the various concepts, theoretical strategies, modes of validation, etc., that go to make up the specificity of any science. Hence, the *positive* nature of this
unconscious. It is not that which is repressed, deflected or
left out of scientific consideration, but the positive "conditions of existence"[33] of science understood as a discursive
practice.
Foucault's archeologies sought after that end to uncover

the unconscious regularities of discourse—the "complex group of relations that function as a rule . . . [and] lays down what must be related, in a particular discursive practice, for such and such an enunciation to be made, for such and such a concept to be used, for such and such a strategy to be organized."[34] As such, these rules of formation are distinct from the grammatical, logical and psychological relations that operate in discourse.[35] The specific level Foucault seeks to articulate concerns the pragmatic relations that organize discourse into a field of specific possibilities of enunciation, predetermining both the forms of objects capable of being enunciated and subjects capable of enunciating. He describes these relations as occurring at the "limit of discourse" insofar as they concern "not the language used by discourse" and its specific concepts, words or propositions, but "discourse itself as a practice." "They determine the group of relations that discourse must establish in order to speak of this or that object, in order to deal with them, name them, analyze them, classify them, explain them, etc."[36]

In sum, power in Foucault's account is at once a condition, effect and internal regime of knowledge. As a condition, relations of power make possible the deployment of certain types of knowledge. The practice of the disciplines and of the administration of sex form social matrices that allow specific forms of knowledge to emerge and be socially instituted. They make it both possible and necessary to legitimately speak of an individual's character and inner desires with the authority of science. As an effect, knowledge enhances the performance of power and increases its sophistication. The detailed forms of examination, classification, diagnosis, interpretation, etc., immediately carry along and articulate the administration of life that forms their historical condition. They are not just a superstructural effect, but an essential part of its exercise. Power is not blind. It may be anonymous, but its government is strategic and articulate, and as such, implies a form of knowledge appropriate to its exercise.

Finally, power is immanent to knowledge. It constitutes an internal regime which determines the various methods, theoretical options and forms of justification that will be acceptable at any given time and place. This aspect of Foucault's thesis is clearly the most epistemologically unsettling. For one might easily accept that power is a condition and effect of knowledge and still insist that this is a matter of its discovery and application, but not of its justification as true. Truth emerges in the murkiest of circumstances and is often put to the most undesirable of uses. But one must clearly distinguish the context of discovery (and also application) from the context of justification. For, whereas the discovery may vary from circumstance to circumstance, the justification of truth is a matter of timeless ideal relations between propositions and their objects. The epistemological comfort provided by this traditional distinction is boundless inasmuch as it allows one to both recognize and ignore the contingencies of history in the production of knowledge. Foucault's ideas suggest that it is also an illusory comfort which too easily forgets that contexts of justification have their own histories.

"Each society," Foucault writes,

> has its own regime of truth, its "general politics" of truth: that is, the types of discourse which it accepts and makes function as true; the mechanisms and instances which enable one to distinguish true and false statements; the means by which each is sanctioned; the techniques and procedures accorded value in the acquisition of truth; the status of those who are charged with saying what counts as true.[37]

The distinction between a context of discovery and of justification is fine as far as it goes. But insofar as it is intended to set up a rigorous division between the epistemologically irrelevant circumstances of discovery and historically transcendent rules and procedures of justification, it fails to do justice to the social-historical formation of such rules and procedures. As one aspect of this historical formation, power sets limits on what sorts of statements and experiments can count as legitimate and what sorts of evidence can be entertained as verifying or falsifying specific sorts of theories.

Only, for example, with the rise of the sciences of the individual in the context of the administration of life does talk about entities like "character" and "desire" assume an epistemic value as legitimate scientific discourse. Only with the clinical codification of confession does the practical necessity of granting the experimental validity of introspection even arise as a problem.

Foucault's ideas converge here with Thomas Kuhn's work on the role of paradigms in the development of science, inasmuch as his idea of a paradigm, like Foucault's regime of truth, cuts across the traditional distinction between discovery and justification.[38] "Paradigms," Kuhn writes, "differ in more than substance. . . . They are the source of the methods, problem-field and standards of solution accepted by any mature scientific community at any given time."[39] Changes in the accepted scientific paradigm result in changes in the way science is practiced, reformulations of the range of problems considered legitimate for scientific study, and even in the replacement of one set of data with another qualitatively different set. Kuhn characterizes this last aspect of paradigm change as a change in the very world in which the scientist operates. His point here is that whereas Aristotle, for example, could only see a swinging stone as an instance of constrained fall, Galileo, operating with a different paradigm, saw a pendulum. And these differing conceptions of what there was made possible different observations, measurements and describable regularities.[40] Similarly, Foucault argues that the character type we know as the "delinquent" only emerges as a possible object of knowledge with the whole range of techniques of surveillance and documentation that formed disciplinary power. The delinquent is not an objective reality to which older penitentiary methods were blind, but a correlate of the disciplinary practices which made it both possible and necessary to describe individuals in terms of underlying character traits that inclined them in the direction of criminal behavior.

Kuhn's paradigms and Foucault's regimes of truth are not, of course, identical notions. Most importantly, they differ in terms of the relative degree of nonepistemic relations they encompass. A paradigm encompasses such non-epistemic factors as the material instruments available to a science, but stops short of taking in other more politically loaded factors[41] that the notion of a regime of truth is meant, in principle, to capture. Foucault's concept is intended to circumscribe a level at which politics is intrinsic to the formation and deployment of knowledge—a "political economy of truth."[42] As such, his work also constitutes a rejection of the classical Marxist distinction between ideology and science. All science is ideological inasmuch as it is "one practice among others" constituted in and constitutive of historically specific relations of power. But this does not imply "error, contradiction, and a lack of objectivity."[43] Truth, error, objectivity and the lack of it are themselves possibilities which only emerge on the basis of specific regimes of truth. "The problem," Foucault writes, more-or-less summarizing the aims of his historical-epistemological project,

> does not consist in drawing the line between that in a discourse which falls under the category of scientificity or truth, and that which comes under some other category, but in seeing how effects of truth are produced within discourses which in themselves are neither true nor false.[44]

The Problem of Truth

What, though, in all of this is to become of truth? The very way in which Foucault has cast the problem would appear to determine a sceptical conclusion. Truth is an effect of historically divergent discursive regimes. And these discursive regimes institute power relations in and through the knowledge they make possible. As such, it would appear that knowledge is a mere means in the service of power. Claims to truth and validity would be no more than a subterfuge concealing the real operations of subjection and coercion which the practice of knowledge sets into motion. On this reading, Foucault is continuing Nietzsche's project of disclosing the will to knowledge as an effect of the more fundamental will to power. Power is at the heart of knowledge and is the secret of its pursuit. "Truths," as Nietzsche put it, "are illusions about which one has forgotten that this is what they are. . . ."[45]

Such a Nietzschean reading[46] of Foucault's account of power/knowledge is rather extreme. But it succeeds in getting at the most disturbing and unsettling aspect of his analysis. For all of Foucault's work in this area is aimed at unmasking the political realities of our epistemic practices. In calling his studies "genealogical," he intentionally invokes the legacy of Nietzsche's attempt to chronicle the historical descent of our most cherished values. "The very question of truth . . . does this not form a history, the history of an error we call truth?"[47] In his programmatic address to the College de France in 1970, this Nietzschean train of thought emerges most forcefully in his discussion of the opposition between the true and the false as a historically constituted system of discursive exclusion—as a historically developed will to truth. Beginning with the Greeks (Plato, roughly) true discourse was conceptually distinguished from the exercise of power and the extension of desire. As a result of this, truth begins to conceal the will to truth that pervades it. Its material linkage with power and desire is forgotten. "True discourse, liberated by the nature of its form from desire and power, is incapable of recognizing the will to truth which pervades it; and the will to truth, having imposed itself upon us for so long is such that the truth it seeks to reveal cannot fail to mask it."[48] Knowledge as a means and mask of power—such are the extremes to which this reading leads.

From this perspective, Foucault's work begins to look something like intellectual guerilla warfare. Playing the game of the rationalist to the hilt, Foucault seeks to sabotage our epistemic practices—to undermine reason from within. And he has indeed characterized the task of the intellectual in terms of "a battle about the status of truth and the economic and political role it plays."[49] The content and truth value of his ideas would be, on this score, irrelevant to their primary function as strategically placed weapons. Carrying this perspective to its logical(!) conclusion, Gilles Deleuze has sought to reformulate the status of Nietzsche's aphorisms as "a play of forces," that produce their effects outside any horizon of meaning.[50] Meaning, like truth, is only a tactic utilized for a particular effect. It is all a matter of attaining a point where "language is no longer defined by what it says, even less by what makes it a signifying thing, but by what causes it to move, to flow, and to explode—desire."[51] Desire is understood here not in terms of a lack and its representation, but as a positive production and disruption of a material field. Perhaps Foucault's works should be taken, then, as discursive productions of desire and disruptions of the constraints to which reason artificially subjects desire. His principle irony[52] would be to have done this by having played the game of reason better than most of the rationalists to which his writings are addressed.

Such irony cannot, however, be coherently maintained. Though there is certainly a political level to Foucault's work which may not be overlooked (and his writings have had definite material effects in the various political, philosophical and cultural fields in which they have been received) if his works merely persuade one of the folly of reason, then that very persuasion is folly. Reducing knowledge to a tactic in games of power is ultimately another form of the empirical treatment of knowledge. Reason has again become a bone, or perhaps in this case, a club. For the level at which we think we are being rationally persuaded by lines of justification that appear valid is only a veil that hides the reality of coercion and constraint. Reason is only power, continued by other means. As such, it only possesses the de facto necessity of an ordering of the practical field that produces a particular range of possible actions—reason as an instance of government. But then there are no longer reasons for acting reasonably and any arguments which could show that knowledge is a mask for power might as well be ignored. For as arguments, they undercut their own claim to validity. But as weapons, they only succeed in governing our actions insofar as we can be persuaded of their validity as arguments. Their only value as weapons lies in their strength as arguments which, as arguments, they undermine. Either way, nothing is accomplished.

If pushed hard enough Foucault's more Nietzschean tendencies clearly self-destruct. Foucault himself, however, rarely pushes things to such extremes. The vast majority of his efforts are not, after all, sweeping aphorisms designed to jolt and shock our received philosophical sensibilities, but carefully constructed historical descriptions and self-consciously–restricted theoretical accounts that disturb us precisely insofar as they document or suggest relations between power and knowledge that demand new ways of thinking about what it is *to know*. In an interview given shortly before his death in 1984, Foucault himself came to unequivocally deny the suggestion that power and knowledge were in any sense identical. Attempting to clarify his position, he says,

> On a donc des structures de pouvoir, des formes institutionelles assez voisines: internement psychiatrique, hospitalisation médicale—auxquelles sont liées des Formes de savoir différentes, entre lesquelles on peut établir des rapports, des relations de conditions, et non pas cause à effet, ni *a fortiori* d'identité. Ceux qui disent que pour moi, le savoir est le masque du pouvoir ne me paraissant pas avoir la capacité de comprendre.[53]

There are relations and connections between structures of power and forms of knowledge, the former conditioning the latter, but not as cause to effect. Clearly, Foucault had come to radically qualify his earlier Nietzschean tendencies. The problem remains, though, of how to conceive of this conditioning. Foucault does much to establish *that* power and knowledge are connected in various ways, but leaves us largely in the dark as to the precise status of these connections. The classical Marxist paradigm of infrastructure and superstructure fails in that power is in no way external to knowledge. Much of Foucault's work is aimed precisely at demonstrating the inadequacy of that way of conceiving things. The Nietzschean model of knowledge as a mask of power is the next obvious move. And, as we have seen, there is reason to believe Foucault's initial reflections stayed fairly close to this paradigm. But its internal incoherence as an epistemological position, coupled with Foucault's own explicit denials that he *ever* intended to treat knowledge as a mask for power, let alone identify the two, leads one to abandon this model as well.

Foucault's Positivist Account of Practice

This issue has its theoretical precedent in Foucault's earlier attempts to think the connection between discursive and nondiscursive practices, which Dominique LeCourt has singled out as the Achilles' heel of Foucault's *Archeology of Knowledge*. Foucault's theory, LeCourt writes, "does not enable us to think the *unity* of what it designates except as a *juxtaposition*."[54] This problem stems, no doubt, in part from Foucault's early emphasis on deriving the unity of a discourse from the rules of formation that govern its practice.[55] For the status of these rules was always enigmatic.[56] But equally at fault, and more important for my purposes, is Foucault's conception of practice.[57] Conceived exclusively from a perspective of exteriority, in which all reference to the subjective or lived side of practice is excluded, practice is understood as one positive, analytically observable event among others. Only its empirical presence in a materially dispersed field remains. As so conceived, the unity of the discursive fields themselves, let alone their articulation upon nondiscursive practices, can only be a matter of empirically discernable juxtapositions. From such a descriptively impoverished perspective, one is limited to observing the rulelike regularities these events appear to obey. All that is left are the coordinates, so to speak, of their empirical correlation.

As talk of power relations comes to replace that of discursive rules in Foucault's work, the perspective of exteriority remains privileged. "What is needed," he reasserts in 1977, "is a study of power in its external visage. . . ."[58] The language of exteriority changes from one of rules of formation to relations of constraint and subjection, but the attempt to stand completely outside the practical field and study the de facto connections of materially dispersed events remains the same. Practices are still grasped solely as events and Foucault's understanding of practice remains, as he himself admits, positivistic.[59] Practice, discernable only in its simple material anonymity, is a given; a historical product entering into empirical relations with other historical products. The practical *production* of history, however, is lost. And it is just this incipient positivism that stands in the way of attaining an adequate conception of the connections between power and knowledge. For in order to understand how power conditions our epistemic practices, one needs to know how any practice in general is formed on the basis of power. It is necessary to know, in effect, how individual agents are practically constrained by power relations that they live as a modification of their field of practical possibilities.[60]

To govern, Foucault argues, is "to structure the possible field of action of others"[61]—to produce and delimit, therefore, an individual's future. Clearly, this is a matter of relations of exteriority, of organizing a material field of action. But there is also an implicit reference to action as a lived appropriation of this field. Power acts through structuring someone's field of possibilities and determining in advance the sorts of choices available for the agents who must live in terms of this field of possibilities. What power conditions, therefore, is an individual's freedom. Foucault himself came to underscore this point in the article just cited. He writes there, "When one defines the exercise of power as a mode of action upon the actions of others . . . one includes an important element of freedom. Power is exercised only over free subjects, and only insofar as they are free."[62] But freedom is no longer just a matter of relations of exteriority. The aims and projects of the individual must now be taken into account. There are no longer merely a number of discernible events dispersed in some more-or-less regular manner, but a number of individual relations to this field of dispersed events in terms of the concrete projects it makes possible.

There is, in other words, a reference to the kind of interiority that Foucault has otherwise been at such pains to avoid.

In the second volume of *The History of Sexuality*, *The Use of Pleasure*, Foucault begins to explicitly come to terms with this dimension of interiority. He is concerned there with the ways individuals produce themselves as specific sorts of subjects in and through socially regulated practices. "It seemed appropriate," he writes, "to look for the forms and modalities of the relation to self by which the individual constitutes and recognizes himself *qua* subject."[63] Clearly, in Foucault's case at least, "the fog emanating from Paris in recent decades," which Charles Taylor describes as completely obscuring a proper grasp of the role of the subject in the production and maintenance of social structures, seems to be clearing somewhat.[64] But despite the distinct cracks in Foucault's positivistic tendencies, we look in vain for anything like a positive articulation of free productive action. Freedom slips in the back door, as it were, as a necessarily "agonistic"[65] quality of power. And for all the novel emphasis on self-constitution in *The Use of Pleasure*, the predominant theme is still an analysis of sexual practice as a constituted tradition deploying possible sites and modes of self-constitution, and not on practical self-constitution in and of its own right. He still lacks, therefore, an account of social practice which would allow an adequate understanding of how our epistemic practices allow for the conditioning of power in the way they deploy themselves in relation to power. As power implies freedom, it also implies an account of action adequate to that freedom; an account of autonomy that is proper to practice in general, and our epistemic practices in particular, consistent with their heteronomous relation to power. For such an account it is necessary to turn to Sartre and his understanding of praxis as totalization.

Chapter 4

Power, Praxis,
and the Practico-Inert

The key to Sartre's later philosophy is to be found in his account of *praxis*. Action has, of course, always been a central concept in his work. Consciousness is understood in *Being and Nothingness* as "pure spontaneity"[1]—freedom determining itself in the light of its own projection of future possibilities. But action, in this context, was always the consciousness of action, never a real, which is to say, material, modification of the world. Only as praxis does the *consciousness* of action subordinate itself, in Sartre's work, to that action of which it is conscious—action as labor, understood in Marx's sense as "a process between man and nature . . . by which man, through his own actions, mediates, regulates and controls the metabolism between himself and nature."[2] Sartre's account of praxis is, thus, an attempt to come to terms with human existence in its materiality as that historical process through which human beings produce themselves as a function of their regulated modification of their natural environment. His shift to a philosophy of praxis reflects this new concern with understanding the material production of history in terms of the practices of the individuals who live through it, and with establishing the *practical* intelligibility of the social-historical world on that basis.

Praxis as Totalization

The thesis of the practical intelligibility of history refers immediately to the question of the proper intelligibility of praxis itself. And this, Sartre argues, is to be found in understanding praxis as a material totalization of its environment. Every activity involves the formation of a practical field in the light of specific needs or aims and the transcendence of the inevitable obstacles that emerge on the basis of that field through a material modification of it. It is always an active, ongoing synthesis of its milieu—the production of a practical totality that exists *as* a totality only as a function of the practical totalization that sustains it. For a practical field only exists as a unity of instrumental relations, and this unity disappears with the praxis for which it is functionally significant. Considered apart from the labor that works it, a factory is an indefinite multiplicity of steel and glass where every part stands in some external relation to every other. Only in the light of the praxis that utilizes it to some end is a factory really a factory; a tight complex of production lines all coordinated with each other and regulated in terms of the product for which they are the means. To say, then, that praxis is a totalization is to say that

> it is a developing activity, which cannot cease without the multiplicity reverting to its original statute. This act delineates a practical field which, as the undifferentiated correlative of *praxis*, is the formal unity of the ensembles which are to be integrated; within this practical field, the activity attempts the most rigorous synthesis of the most differentiated multiplicity.[3]

Sartre understands praxis as synthesis. It is an integration of a material multiplicity into a totality distinct from the sum of its parts but present in them all as their practical significance in relation to each other and to the goals of that praxis. In this way it transforms the "exterior" relations of a material multiplicity existing side by side each other into a network of "interior" relations where each part is what it is (in its practical significance) only through its relation to all the others. Sartre often speaks of their transformation as an "interiorization of exteriority" and an "exteriorization of interiority," where the first moment indicates the practical integration of a material environment and the second, the fixing of these practical relations in matter. Through the totalizing movement of praxis, material relations become practical and practical relations, material. Praxis, one might also say, objectifies itself, insofar as it produces or reproduces a practical totality that is the material embodiment of its needs and interests. Through its regulated modification of the environment, it produces a material milieu structured in terms of its goals. Practical intentions are objectified as the material possibilities of the practical field to which one is engaged. Objectification, interiorization and synthesis are, therefore, all ways of speaking about the same process which Sartre designates by the term *totalization*.

This practical totalization of a material field is regulated by and subordinate to the objectives that are to be realized. The projection of a goal, of a future state in which one's needs or interests are fulfilled, is crucial to praxis. For it is in terms of this future state of affairs that the present is evaluated and modified. The future is the regulative basis of the present insofar as the present state of affairs assumes its significance as a practical field only in terms of the projected end to be achieved. The tools I have at my disposal, for instance, will only appear as adequate or inadequate in relation to the task I set for them. To totalize, therefore, is to temporalize—to project a future state of affairs on the basis of one's material possibilities in terms of which the present state of affairs is to be modified. This temporalizing dimension of praxis presupposes, as well, the existential structures of the project. Praxis is a negation or transcendence (*dépassement*) of the given state of affairs towards an objective that is not yet. I negate and transcend my present situation by acting to bring about another. This transcendence is, of course, conditioned by the historical circumstances that make it possible and structure its course. Practical transcendence, because it is identical with praxis itself, is limited to the specific possibilities that are materially adumbrated in a society at any given moment. And yet, for precisely this reason, praxis cannot be defined simply in terms of those past or present conditions, but must be taken in its relation to the future it aims at on the basis of these conditions. "The most rudimentary behavior," Sartre writes, "must be determined both in relation to the real and present factors which condition it and in relation to a certain object, still to come, which it is trying to bring into being. This is what we call *the project*."[4]

Comprehension

Sartre's understanding of praxis encompasses what one might call the "material life of the agent." To act is to live through material circumstances in a singular way where such "living through" may be construed as neither subjective nor objective, but a "moving unity of subjectivity and objectivity. . . . "[5]—a material production of the self as a practical relation to the world, to others, and to itself on that basis. Praxis embodies a lived experience (*le vécu*) of the world in which it acts. Sartre gets at this notion by describing it as "life aware of itself, without implying any thetic knowledge or consciousness."[6] In his or her practical engagement within the world, the agent experiences that world, and him- or herself in the world, in a way which is fundamentally different from a thetic or propositional knowing. Sartre elsewhere describes this practical nonknowledge as comprehension. "To exist, to act and to comprehend," he writes, "are one and the same."[7] Praxis is, in and of itself, a comprehension of its practical field inasmuch as it implies a lived understanding of its endeavors and the situation in which they are carried out. When my companion moves to open the window in a hot room, I understand the action without having to spell it out for myself, in terms of the room as an instrumental context organized by our action in the light of specific objectives. I live the heat as stifling our task there and comprehend the other's action on the basis of that practical familiarity with the material conditions and objectives we share, and just "see" that he or she is letting some air in.[8] "Comprehension," Sartre writes, "is simply the translucidity of *praxis* to itself, whether it produces its own elucidation in constituting itself, or recognizes itself in the *praxis* of the other. In either case, the comprehension of the act is effected by the (produced or reproduced) act. . . . "[9]

A helpful parallel may be drawn here to Gilbert Ryle's distinction between "knowing-how" and "knowing-that."[10] It is possible, for example, to know a lot about playing chess, riding a bicycle or being rhetorically persuasive without being particularly good at any of these things. Conversely, it is possible to be very good in all these areas without being able to say exactly what it is that makes one so good. In the first case, one knows-that (. . . the game of chess has so many strategic possibilities, riding a bicycle obeys certain laws of aerodynamics, rhetorical persuasion involves certain principles, etc.) without knowing-how (. . . to competently *do* any of these things). In the second, one knows-how without knowing-that. Our comprehension of our companion's gesture at the window is, likewise, a matter of knowing-how to get about a room and get things accomplished there, as opposed to knowing-that "this room is the sort of place that is likely to get too hot to work in and that one can often simply open a window and ventilate it to cool it off and that, as a matter of fact, people tend to do just this rather than sitting there and being miserable." Know-how is a matter of practical skill rather than having a set of facts at one's disposal. There need be no analytical knowledge of the situation, but only an intuitive grasp of it in terms of one's objectives there. Someone with practical expertise at chess, for instance, need not count out all the possible moves and countermoves and consider their relative values, as a digital computer must. They simply "see" strengths and weaknesses on the board and act accordingly.[11] Their skill at the game constitutes a practical comprehension of it—a knowing-how to play.

Comprehension is a matter of intuitively grasping a situation on the basis of one's skill at dealing with it. It is, therefore, completely a matter of practice. To act is to project a future on the basis of which present circumstances are totalized, which is to say, grasped as a totality; as a chess board with strengths and weaknesses or as a room needing ventilation. Our practical totalization of a material field comprehends that field in its totality *as* a global field of action. It is this totalizing dimension of praxis which makes possible a global or intuitive apprehension of a situation without having to "count out" all of its specific elements. One may distinguish in this way two related senses of *comprehension*, both of which refer to our practical engagement within a situation: comprehension as the totalizing movement of praxis that produces a practical field on the basis of the material circumstances at its disposal, *and* comprehension as the intuitive, nonanalytic perceptual or discursive grasp of the practical field in the light of one's ongoing totalization of it. Both senses must be preserved and thought together if one is to grasp comprehension as a form of practical knowledge—an ability to act *and* to elucidate oneself and one's situation on the basis of that action. Our chess expert knows how to skillfully manipulate his material field and perceive and speak of it in a global way in terms of the strengths and weaknesses of the board. Flaubert knew how to produce himself as what Sartre calls a "passive agent" and grasp himself as such, in an indirect way, in his writings.[12] When Sartre speaks of *comprehension* he refers to both these dimensions at once—to "activity itself as self-elucidating."[13]

Another way of developing this point is to think of praxis as embodying a practical interpretation of the world. In the course of its own realization, self-elucidating praxis produces a determinate sense for the world by producing a practically significant context in which the world can make sense. Nothing makes sense outside of some context or situation in which it is taken *as* something, in the light of the particular objectives and interests which are relevant there. There is no such thing as a pristine or 'value-free' encounter with the world.[14] And these practical contexts are themselves produced in and through the practical totalizations which sustain them. "Meaning," Sartre writes,

> can be defined . . . as the synthetic totalization of scattered chance occurrences by an objectifying negation, which inscribes them as necessity freely created in the very universe in which they were scattered. . . . In other words, man is that being who

transforms his being into *meaning*, and through whom *meaning* comes into the world.[15]

By this, Sartre does not intend to resolve the being of things into their meaning. Any hint of idealism is overturned in his insistence elsewhere that "significations are *composed* of matter alone."[16] Meaning is a material relation. But this relation is itself produced or sustained by praxis as a material totalization of the practical field in which such relations subsist. For relations of signification are necessarily interior relations between elements that assume their significance only as a function of their relation to other elements. Sartre agrees, then, with Saussure's thesis that significance is constituted by a network of differential relations.[17] Red is only red by virtue of its difference from blue, green, etc. But such differential relations are instituted through praxis.

> Nature knows only the independence of forces. Material elements are placed one next to the other and act one over the other. But the lines of force are always external. It is not a matter of internal relations, such as that which poses masculine in relation to feminine or plural in relation to singular: that is, of a system in which the existence of each element conditions that of all the others. If you admit the existence of such a system, you must also admit that language exists only as spoken, that is, in action.[18]

As it is with language, so it is with any signifying system; it exists only in practice, only in the actions that realize that system as a field of practical possibilities.

In this way, praxis is, in and of itself, an interpretation of things—a determination of something *as* something. As Heidegger equates interpretation with "the working out of possibilities projected in the understanding,"[19] so Sartre might equate it with the realization of possibilities projected within practical comprehension. To act in a historical situation is to interpret that situation—to carry on the ongoing collective interpretation of the world in which one's praxis is integrated. It is to produce a way of acting and speaking (which is itself a way of acting) in terms of which the world will be experienced. Praxis is a comprehension of its practical field precisely insofar as it is a practical interpretation of it. Its totalizing movement realizes a material network of practical significations that are comprehended/interpreted precisely insofar as they are lived by praxis in determinate ways. And whereas we may be accustomed to thinking of an interpretation of a particular text or of a language as limited, ultimately, by the *facts* of the matter, at this level of what we are calling "practical" interpretation, we must agree with Nietzsche, when he writes, "Against that positivism, which halts at phenomena—'There are only *facts*'—I would say: No, facts is precisely what there is not, only interpretations."[20] For praxis, as a determination of sense, fixes the range of what can count *as* a fact, inasmuch as facts have sensible content. The only limitations to practical interpretation are those imposed by the historical possibilities of the material field in which one finds oneself, which are, of course, a matter of past interpretations/totalizations of that field: of the way in which previous communities have productively modified the environment *they* had to deal with. The only limitation to our practical interpretation of ourselves and our situation is, therefore, that of other practical interpretations which form the historical foundations for our interpretive endeavors.

Counter-Finality and the Practico-Inert

Thus far, praxis has been examined only in terms of the active production of history. An adequate treatment, however, must also take into account the way in which the history that we produce nevertheless escapes us. For the two, the production of history through praxis and the way in which that history escapes our control, are inextricably bound together. Or, as Sartre puts it, "if History escapes me, this is not because I do not make it: it is because the other is making it as well."[21] History and my own actions as well, insofar as they are totalized within history, escape me to the extent that I share my field of action with others. Our multiple actions combine there to produce material effects unintended by anyone. These, then, modify the objective sense of everyone's praxis, imposing new goals and ends that no one, individually or collectively, has projected. Sartre describes these new objectives as "counter-finalities," ends that are other than those intended by the agents themselves. They define a "primitive type of alienation,"[22] prior and irreducible to exploitation,[23] in which historical events "steal" our praxis from us and we find ourselves accomplishing things we never imagined.

In the *Critique*, Sartre gives two examples of this phenomenon. In the first he describes how the multiple effects of Chinese peasants working separately at clearing their land for cultivation led to a systematic deforestation of the countryside, which consequently brought about a series of devastating floods which undid collectively what they were pursuing individually.[24] In the second more complex case, he discusses the Spanish import of precious metals in the sixteenth century and the economic impoverishment to which it led. With the discovery of a new amalgamation process, the production of precious metals increased drastically, as did the Spanish import of these metals. But as more and more gold and silver were accumulated by individuals seeking to increase their wealth, a general inflation set in, which undercut those individual efforts. Responding to this situation by lowering the wages of their employees in an attempt to control rising costs of production, employers only succeeded in lowering the working class's standard of living to such a point that it exposed them to various famines and epidemics. This, in turn, led to a labor shortage which brought about an increase in wages as employers competed with one another over scarce labor-power. Once again, the actions of the individuals involved led directly to the subversion of their own aims and objectives.[25]

Both scenarios present not merely the failure of action but the turning of action against itself[26]—"a state in which there is a constant transformation of man's exigencies in relation to matter into exigencies of matter in relation to man."[27] In this way, the practical field is transformed from an instrumental context *in the service of* praxis into an arena of inert processes to which praxis is subjected—what Sartre calls the "practico-inert." Here it is not so much the individual agents who act, as it is worked-matter which acts through these agents. Praxis is transformed into a means of the practico-inert, as a directed realization of its inert possibilities. A factory, for example, designates its mode and rate of work in advance according to the requirements of the machines and the marketplace, and an economic milieu marks out a place for each of its workers according to the "needs" of the specific forms of production carried out there. "The working woman," Sartre observes,

> is expected in bourgeois society, her place is marked out in advance by the capitalist "process". . . . Her life and destiny can be determined *before she gets her job*, and this prefabricated reality must be conceived in the mode of *being*, in the pure materiality of the in-itself. The role and attitude imposed on her by her work and consumption have never even been the object of an intention; they have been created as the negative aspect of an ensemble of directed activities . . . or, in other words, as a result of *counter-finality*.[28]

In this way, the practico-inert forms a material destiny for praxis. It designates a form and order to one's practical endeavors which have never been prescribed by anyone but the anonymous exigencies of the field itself. It is not as if a group of individuals consciously organize their forms of life and then submit to it. One rather submits along with everyone else to a set of exigencies that are maintained by virtue of everyone's practical separation from everyone else. For one belongs to the practico-inert not as a member of a group that is trying to realize some commonly held objective, but as an isolated member of a series, in which one's position in the series is strictly defined by the predetermined structure of the series itself. Sartre's examples of practico-inert collectives—riders lined up for a bus, the audience of a radio broadcast scattered among various homes throughout the country, the multiplicity of buyers, sellers, producers and consumers conducting their separate business in the free market—all underscore this form of serial unity in which one is united to the other precisely through one's separation and isolation. One enters the marketplace as another isolated consumer confronting another isolated seller. One lines up for the bus as another bus rider who merely takes his or her place behind the other who took their place in the same way. Everyone acts and conditions each other *as an other*. We act not in terms of our capacity to come together and organize things for ourselves, as free agents acting on our own concrete needs and desires in reciprocity with others, but as another bus rider lining up one after another, another radio listener among others, another consumer confronting another seller. One acts as the others do, linked to all the others by a bond of exteriority (their sharing the same practico-inert field), which is also a practical inability to change the practico-inert field itself. For insofar as one acts as an isolated bus rider, radio listener or consumer, one's only choice is to play along in terms of the specific possibilities and requirements that predefine the field in question. To this extent, one's action becomes, as Sartre has it, a form of "passive activity" insofar as it is a passively directed form of conduct, which only serves to maintain the system of practico-inert possibilities to which it submits.[29]

The practico-inert constitutes a "fundamental level of social being"[30]—a level at which a multiplicity of individuals condition or direct the conduct of each other by virtue of their belonging together in the same material field. It forms what Foucault would call a form of "government" insofar as everyone's action, through the counter-finalities they set in motion, leads to a "structur[ing of] the possible field of action of others."[31] The practico-inert is, therefore, in Foucault's sense of the term, a network of power relations governing the conduct of individuals at a very rudimentary level. Indeed, the parallels between the two concepts are quite striking. The practico-inert, like power, is a field of relations[32] that only exists in action, as a symbiosis of worked-matter and living praxis. Its power to constrain and

organize conduct is not derived from any classically conceived source of political authority (indeed, in its reemergence within the institutionalized group, it is the basis
of political sovereignty)[33] but emerges "immanent to the
sphere in which it operates"[34] as a function of the material
inertia of social practice itself. In this way, it can be seen to
traverse the social body as a whole in the "micro-practices" of
everyday life (riding buses, buying and selling commodities,
etc.). And, most significantly of all, it constitutes an intentional, but nonsubjective level of social existence insofar as it
is a field of counter-finalities; of intentional goals and objectives in which "the logic is perfectly clear, the aims decipherable, and yet it is often the case that no one is there to have
invented them, and few who could be said to have formulated them."[35] What Foucault has said of power could just as
well, and without qualification, be said of the counter-
finalities of the practico-inert: "People know what they do,
they frequently know why they do what they do; but what
they don't know is what what they do does."[36]

Contingency Lived as Necessity: Norms

Sartre's account of the practico-inert ought, therefore, to
provide a renewed perspective on the relation of power and
social practice which was so problematic with Foucault. For
his seemingly paradoxical emphasis on inert practice or passive activity is oriented toward dealing with the problem of
how individuals are conditioned by their material situation
and yet remain self-determining agents actively constituting
their lives on that basis. It is a question of formulating a
notion of practical autonomy that is consistent with the heteronomy of historical conditions; of understanding "how we
ourselves make something of what has been made of us."[37]
Specifically, it is necessary to understand how the practico-
inert's production of the individual as a *means* toward realizing the counter-finalities of the material field both utilizes *and*
preserves the individual's own practical production of his or
her self as an irreducible moment in that process. As Sartre
emphasizes, "Freedom, in this context, does not mean the

possibility of choice, but the necessity of living these constraints in the form of exigencies which must be fulfilled by a
praxis."[38] We live the practico-inert not as a field of possibilities for self-determination, but as a network of material
exigencies, of needs and demands inscribed in matter to
which we must submit.

The exigent character of the practico-inert holds the key
to the problem. For it is a hybrid product of the totalizing
freedom of praxis and the inert constraints of worked-
matter.

> Material exigency comes to the machine through man
> to precisely the extent that it comes to man through
> the machine. . . . exigency is *always* both man as a
> practical agent and matter as a worked product in an
> indivisible symbiosis.[39]

The requirements of a particular machine to be worked at a
certain rate, with a particular level of skill and knowledge of
its operation, only exist as demands in relation to the complex social network of production in which it functions. Its
exigent character does not inhere in it as a material object
divorced from the praxis that works it. It demands something of us only in the way it is situated in relation to the
practical field as a whole and the social ensemble designated
by that field. Material exigencies only emerge through the
praxis which works with that material in terms of the conditions it places on that work. In this way, they come "to the
machine through man to precisely the extent [they come] to
man through the machine." Their status is practico-inert.
That is, they exist only in terms of the practices that sustain
them as a dimension of material inertia at the heart of
praxis—as a demand on its future.

The constraints of the practico-inert, its power to organize and govern conduct, are lived, therefore, as practical
norms—categorical imperatives imposing untranscendable
duties on the individual:[40] "Thou *shalt* be at work at 9:00 A.M
and work in a prescribed manner till 5:00," "Thou *shalt not*
drive home on the wrong side of the road," etc. At the level
of our serial individuality, of our separate, day-to-day,

practico-inert lives as any other worker or commuter in relation to any other worker or commuter, we encounter an in-
numerable array of such prescriptions. They govern our conduct precisely insofar as they determine an anonymous
future or telos for our action which is given as "having-to-be"
realized, as practically imperative. Sartre himself is emphatic
concerning their categorical quality. For the exigencies of the
practico-inert are not presented hypothetically, with a structure of, "If you want Y, then you ought to do X." It is not a
question of, "If you want your wages . . . ," or, "If you don't
want to be fined . . . ," as if one were being threatened into
submission.[41] Things *just are* a certain way and one is expected to behave appropriately.

> In the milieu of organic life as the absolute positing of
> itself the sole aim of *praxis* is the indefinite reproduc-
> tion of life. Insofar as the means of subsistence are
> determined by society itself, together with the types
> of activity which will allow them to be procured ei-
> ther directly or indirectly . . . the vital tension of the
> practical field effectively results in exigency being
> presented as a categorical imperative.[42]

The practico-inert, as with every field of practical endeav-
or, is a fusion of fact and duty. De facto historical conditions
are lived as duties by the praxis that assumes them and projects a future on that basis. In discussing Flaubert, for instance, Sartre draws attention to how social structures
which, from the perspective of the historian or sociologist,
are contingent facts,[43] prescribe a future for Gustave that he
must assume as an obligation. He writes,

> Bourgeois, son être-bourgeois est défini par la totalité
> des carrières qui représentent à la fois ses chances et
> son devoir de se faire le bourgeois qu'il est. . . . Dans
> toute activité humaine le fait et le droit sont insép-
> arablement mêlés.[44]

The historical possibilities of our class for a range of careers
or, for that matter, of any tightly structured field of possibilities which are bound up with the conditions of one's
livelihood, are never possibilities which we may or may not

choose to realize, as we may or may not choose to buy a Coke or a Pepsi. They *are* possibilities, but possibilities which, in some form or other, we are *obliged* to realize. They impose themselves neither as mere invitations to nor as coercive violations of freedom, but rather as obligations on freedom. Praxis conditions its social-historical conditioning through having to appropriate its de facto milieu as a normatively structured field of practical obligations.

Sartre's idea of the practico-inert as a field of lived imperatives provides the beginnings of an answer to the question posed in chapter 1 concerning necessity. For the imperatives of the practico-inert constitute a level of normative necessity at the heart of historical contingency—of contingency *lived as* necessity. Sartre elaborates on this idea in his essay on Kierkegaard:

> The contingency of our being is the beginning; our necessity only appears through the act which assumes this contingency in order to give it a *human meaning*, in other words to make of it a singular relationship to the Whole, a singular embodiment of the ongoing totalization which envelops and produces it. . . . Thus the web of subjective life . . . is nothing other than the freedom that institutes the finite and is lived in finitude as inflexible necessity.[45]

The situation in which we find ourselves is always a bundle of historical and material accidents. My body, my family, and my class are all contingent events which need not have occurred as they did. There is no reason for one's bourgeois or working-class origins. They are simply accidents of birth. But once they are practically appropriated as the conditions upon which one produces oneself in this or that way, they assume an irreducible significance. Working-class origins become a practical limitation (one cannot afford the cultural possibilities accessible to others of bourgeois origin) and positive determination of a style of life ("We shall think *with* these original deviations, we shall act *with* these gestures which we have learned and which we want to reject."[46]), and in this way come to define a sense or direction for one's life which one is *obliged* to come to terms with as a *free* agent. Thus, the contingency of historical circumstances is lived as the necessity of a practical obligation—of a freely assumed 'indebtedness' to those circumstances which affords no court of appeal.

> Necessity . . . resides neither in the free development of interiority nor in the inert dispersal of exteriority; it asserts itself, as an inevitable and irreducible moment, in the interiorisation of the exterior and in the exteriorisation of the interior.[47]

It should come as no surprise, then, that "the first practical experience of necessity"[48] would be formed in terms of the counter-finalities of the practico-inert. For it is there that Sartre's critical investigation first encounters an end which is imposed on praxis from the outside. Considered abstractly (that is, apart from their dialectical connection), the "inert dispersal of exteriority" exhibits only the rigidity of more-or-less strict, but always contingent, associations, while the "free development of interiority" only manifests a translucid projection of ends which depend on the whims of our needs and desires. Only with the interiorization of inert exteriority and the exteriorization of this interiorization as a concrete material praxis, totalizing *and* totalized by its material field, does one discover goals and objectives that function as imperatives. Indeed, Sartre goes so far as to identify ethical values with the interiorization of practico-inert exigencies[49] and, more importantly, for this investigation, to include "'scientific' necessity—that is to say, the modality of certain chains of exact propositions"[50]—under this general rubric as well. Both ethical and epistemic necessity are, for Sartre, instances of the conditions of praxis lived as normative obligations on that praxis. Both senses of "getting things right" only emerge as inert determinations of our practical appropriation of material circumstances.

Autonomy and Heteronomy as Two Dimensions of Praxis

To return to the initial question, it is clear that the practico-inert production of the individual as a means to *its* ends cannot be accomplished at the expense of freedom, but in fact, presupposes freedom as its unwitting accomplice.[51] Reframing the discussion in terms of Foucault's concept of power, the individual's free practical production of him- or herself is seen to be an *irreducible* moment in the operation of power that governs them. Restricting the context even further to the social practice of knowledge, Sartre's position only serves to reinforce Foucault's basic thesis that knowledge can be used by and serve to articulate the deployment of power. As with any praxis, knowledge is always susceptible to being caught up in and utilized as a means in a network of counter-finalities which subvert its best intentions. But there is no longer any question of its reduction to a *mere effect* or subterfuge of power, for power governs the practice of knowledge only insofar as it is interiorized by that praxis as a set of imperatives according to which it must constrain itself. There is preserved in this account a sense of autonomy proper to knowledge as "an action which gives itself its own rules by revealing them as exigencies in the object,"[52] consistent with its heteronomous relations with power.

Through conceiving praxis as a material totalization, as an interiorization of exteriority and exteriorization of interiority, the dichotomy of autonomy or heteronomy is undercut. Their disjunction is rendered inclusive in terms of the dialectical relation of the interior and exterior dimensions of praxis. As a way of "making something out of what has been made of us," praxis includes both its determination as a material being among other material beings *and* its own self-determination on this basis as a practical totalization of its material circumstances. In this way, the nonepistemic dimensions of the practice of knowledge can be properly recognized as determinations of that knowledge without reducing knowledge to an empirical product of these historical contingencies. Knowledge maintains its autonomy as a *responsible* practice able to give a rational account of itself in terms of its own epistemic norms. For though the practice of knowledge is sustained by and sustains relations of power; though its very form and style of operation are determined by and determinative of a form of "government," its *norma-*

tive regulation of itself constitutes a level of rational self-determination that must be accounted for on its own terms, as a process of giving and asking for reasons. Certainly, one may abstract from this interior dimension, as Foucault does, and simply analyze the external relations of constraint and subjection instituted through its practice. But if that practice is to be understood as power *and knowledge* together, directly implying each other in a process which reduces neither to the other, one must recognize the interior dimension of the practice of knowledge—its rational self-determination according to its own epistemic norms—as a methodologically irreducible level in its analysis. Giving and asking for reasons must be analyzed as an autonomous process proceeding according to its own *normative* principles. Granting this, however, the political economy of knowledge may still be analyzed through asking how the de facto constraints of power are interiorized by the practice of knowledge as it responds to and develops in terms of the exigencies of its particular historical situation, and how that practice exteriorizes itself as a material enhancement of and/or deviation within the power relations that condition it.

In short, one must refuse to collapse an analysis of the self-determination of a practice according to *norms* into an empirical description of the *facts* of its social-historical constitution. In this way it can be seen how knowledge, precisely insofar as it is rational, is conditioned by and sustains particular relations of power, without being reduced to a mere effect of these contingent historical states of affairs. Through adopting a dialectical model of the relation of power and knowledge, this most immediate sceptical challenge to Foucault's analysis may be defused by rejecting any temptation toward an empirical treatment of reason. Knowledge maintains its autonomy as a product of rational inquiry. Its heteronomous relations with power, far from erasing this autonomy, presuppose it, just as the operations of the practico-inert presuppose the autonomy of free practical agents.

All this is not to say, of course, that Foucault *would* have had anything to do with any of this. Foucault's hostility to dialectical thought and his linking of the crucial notion of totalization with the preservation of "continuous history [as] the indispensable correlative of the founding function of the subject,"[53] would, no doubt, prevent any easy rapprochement between his approach and that of Sartre. And though I would argue that Foucault misunderstood this notion as Sartre employs it, particularly in overlooking the way in which totalization is always effectively detotalized by the social and material field in which it finds itself,[54] still, this is neither the time nor the place to argue that Foucault *could* have accepted Sartre's position. The point is simply that Sartre's notion of praxis makes possible an understanding of the relation of power and knowledge that is capable of preserving Foucault's basic thesis of a "political economy of truth" while undercutting the most obviously sceptical epistemological implications of that position. For, as noted in the last chapter, it is Foucault's incipient positivism which forces him to approach knowledge as a sociological fact, correlated in certain determinate ways with another sociological fact— power. Conclusively abandoning this positivism allows access to a different way of conceptualizing their relation that avoids treating knowledge as a set of de facto discursive regularities controlled, in some way or other, by power. Through understanding knowledge as a normatively self-regulating social practice, determining itself on the basis of power relations it must conserve as much as it surpasses, it is possible to preserve an irreducible dimension of necessity at the heart of historical contingency and begin to grasp how knowledge may be described simultaneously, without inconsistency, from both a political and epistemic perspective, as power *and* knowledge.

Chapter 5

Knowledge as
a Social Practice

From Foucault we receive an account of the relation between knowledge and power which undercuts our traditional conception of knowledge as the "pure reward of free spirits." From Sartre we receive an account of praxis which is capable of handling this relation in a nonreductive fashion. Together they present an account of knowledge as a social practice, regulating itself in terms of epistemic norms formed on the basis of nonepistemic conditions. Power, as a mobile set of practico-inert relations that form the material basis of our social being, conditions the practice of knowledge in the three ways considered in chapter 3; as condition, effect and internal regime. The practice of the examination, for instance, and the truths about the individual it produces, are made possible by the practico-inert exigencies of the disciplinary technologies whose operation it refines and focuses. The material, nonepistemic requirements of the hospital, workplace, school and prison are interiorized in the epistemic practices formed there as norms which reproduce, as it were, their relations of power in terms of positions of epistemic authority—determinations of who may say or claim to know what under what circumstances. The power that subordinates the subject of discipline to an analytical grid of discrete motions and performances is interiorized as the epistemic appropriateness of restricting knowledgeable utterances to a correlative grid of "objective" behaviors and test scores. The power that incites the individual to speak of his or her pleasures and desires is interiorized in terms of an expansion of evidential norms to include subjective accounts as symptoms of underlying psychological pathologies. In both cases, the material exigencies of an emerging technology of government demand certain forms of knowledge appropriate to their operation, and these exigencies are interiorized as norms governing the practice of that knowledge.

In a passage I have already referred to, Sartre writes,

> It would be easy to show how so-called "scientific" necessity—that is to say, the modality of certain chains of exact propositions—comes to science *through* practice and *by it* as the limit negation, through exteriority, of the dialectic, and how it appears by means of free dialectical research as its real and always Other objectification.[1]

The necessity of a set of scientific propositions, the epistemic appropriateness of their form and sequence, is a practico-inert limit of scientific practice—its free appropriation of material limitations as normative duties. Power, therefore, conditions knowledge by making it possible, is interiorized by knowledge as epistemic norms regulating the production of scientific discourse (as, that is, internal regime), and is exteriorized in terms of a more efficient operation of power itself.

Two Senses of Normative Necessity

The form which the practice of knowledge may take, however, varies with the status of the norms it employs and the mode of necessity it institutes. In an unpublished manuscript only recently discovered and summarized by Robert Stone and Elizabeth Bowman,[2] Sartre distinguishes between alienated norms that prescribe a future that merely repeats the past practices of others, and norms that "prescribe acts, and hence futures, that are given as unconditionally possible."[3] Thus far I have considered only the first sort of norm. Sartre calls them values or imperatives[4] and limits their status to that of practico-inert exigencies, lived by praxis as an obligation of worked-matter on its future. Such alienated norms presuppose, however, their unalienated variety,

which is identical with the normative structure of praxis itself positing its own ends on the basis of its material needs.

Need, as the most elementary structure of practical transcendence, is at the root of normative necessity.[5] Positing its
ends in terms of the satisfaction of need and regulating itself
on this basis, praxis gives itself norms as the unconditioned
possibility of making itself, not in terms of the material exigencies of the practico-inert, but in terms of the autonomous
satisfaction of its *own* needs. Sartre writes, "La véritable éthique fond et dissont les morales aliénées, en ce qu'elle est le
sens de l'histoire: c'est- à-dire le refus de toute répétition au
nom de la possibilitié inconditionnée de FAIRE L'HOMME."[6]
This more fundamental sense of the normative may not be
defined, however, in terms of any formal set of rules of conduct derived, as it were, from the "essence" of praxis as
opposed to the traditions of history.[7] It is, rather, the very
movement of praxis determining itself as "the unconditioned
possibility of making man"—praxis as autonomous self-
determination.

This dimension of the normative both grounds and dissolves the alienated imperatives of the practico-inert in that,
(1) it is structurally presupposed in those imperatives. The
free self-determination or autonomy of praxis is a condition
of any inert system of alienated values. Autonomy is never
canceled or destroyed in its alienation, but only used and
inverted toward *other* ends. And, (2) it is this very movement
of free self-determination that, through becoming a revolutionary praxis, is capable of overturning its practico-inert
destiny and producing itself in the light of its own ends. This
last sense of the normative as revolutionary praxis ties in
with the second experience of necessity[8] Sartre uncovers in
the *Critique*, that of the group as "the equivalence of freedom
as necessity and of necessity as freedom," of "freedom . . . manifested as the necessity of dissolving necessity."[9] For the group, as Sartre understands it, emerges as a
practical organization of a social ensemble *against* their isolated, serial destinies in the practico-inert. It is, therefore, by
definition, a revolutionary struggle against the alienated
norms of practico-inert existence. The freedom of every iso-

lated, serial individual[10] which is used and distorted by the practico-inert, is reconstructed at the more complex level of the group as insurrection, aimed at the dissolution of its alienation. It is not, for this reason, the same as the freedom of individual praxis, considered abstractly, as a solitary production of a practical field in the light of its needs. The freedom of the group, its praxis, must be a coordination of its various individual tasks and subordination of isolated partial objectives to the common end, interiorized by all as their own. The common end must be freely adopted by everyone as "the necessity of dissolving necessity," and so, as a normative project of unconditional self-determination at the level of the group as a whole.

The solitary freedom of the serial individual to be used according to *other* practico-inert exigencies is exchanged for freely adopting the necessity of the group praxis as a possibility of collective self-determination. This collective[11] necessity is instituted in terms of what Sartre calls "the pledge"—a kind of oath of allegiance in which everyone "swear[s] so as to make the Others swear . . . so as to guarantee oneself against the possibility that they will disperse . . . [and] in order to protect oneself against oneself in the Others."[12] The pledge is a guarantee both to oneself and to the others that one will not abandon the group. Structurally, it is just that level of group praxis in which everyone is obligated to everyone else to maintain their commitments to the group. As such it need never be explicitly instituted as an oath, but may only be embodied in a practical milieu of "fraternity and fear"[13] in which the others are granted a power over one's life and everyone can, more or less, count on everyone else as a comrade in and through that power. In this way, a new form of inert exigency is produced in that

> I become in everyone the *transcended condition of free praxis* (sure of myself and of the Others, no one need concern himself with anything outside his specialized task) and, in so far as this free common *praxis* returns to me as a condition of *my own freedom* (I, too, must

rely on them in performing my task, either on my own or in a sub-group), it constitutes the untranscendability of being-in-the-group as *an exigency*.[14]

The exigency of the pledge makes possible and is further elaborated by the distribution of concrete functions in organized groups and the network of reciprocal rights and duties this implies (my right to expect others to carry out their functionally designated duties and vice versa).[15] A complex structure of inert reciprocities[16] is formed as the social condition of one's functionally designated praxis. One's task is conditioned by its relations with all the others and given to one as one's duty to the group. One must be careful, though, not to confuse this sense of necessity with that of the practico-inert. Clearly, they resemble each other in that they are both inert determinations of praxis which arise on a strictly social basis. As Sartre writes, "It would be absurd to suppose that an individual freedom could be limited *by itself* . . . since *praxis* is the transcendence of conditions. . . ."[17] All practical necessity is a function of my relation to others. The very idea of a *solitary* praxis giving itself its own norms outside all social conditions is tantamount to a pure freedom willing itself to be whatever it desires, irrespective of any limiting conditions—an imaginary freedom. Even the "unconditioned possibility" of autonomous self-determination is, for Sartre, a social possibility. "L'histoire n'a de réalité que par la possibilité inconditionnée pour l'homme de se réaliser dans sa pleine autonomie: comme praxis, dissolvant en son sein le practico-inerte à mesure qu'il se produit. Comme praxis de tous les hommes associés."[18] And as inherently social, all necessity shares a dimension of alterity[19] in which each individual is conditioned in his or her individuality as an *other* in relation to all *others*. But, whereas, this alterity is a function of material contingency at the level of the practico-inert, in the group "alterity is a relation defined by a rule, in conformity with a praxis. . . ."[20] The alterity of one's functional membership in an organized group is produced according to a practical rule where one's dependence on the others is no longer a practical impotence to escape one's inert destiny, but a practical empowerment to achieve common ends impossible in isolation. The practico-inert limitations of the serial individual are overthrown in favor of the "enriching limitation[s]"[21] of the "common individual"—the individual as a member of a group carrying out functionally defined tasks coordinated in relation to a common end.

Both the serial and the common individual act on and interiorize inert conditions which limit their endeavors, and are lived as normatively prescribed futures. But, for the serial individual, activity is a means of the passive exigencies of the practico-inert. For the common individual the passivity of the distribution of roles that condition his or her specific function in the group is a means in the development of the group praxis which each interiorizes as his or her own. In the first case, activity is a means of passivity, whereas in the second, passivity is a controlled moment of free activity. Sartre writes,

> the conditioning of functions by each other (once their synthetic, reflexive determination is complete) takes place in exteriority, as in the physical world. However, it is important to recognize that this skeleton (of inert reciprocities) is sustained by all the common individuals and that it is always possible for the group, as totalising action, under the pressure of new circumstances, to dissolve it entirely. . . . this necessity, as exteriority structuring interiority, is simply the obverse of the practico-inert: the latter effectively appeared as passive activity, whereas the former constitutes itself as active passivity.[22]

The active passivity of the group, inertia structured and controlled according to the needs and objectives of the group praxis, is the only possible realization of norms as instances of autonomous practical self-determination, "comme praxis, dissolvant en son sein le practico-inerte à mesure qu'il se produit. Comme praxis de tous les hommes associés." For it is only as action in common that autonomy can be realized without alienating itself in the counter-finalities of worked-matter.[23] It is only in and through the constraints of the reciprocal rights and duties of the group that freedom is realizable *in practice*.

Knowledge and Belief

The practice of knowledge may, therefore, be organized along either of these lines: as the alienated practice of a practico-inert collective[24] or as the revolutionary practice of a group struggling against the practico-inert. This practical distinction, moreover, gives rise to an *epistemic* distinction which Sartre fleshes out as that between mere belief and knowledge proper.[25] Sartre would, no doubt, find the discussion so far of both these forms *as knowledge* (without qualification) misleading. Alienated 'knowledge' is only a form of systemic credulity, an arrested moment in the production of knowledge proper.[26] The practice of knowledge presupposes belief as a surpassed moment in its production, but in its nonalienated realization, "rigorously excludes belief."[27] In speaking of the practice of knowledge *in general*, therefore, one must be careful to distinguish its arrested instantiation as belief from its full realization as knowledge proper.

Sartre's most extensive discussion of this distinction can be found in his account of Flaubert's *"maladie de la Vérité"*,[28] his "disease of Truth," in *The Family Idiot*. He characterizes Flaubert there as an individual practically incapable of engaging in the enterprise of knowledge proper. Gustave is trapped in a world where things are taken completely on the authority of others. He submits to the declarations of others, unable to actively or critically appropriate them for himself in the light of evidence. He "tastes" things but does not know them.[29]

> Not that the thing is not there, nor that he doesn't see or touch it; he enjoys it with all his senses. But he fails to unveil [dévoile] it as *object* since he doesn't engage

in the enterprise of attempting to classify it in the herbarium of knowledge.[30]

The object as classified in the "herbarium of knowledge" eludes him to the extent that self-affirmative praxis is impossible for him. For, as Sartre explains it, Flaubert was never valorized by his family as someone with a "mandate to live,"[31] as one with a mission and worth in relation to that mission. Consequently, he is unable to affirm himself in reciprocity with others and "can under no circumstances consider himself a solid link in a chain of collective operations,"[32] such as that collective operation that is knowledge. He learns the language of knowledge by rote and mimics its exercise. But it always remains for him the property of others. He must submit to it when questioned by adults, but it does not engage him actively, for he is unable to submit their authority to the critical test of evidence, by affirming himself in reciprocity with them as competent to critically examine their claims. He replaces evidence with "pathic enjoyment,"[33] with a faith "proportional to the importance of the speaker, that is to say to his affirmative power."[34] The knowledge of others is suffered by Flaubert as the authority of belief.

Flaubert is, of course, an extreme example of someone trapped at the level of belief, unable to know anything at all. Belief is usually a more-or-less *provisional* aspect of knowing as when we, say, believe on the authority of a doctor that our condition will improve in a week or so if we stay in bed, drink plenty of fluids, etc., but will seek second opinions and more information so as to critically assess our doctor's judgement, if we get worse. Still, Flaubert's case is useful in highlighting the general structure of belief qua belief, of which the most salient point is its uncritical reliance on *authority*. Authority is a practical relation which I have not yet discussed for it represents the reemergence of seriality and impotence in an organized group and its consequent transformation into what Sartre refers to as an "institutional group."[35] The institutional group, for Sartre, is at the dividing line between the group and its deterioration back into a practico-inert collective. It is, as it were, the group in the process of petrification, where "goals lose their teleological character . . . [and] without ceasing to be genuine goals . . . become destinies."[36]

Authority is, therefore, a more complex version of the sort of alienation found in the practico-inert. It may be described as a concentration of sovereignty into the hands of a single or fixed set of common individuals. In the group, prior to the emergence of *authority*, sovereignty belongs with everyone as their reciprocal regulatory power over each other through the common praxis. That is, every member of the group is a "third party" to everyone else, integrating them as the means to a common end they have all adopted. But this regulatory action is not isolated. It is repeated in the praxis of all group members, totalizing the group (and recognizing themselves as totalized by others as "in the group") in the light of their shared objectives. Sovereignty is, thus, better described as "quasi sovereignty"[37] inasmuch as everyone's praxis both *regulates* and *is regulated by* the praxis of the others. At a practical level this implies an absence of leaders in the sense of those whose orders are to be obeyed. Because of the reciprocity of the group, mediated by the common objectives they share, "orders" are "simply the common *praxis* becoming, in some third party, regulatory of itself in me and in all the other third parties, in the movement of a totalisation which totalises me and everyone else."[38] Insofar as we are all *the same*, as members of a group working toward objectives held in common, the other simply accomplishes through the order given "over there" what I would do myself if I weren't "over here."

Sovereignty is institutionalized as authority when the exigencies of the functional organization of the group begin to overpower the praxis of the individuals who have produced them. As new counter-finalities emerge in the group, function is transformed into destiny and the impossibility of change. In this process of group petrification, sovereignty ceases to be fluid, moving from place to place as the needs of the group praxis demand, and becomes installed in permanent positions of power over others. Authority is, therefore, the death of reciprocity in that I am regulated by those with authority, but they are not regulated by me.

Belief, similarly, implies an absence of reciprocity. I take on authority what I have been told. The other's claim is regulative for me, but I no longer assert a regulative claim on the other, for that would entail an "end to authority,"[39] as Sartre understands it, in a critical examination of that claim in the light of evidence. At the level of belief, ideas are merely serial commodities whose epistemic value is only the degree of credibility they can be exchanged for in the other.

> These are the rules of belief: what everyone believes of the Other is what the Other conveys in so far as he is Other (or in so far as the news comes to him already from an Other). In other words, it is negative information in that neither the person who receives it, nor the one who gives it, could or can verify it.[40]

The serial ideas of belief are, therefore, not so much thoughts[41] as they are commodities in circulation, never intended to serve as a "unifying unveiling of objects in the dialectical temporalisation of action,"[42] but only as an inert bond between serialized individuals. Sartre mentions racist ideas as an example.[43] Inevitably repetitious and vague in what little content they have ("*They*"—plug in whatever racial or ethnic group is currently in disdain: Blacks, Jews, Arabs, etc.—"are dirty, are lazy, cheat, can't be trusted, . . . "), their indubitability to the racist is simply the degree to which none of the others ever questions them. Indeed, they do not function as claims which might be open to question; which is why questioning racism at an intellectual level never does any good—it is simply irrelevant. They function as practico-inert exigencies, which realize an inert unity for the collective in and through the obligations of typical sorts of conduct they impose. Nothing more than this unity in exteriority is ever achieved, for they do not function as a basis for the critical reciprocity of a group praxis. Detached in this way from the possibilities of group reciprocity, the "rules of belief" can only be those of alterity and 'validation' will necessarily rest on the authority of others—on what "they" believe.[44]

Knowledge, in its proper sense, involves an "elimination of all alterity"[45] and the democratization of authority in the reciprocity of a critical practice based on evidence. Like the revolutionary praxis of the group, knowledge begins with alterity; in this case, the alterity of belief or 'received opinion'. As Sartre notes,

> You have to begin with credence or to deny man—you make a fool of yourself in the beginning, but so what? . . . This first moment, one man's confidence in another—is immediately passed over [*se dépasse*] on the way to reciprocity: I sovereignly affirm what is sovereignly affirmed to me. However, I would continually be taken in by lies, fallacies, if I did not have at my disposal [—in principle if not in each case—] genuine *reducing agents* [*réducteurs*].* Or rather, I have only one, though it varies constantly: evidence. This means that I reclaim the affirmation from the Other, according to its requirements [*exigence*] but in the presence of the thing, through my intuition of it. Belief automatically disappears—it yields to the act. Now I *know*. . . .[46]

Knowledge is formed as a practical operation carried out on the collective ground of belief. We must begin with what others have said—with knowledge as a historically sedimented tradition encompassing both the 'stock of knowledge' or 'received opinion' taken for granted by the community one is engaged to as well as the epistemic norms which have governed the acquisition and validation of that "stock." As with any praxis, the conditions of our epistemic practices are historical. But again, as with any praxis, the important thing is not only what others have made of us, but what we are able to make of what they have made of us. The second essential moment of knowledge is, therefore, our practical appropriation of the tradition in the light of evidence.

Evidence, like knowledge itself, has two components: (1) the exigencies of the belief submitted to critical examination;

and (2) an intuition of the object of concern, which Sartre describes elsewhere as a practical unveiling (un dévoilement pratique).[47] This two-sided character of evidence is echoed elsewhere in the *Family Idiot*, where he speaks of "truth as an enterprise" of "ces clartés actives—intuition et serment mêles—que *décident* ce qu'elles *constatent*."[48] That evidence which decides what it establishes or verifies is a mixture of intuition and *serment*, the French word translated in the English edition of the *Critique* as "pledge." Evidence requires an intuitive unveiling of "the things themselves,"[49] but this unveiling is a practical enterprise determined by the epistemic norms of the group one is pledged to. Sartre's point here is, I believe, simply that no intuitive presence can, in and of itself, count as evidence for one's belief. It is also necessary that it be the *right* sort of thing that our community would acknowledge as *appropriate* to count as evidence. My intuitive presence to a grey pair of pants will not count as evidence for the assertion, "There is a grey pair of pants," if I know myself to be color blind. None of my color-relevant perceptions will, in that case, carry much, if any, epistemic value at all. And no one's intuitive presence to a screen with various spots of light on it will count as evidence for much of anything unless they have been trained to decipher those spots of light in an appropriate way as "planes in the sky," "incoming missiles," or what have you. Intuitions require norms that determine whether or not they are appropriate to count as evidence for some range of assertions. Sartre's theory of evidence here reflects a move away from his earlier phenomenological equation of knowledge and intuition, understood as "the presence of the thing (Sache) 'in person' to consciousness."[50] Evidence is more than Husserl's "mental seeing of something itself."[51] It involves a reference to the exigencies of the specific belief under consideration, and so to the epistemic norms of one's pledged group which determine appropriate procedures for examining that belief, as well as the range of possible intuitions which may count as evidence for it. It would appear, therefore, that Sartre has joined with Sellars in abandoning the "myth of the given."[52]

"Truth," Sartre writes, "is normative because fidelity to

logical 'principles' is only a form of fidelity to the pledge."[53] The epistemic norms of the group I am pledged to, everything from the logical principles that prescribe certain forms of inference to the degree of reliability it affords its scientific instruments, provide a basis upon which we may share a body of evidence and examine in critical reciprocity our shared beliefs, and even, should it become warranted, those norms themselves. If we should, for instance, find certain rules of evidence to be so restrictive that they do not permit significant questions to be adequately decided, we may come as a group to discard or enlarge those rules, on the basis of the evidence (or *lack* thereof) they make possible. There is, therefore, a dialectical relation in evidence between the pledge and intuition that makes possible *both* knowledge as a shared tradition *and* knowledge as a critical-reciprocal transcendence of that tradition. This, in turn, allows one to understand how epistemic norms may possess a sense of *authority* (though I doubt Sartre would call it that) that is not alienating, precisely because that authority rests on and makes possible a critical and reciprocal appeal to evidence in the light of which it may be assessed. The epistemic norms of a community engaged in the practice of knowledge, in its proper sense, has the same status as pledged inertia in a group—it is a form of active passivity, inertia directed and controlled by the practice of all the common individuals who together constitute that group. As a social practice, knowledge is, therefore, a rule-governed endeavor that makes it possible for those participating in it to determine its structure and content for themselves through a practice of critical reciprocity that may put the authority of any claim in question—which means that, in principle, it opens up the authority of every claim to the questions of any participant in that practice.

Critical Reciprocity and the Politics of Knowledge: Lyotard

As discussed at the end of chapter 4, Sartre's account of praxis allows one to describe *knowledge* from both an epistemic and social-political perspective as a social practice which simultaneously institutes relations of power and knowledge. Such a nonreductive, hybrid description is to be found in his account of knowledge as the "elimination of alterity" in the praxis of a group. "Truth is *both* a controlled, practical decoding of objectivity *and* a determination of sociality in interiority . . . the first fixes certain abstract conditions for an integration which is the only possible source of its concrete meaning."[54] Knowledge is both a critical-intuitive relation to objectivity on the basis of epistemic norms *and* a practice of mediated reciprocity in the group which, to the extent it is possible, eliminates alterity and allows for a heightened integration of everyone in the group, in terms of the common praxis to which they are engaged. These two descriptive registers are not, moreover, parallel to one another, as if one might go back and forth between a purely epistemological and purely sociological description, the one never encroaching upon the logical space of the other. The social-political organization of knowledge is immediately an object of epistemological concern and the epistemological status of knowledge is immediately a social-political affair.

This is most apparent in the relation between reciprocity and evidence. Possessing evidence for one's claims is clearly a matter of epistemological significance. It belongs without question to the 'context of justification'. Reciprocity, on the other hand, is a practical reality with social-political significance for the group that institutes it. But the political practice of reciprocity in a community is essential to a practice of knowledge which would substitute an appeal to evidence for an appeal to authority. Reciprocity in the practice of knowledge implies evidence—the right to ask for and the obligation to give reasons for one's claims—and evidence implies reciprocity—an opening up of the authority of one's claims to the critical examination of others. A lack of evidence for one's claims *is* the alienation of one's beliefs to the others and this alienation *is* a lack of evidence. The power relations that Foucault analyzes as an internal condition of knowledge are interiorized as either practico-inert or group norms, and this practical, political difference marks an epistemological difference between belief and knowledge proper that serves simultaneously as a basis for political *and* epistemological critique.

This point may be seen more clearly in the light of the political questions raised by Foucault's analysis of power-knowledge. For if power and knowledge are connected, the practice of knowledge raises not only the sorts of epistemological questions I have primarily addressed here as to how knowledge maintains a sense of autonomy under such heteronomous conditions, but political questions regarding how we ought to proceed in concrete social-historical circumstances with our "games of truth."[55] If knowledge is necessarily a moment in the deployment of power, we need to be able to draw political distinctions between just and unjust epistemic regimes, to form responsible judgments that concern not only the epistemic coherence of such regimes, but their political value as well. And it is here that Sartre's understanding of knowledge as a social practice, capable of totalizing the power relations that condition it in either a milieu of authority or reciprocity, is particularly helpful. For it is the reciprocity, or lack thereof, of the epistemic regime in question that simultaneously allows one to distinguish critical knowledge from doctrinaire dogma and an authoritarian deployment of power from a democratic one.

The role of reciprocity in any adequate assessment of the politics of knowledge may be seen concretely in terms of what Jean-François Lyotard has analyzed in *The Postmodern Condition* as the contemporary tendency to legitimate or justify the worth of knowledge through its economic or political "performativity." With the increasing technological complexity and costs of research, the practice of knowledge has come increasingly under the domination of those who have the money to fund it, principally private corporations and the State. This in turn makes the legitimation of knowledge increasingly a matter of establishing its economic or political worth, its capacity to perform by way of contributing to the economic or political power of those who fund it. As Lyotard succinctly notes, "no money, no proof—and that means no verification of statements and no truth."[56] Performativity could be said, then, to establish the pragmatic limits of acceptable scientific discourse—a limit which culminates in "the decision maker's arrogance . . . 'Adapt your aspirations to our ends—or else.'"[57]

As a way of challenging this coercive and authoritarian state of affairs, Lyotard proposes to think of the legitimation of knowledge in terms of its potential for "paralogy"—its capacity to anticipate anomalies, generate novelty, and generally, to creatively expand the limits of acceptable "true" discourse. The essential effect of his suggestion is to fundamentally rethink what it means to secure the worth of our epistemic practices. Rather than looking to justify our established rules of inquiry, we should think of the worth of an epistemic practice in terms of its ability to foster experimental modes of thought that transgress those established rules in creative ways. The performative stability of knowledge is subverted in this way through a permanent "petition"[58] to transgress the rules that define the limits of acceptable epistemic discourse, in search of novel and imaginative discursive possibilities. The claims of power are to be challenged, then, through the institution of a kind of permanent epistemic revolution.

Lyotard's analysis of performativity and his ideas concerning paralogy demonstrate the necessity of a critical analysis of the politics of knowledge, an analysis that would establish a basis for a political challenge to the claims of power intrinsic to knowledge as a social practice. His own proposals, however, are inadequate to that end. For power is not necessarily subverted through giving an unqualified license to novelty, experimentation, and the transgression of rules. As Foucault correctly emphasized, power does not reside in a static set of institutions or prohibitive injunctions. It is, rather, the fluid product of a multiplicity of actions; a concatenation of the diverse constraints which a multiplicity of actions have on each other. And as sexual novelty, experimentation and the transgression of mores did not, as Foucault argues, liberate sexual desire from power, so neither would such a strategy liberate the social practice of knowledge. Rather, just as sexual paralogy was co-opted by the normalizing discourse of the social sciences which provided a psychological ethic of sexual liberation in terms of the "true" expression of desire,[59] so it is not hard to imagine scientific paralogy becoming co-opted by the demands of performativity, which could easily encourage a boundless innovation with epistemic norms in terms of an ethic of increased performance.

Lyotard's concerns suggest, however, that a discursive practice that is accepted without question, that is subordinate to the "the decision maker's arrogance," that is imposed, in short, only on its own authority, is both epistemologically and politically illegitimate.[60] This, in turn, brings us to the issue overlooked in Lyotard's proposals—that of reciprocity as a nonauthoritarian totalization of the power relations that condition any epistemic regime. For the capacity to ask for evidence for an epistemic claim and the obligation to give it upon request—the practice of giving and asking for reasons—is, at a pragmatic level, a rejection of the demands of authority and the imperatives of power. The emergence of such epistemic reciprocity is both a demand for *reasons*, at the level of the adjudication of truth claims, and for *justice*, at the level of the practical relations that obtain between those who put forward such claims and those who would question them. The inadequacy of Lyotard's concept of paralogy as a challenge to authority lies in its inability to coherently raise this demand for epistemic reciprocity. Through a myopic preoccupation with fostering experimentation and change, Lyotard completely disregards the character of the *practical relations* which are instituted in that experimentation and change. Change is, after all, sometimes for the worse. Sartre's understanding of knowledge proper as a practice of reciprocity provides a critical basis for this judgement. Change is for the worse when it significantly erodes the capacity of an epistemic community to reciprocally challenge one another's claims. Legitimating the contemporary production of knowledge in relation to its performativity is illegitimate, both politically and epistemologically, in that it places the norms of inquiry outside the range of critical and reciprocal accountability.

This suggests that Sartre's distinction between knowledge proper and mere belief, between a practice that totalizes power as relations of authority and a practice that totalizes power as relations of reciprocity, may serve as a more adequate model of epistemic legitimation than Lyotard's one-sided notion of paralogy. In fact, when Lyotard comes, at the end of *The Postmodern Condition*, to propose giving the public free access to all data banks, his proposal evokes primarily not the fostering of paralogy, but the institution of a form of reciprocity. For the aim of the proposal is to allow groups to raise questions of a body of knowledge that would otherwise be authoritative; to, as he says, "aid groups discussing metaprescriptives by supplying them with the information they usually lack for making knowledgeable decisions";[61] to, as I would put it, create the conditions for the possibility for groups to determine *for themselves* the modes and strategies of a discursive practice most appropriate to their specific aims and objectives. If groups and communities are to be able to challenge the claims of power in the practice of knowledge, it is not enough to legitimate innovation and experimentation, even at the level of the rules that regulate our epistemic practices, but to create the conditions necessary for groups to question authority; to demand reasons for claims that are promulgated as true; to be able to determine for themselves, in reciprocity, the forms of epistemic discourse appropriate to their pragmatic objectives and concerns. This would not sever the connection between power and knowledge. But it would create the necessary pragmatic conditions for a permanent critique of the claims of power, whatever they may be and however they may arise. Legitimate knowledge creates those conditions in a community through instituting, as Sartre puts it, "truth as a communal enterprise and a demand for reciprocity. . . ."[62]

Truth, on this account, may be construed both as an effect of the epistemic practices of the group, in that the institution of reciprocity makes it possible (and necessary) to *justify* one's claims as true on the basis of evidence, *and* a condition of those epistemic practices, in that the production of truth makes possible a dissolution of alterity, and consequently an enhanced integration of the group as an ensemble of individuals who relate to each other in critical reciprocity on the basis of that shared truth.[63] And, in this way, we are brought back to the issue of historical relativism with which we began. For though a Sartrean account of knowledge as a social practice avoids the immediately self-defeating relativism of epistemological empiricism in its preservation of a sense of rational necessity at the heart of historical contingency, the question still remains as to how truth, in any sense, might transcend the historical limitations of a given epistemic practice and emerge as "a case of validity in the timeless realm of Ideas."[64] The status of truth seems to be entirely social and practical, integrated inextricably with the historical practice that produces it. We have seen how the question of the being of knowledge may be resolved in a way which avoids the pitfalls of empiricism. We still want an answer to the other half of the problem—the question of the knowledge of being and its precise epistemological status. It is to this question that we must now turn in part 3 in order to assess the overall coherence of Sartre's epistemological position as both an account of knowledge as a social practice *and* a critique of dialectical reason as the "non-theoretical foundation"[65] of any theoretical knowledge.

Part III

Questions of Method

Chapter 6

The Case Against
Method: Rorty and Feyerabend

Sartre's account of the being of knowledge as a social practice seems to raise as many problems as it solves. Though a sense of rational necessity is rescued from the quagmire of historical contingency, this is accomplished only by apparently equating the rational necessity of a justified claim to truth with the historical necessity of a self-determining social practice. In this way, the question of the being of knowledge leads to that of the knowledge of being. For what epistemological status can now be granted to Sartre's account of the practice of knowledge itself? On its own terms, it would seem that the validity of any theoretical claim, including its own, is simply a matter of whether it is justifiable in relation to the particular norms that regulate the epistemic practices in terms of which it is produced. As a social practice, must not the validity of any claim to knowledge be relative to its own practical aims and objectives? Sartre's *Critique* is meant to establish dialectical reason as a universal method for the human sciences. But what sense can be made in that account of methodological constraints on the practice of knowledge other than that of a set of norms which that practice gives to itself in the light of its own interests? And surely the idea of *one* set of norms that would serve every interest which might ever arise in the human sciences is improbable at best, and at worst, incoherent. For if knowledge is a social practice, it is that practice which constrains the limits and validity of any norms which might regulate it, not vice versa.

The very idea of method is, from this perspective, nothing more than a pragmatic expediency in the social production of knowledge. Knowledge *is* practice and, as such, is constrained only by the limitations of what works. Expounding this point of view in their recent works, Richard Rorty and Paul Feyerabend have argued vigorously for the historical bankruptcy of every attempt to ground the practice of knowledge in any single set of rules or principles. "There is only *one* principle," Feyerabend argues, "that can be defended under *all* circumstances and in *all* stages of human development. It is the principle: *anything goes.*"[1] Feyerabend's point here is not that history shows us *no* instances of methodologically guided practice, but only that every method has its limits. A single scientific method would have arrested the growth of modern science which, by Feyerabend's account, has actually *presupposed* the persistent violation of what are usually taken to be well-grounded principles of scientific practice.[2] And, taking his point of departure from his reading of the history of philosophy, Rorty has argued for the futility of the very idea of epistemologically "grounding" a culture's epistemic practices.

> They [the pragmatists] regard the project of grounding as a wheel that plays no part in the mechanism. In this I think they are right. No sooner does one discover the categories of the pure understanding for a Newtonian age than somebody else draws up another for an Aristotelian or an Einsteinian one.[3]

Grounding a culture's practices is, on Rorty's account, a relatively easy matter. Coming along after the fact, all the philosopher need do is "jack up the practice a few levels of abstraction, and announce that he has grounded it."[4] Rorty recommends that we abandon such meta-practices, leaving our cultural practices on their own to prove their worth, through their own skill and inventiveness. We will look in vain, therefore, for an alternative theory of truth or knowledge in Rorty's pragmatism.[5] To advocate the language of practice in such matters; to say, as does James, that "the true is what is good in the way of belief," is just to say that nothing much more of interest can be said.[6] To say that knowledge is a matter of practice is just to say that it takes good care of itself, without the aid and comfort of an epistemological foundation which would rescue it once and for all from the limitations of its own particular time and place.

The Myth of the Given and Privileged Vocabularies: Rorty

Though grounded in such historical reflection, Rorty and Feyerabend's theoretical posture is clearly not exhausted by it. Their rejection of the transcendental presumptions of reason owes much, in particular, to their criticisms of the empiricist idea of a rigorous distinction between theory and experience—the idea of experience as an epistemological "given" capable of grounding a theoretical discourse without itself presupposing any theoretical assumptions. We can, of course, distinguish theory from experience in a run-of-the-mill sort of way. Our experience of the sky at night is certainly quite different from any of the ideas we might have as to what's actually up there. The question raised here is just whether it makes sense to speak of the factual content of that experience without any reference to those ideas. Is there an irreducible content to that experience that can be *known* without already knowing other things as well? An affirmative answer to this question is a crucial component of what Sellars refers to as "the myth of the given." Returning for a moment to his important essay, "Empiricism and the Philosophy of Mind," we find Sellars arguing there against the idea that "observation 'strictly and properly so-called' is constituted by certain self-authenticating nonverbal episodes. . . ."[7] As simple an observation as "This is green," for instance, possesses its epistemic authority only as a reliable indicator of green objects under certain standard observation conditions. For such a report to count as *knowledge* it is not sufficient to simply be in the perceptual presence of a green object, but to know that those conditions have been met as well: that, for example, the lighting is "appropriate" to such an observation. And from this, "it follows, as a matter of simple logic, that one couldn't have observational knowledge of *any* fact unless one knew many *other* things as well. . . . And to admit this requires an abandonment of the traditional empiricist idea that observational knowledge 'stands on its own feet'."[8]

Sellars's point here is completely epistemological, which is to say that it has no bearing on any psychological or phenomenological theory of how experience is actually constituted. Rorty drives this point home in emphasizing that one may adopt this Sellarsian perspective,

> while cheerfully "countenancing" raw feels, a priori concepts, innate ideas, sense-data, propositions, and anything else a causal explanation of human behavior might find helpful to postulate. What we *cannot* do is to take knowledge of these "inner" or "abstract" entities as premises from which our knowledge of other entities is normally inferred, and without which the latter knowledge would be "ungrounded."[9]

Whatever the 'stuff' of experience may be, its epistemic role as knowledge is a function of its authority to license a specific range of inferences. And this *authority* is irreducible to its constitutive stuff. Only in relation to a background of theoretical assumptions that prescribe limits to the range of what may legitimately be inferred on its basis, does that experience come to count as knowledge. The operative distinction here is between experience as a *causal* condition underlying knowledge (as that which will, as a matter of fact, usually bring about the utterance of a specific sort of report), and experience as a *normatively* appropriate premise in the justification of our epistemic claims. It is only the latter epistemologically significant sense of *experience* that is irreducible to "the given."

But if the idea of experience as a privileged source of epistemic authority is a myth, then the idea of specific vocabularies that are privileged in relation to experience is also a myth. Rorty has argued, for example, that the very language in which we describe our pains as "intense" or "dull," and our ideas as "clear" or "vague"—the language of 'sensation' or 'immediate experience'—is itself only one theory-laden description which could, conceivably, be replaced with another, such as a neurological description that made no reference to the givens of sensation or immediate experience. Not that we could conceptually reduce the content of the one to the other—Rorty's position is not a repetition of the early positivist's dream of a reduction of our confused everyday discourse to the clear and distinct language of science. It is, rather, a question of its potential *displacement* by that discourse.[10] Experience itself, isolated from its theoretical background, is insufficient to authorize any particular descriptive vocabulary. We might just as well use a neurological vocabulary, speaking of the stimulation of our "C-fibers," as that of our ordinary talk of pains and their intensity. To assume we cannot, in principle, is to assume that experience can, in and of itself, count as knowledge. It has been argued, for instance,[11] that such a neurological discourse would, if it completely displaced our ordinary subjective way of speaking, still necessarily entail the sense-content of those expressions, and so in this way retain their descriptive functions in a new linguistic context. The inability to eliminate our ordinary discourse would be based, then, on the persistence of a core of observational facts which would presumably exist apart from any theoretical attitude we might hold in relation to them. But this is, of course, only the given in its most essential form.[12]

If Sellars and Rorty are right that there is no such epistemic core to experience, that *what is known* in experience is as much a function of our theoretical assumptions about that experience as it is of any stuff that might causally underlie it, then the idea of a privileged descriptive vocabulary must be abandoned. That experience seems to demand this as opposed to that way of talking is a function of the theories we hold about that experience which authorize one set of inferences to the exclusion of another. Should another set of theoretical assumptions begin to prove more useful to us, the "obviousness" of the earlier descriptive inferences would disappear, leaving us with the pragmatic question of which way of speaking—which interpretation—serves us best. And here we are back to our cultural practices (in this case the discursive practice of a particular mode of description) proving their worth solely in terms of their own ability to do the things we ask of them. Epistemological questions of grounding give way to pragmatic questions of whether it works or not.

Such a line, Rorty is careful to stress, does not argue *for* the elimination of our ordinary descriptive account of experience. It merely undercuts the necessity of its link with that experience.

> I am not in any sense claiming that the customary vocabulary of introspection is "illegitimate." Rather, I am merely claiming the same "legitimacy" for the neurological vocabulary—where "legitimacy" means the right to be considered a report of experience. My attitude is not that some vocabularies are "illegitimate," but rather we should let a thousand vocabularies bloom and then see which survive.[13]

In this way, Rorty's rejection of the idea of epistemological givenness ties in with the moral he draws from his reading of the history of philosophy. Attempts at legitimating one discourse to the exclusion of others—of "policing" one's culture, assigning rights and privileges here, denying them there—are pointless. The vocabulary of eliminative materialism will fall or fly on its own in terms of its ability to serve the interests that motivate it. We *may* have ethical objections to those interests. Rorty sees no problem with a critique of behaviorism, for instance, in terms of whether we *ought* to be trying to predict and control other people.[14] But to argue that it fails *scientifically* because of its inability to do justice to the intuitions we have of ourselves as essentially more than a mere set of behavioral responses to environmental stimuli confuses the moral force one might concede to such intuitions, with an epistemic force that cannot be conceded to them. For as intuitions, their epistemic authority is relative to a specific range of theoretical assumptions regarding what sorts of beings we take ourselves as—assumptions a behavioral theory would, no doubt, call into question.

Rorty's point here is not that experience has no role at all to play in the formulation, justification or contestation of our theoretical positions. It is just that it plays these roles only insofar as it is already theory-laden. It cannot, therefore, impose untranscendable constraints on the range of theoretical vocabularies we may legitimately employ in relation to it. For this reason, Rorty counsels a laissez-faire attitude toward the marketplace of ideas. In the human sciences, in particular, we should learn to *appreciate* the babble of its divergent tongues. "Why not just say that there are lots of things you can do with people—for instance, dwelling with them, loving them, and using them—and that you should employ different vocabularies depending upon what you want."[15] Trying to describe your relations with friends and family in terms of a network of behavioral contingencies is just as confused as trying to think of the control you must exercise over your employees in terms of human warmth and intimacy. Both vocabularies are "legitimate" in their own pragmatic contexts, and both appear absurd and hopelessly inadequate when they attempt to transcend those contextual limitations by hypostatizing their own values and interests to the exclusion of all others.

"Natural Interpretations" and Incommensurability: Feyerabend

In a somewhat different context, Feyerabend has dealt with these same issues in terms of his criticism of the empiricist prejudice that when observations and theories clash, it is always the theories that must be abandoned. This idea, he argues, ignores the role older theories or ideologies may come to play in the constitution of those observations. An observation may embody what Feyerabend calls a "natural interpretation"[16] which we may, for various reasons, choose to call into question. He notes, for instance, that for many years the observation that a stone that falls out of a tower does not move away from it, but falls in a straight line in relation to it, was taken as a cogent refutation of the Copernican theory of a mobile earth. If the earth moved, so the story went, clearly the tower would move away a certain distance from the stone as the earth continued to move through the

course of the stone's fall. The stone would naturally, therefore, not fall in a straight line, but move in an arc away from
the tower.[17] Galileo's response to this objection was not,
however, to bring Copernican theory in line with the observation, in keeping with sound empiricist principles, but
rather to bring the observation in line with theory. Or, that is
to say, he challenged the epistemic status of the observation
by reinterpreting the motion of the stone as *relative* motion.
Naturally, it appeared that a stone falling from a tower fell
straight down because the whole observational system—the
tower, stone and percipient—was likewise in motion.
Galileo reminded his audience of instances when common
sense acknowledged the lack of equivalence between relative
and absolute motion, when motion was shared by the system as a whole (as on a moving boat, for example). He then
proceeded, with the assumption of a mobile earth, to gener-
alize this lack of equivalence to all cases of observed motion.[18] Under this new interpretation the observation is
brought in line with theory (not vice versa) and its value as a
refutation defused.

Insofar as it is a *mere* perceptual experience, the observation of the stone falling from the tower remains intact.[19] That
is to say, we can at least recognize what is being discussed
when the observation is referred to under both interpretations. But in relation to a new set of theoretical assumptions
(that of a mobile earth) its epistemic value, its authority to
license particular inferences, is completely changed. "We
start," Feyerabend writes,

> with two conceptual sub-systems of ordinary
> thought. One of them regards motion as an absolute
> process which always has effects, effects on our
> senses included. . . . The second conceptual system
> is built around the relativity of motion, and is also
> well-entrenched in its own domain of application.
> Galileo aims at replacing the first system by the sec-
> ond in *all* cases. . . . Galileo's proposal amounts to a
> partial revision of our observation language or of our
> experience. An experience which partly *contradicts*

the idea of the motion of the earth is turned into an experience that *confirms* it, at least as far as "terrestrial things" are concerned.[20]

In changing our observation language, the observation itself also changes. For even the most everyday observations embody interpretations that presuppose theories we may find expedient to disavow. To observe *is* to interpret, in the sense that it is a determination of the epistemic significance of an experience by positing it in a determinate field of appropriate inferential relations. Observations are, therefore, unequivocally related to theoretical questions only insofar as those questions do not call into question the inferential relations within which the observation is 'normally' situated.

In this way we come to see how scientists might be described as practicing their trades in "different worlds." Thomas Kuhn's enigmatic and controversial description refers to a point he shares with Feyerabend concerning the potential incommensurability of different scientific paradigms. Practicing within different paradigms, for example, an Aristotelian will see "constrained fall," where a Galilean will see "a pendulum," when both are looking at a swinging stone.[21] Lacking a mutually shared observation language of sufficient power to offer a point of neutral arbitration between them, exponents of Aristotelian and Galilean paradigms only succeed in disputing with each other in terms of a range of assumptions each finds contestable. Each, of course, points to the *facts* that the other fails to explain. But both have a qualitatively different set of facts they are prepared to acknowledge. "Practicing in different worlds, the two groups of scientists see different things when they look from the same point in the same direction."[22] Incommensurability refers to just this breakdown in contact between competing theories; their inability to find common ground for the rational arbitration of their differences.

Kuhn and Feyerabend both compare it to a gestalt-shift,[23] where there is no continuous transition from the one perceptual gestalt to the other. One either sees the figure this way *or* that, perhaps one *after* the other in rapid succession, but never both together. Seeing the famous "loving cup" as "two people kissing" rules out seeing it as a "vase." Their principles of 'perceptual construction' are exclusive of one another and so prevent their being placed in the same perceptual field where they could be easily compared and judged according to a neutral standard. ("Ah!—this is the *right* perception. The other is clearly distorted, illusory, etc.") Similarly, incommensurable paradigms embody different principles of 'conceptual construction' for their potential domain of facts. When this occurs we may, likewise, find it impossible to place both sets of facts in the same conceptual field where both could be easily compared and judged according to a standard the practitioners of each paradigm would accept. ("Ah!—the motion of the stone is clearly relative. Seeing it as absolute is simply mistaken.")

Feyerabend illustrates this point by comparing the "world-views" of Homeric and post-Homeric Greece. After a short analysis of selective examples of Homeric literature, art and grammar,[24] he notes the lack of any distinction between essence and accident. Things are not 'what they *really* are' plus 'a manifold of appearances'. They are, rather, a paratactic aggregate: an enumeration of parts that form a series with each element given equal importance. A pictorial representation of a child being eaten by a lion, for instance, shows a living, peaceful child in the mouth of a ferocious lion. The "eaten child" is the same as any other, with the addition of the ferocious lion.[25] The elements are simply added together to make the whole. Likewise, Aphrodite may be described as "sweetly laughing" when she is tearfully complaining.[26] Incompatible aspects are simply enumerated together, one after the other, without reference to an underlying essential substrate with which they must be consistent. Sometimes sweetly laughing Aphrodite complains. To know her, it is sufficient to enumerate her various aspects, one after the other. In such a scheme an oar that looks broken in water is deprived of any sceptical force as regards the senses. It is not *an appearance* that deceives us of reality. It is just one of the many varied aspects of oars. "'Broken in water' belongs to the oar as does 'straight to the hand'; it is 'equally real'."[27]

The post-Homeric distinction between essence and appearance brings about a radical reordering of things. Both the elements of the world and their relation to one another are changed. In the one, there are "relatively independent parts of objects which enter into external relations."[28] In the other, there are appearances which form harmonious wholes in terms of the essential reality of the object they manifest. Knowledge of an object, in the first case, is complete with the enumeration of its parts. In the second case, knowledge is never exhausted by such an enumeration. As such, the elements of Homeric Greece may not be combined with the elements of post-Homeric Greece. They are incommensurable in that the principles of construction of the one must be suspended in order to adopt those of the other. The essences and appearances of post-Homeric Greece do not simply *add* to the paratactic aggregates of its ancestors. They *displace* them. Just as in a gestalt-shift, we cannot have both configurations at once.

> We cannot compare the *contents* of A (the world-view of Homeric Greece) and B (the world-view of post-Homeric Greece). A-facts and B-facts cannot be put side by side, not even in memory: presenting B-facts means suspending principles assumed in the construction of A-facts. All we can do is draw B-pictures of A-facts in B, or introduce B-statements of A-facts into B. We cannot use A-statements of A-facts in B. Nor is it possible to *translate* language A into language B. This does not mean we cannot *discuss* the two views—but the discussion cannot be in terms of any (formal) logical relation between the elements of A and the elements of B.[29]

Relativism and Open Exchanges

The idea of incommensurable ways of thought brings us back to the heart of the problem in this essay: relativism. For if there is a fundamental discontinuity between different conceptual traditions, if the firm ground of experience as a theoretically neutral point of arbitration between competing theories has been taken from us, then what is reasonable to assent to, believe in or accept as factual is a matter relative to the tradition in which we happen to find ourselves. This, at least, is the conclusion Feyerabend draws. "Protagorean relativism," he writes, "is *reasonable* because it pays attention to the pluralism of traditions and values. And it is *civilized* for it does not assume that one's own village and the strange customs it contains are the navel of the world."[30] Theoretical and political considerations combine at this point for Feyerabend. A society founded on the supreme value of reason is a closed society, antithetical to the idea of a pluralistic culture where all traditions are allowed to flourish equally in terms of their own standards and values. Feyerabend contrasts this "guided" exchange, where the standards and norms of *legitimate* discourse—discourse with politically significant effects—are determined ahead of time as a precondition for entering the exchange, with an "open" exchange where "the standards that guide the exchange between the various traditions of a free society . . . are . . . determined, improved, refined, eliminated by the traditions themselves. . . ."[31] The rise of scientific rationality to an ever-increasing dominance in contemporary society, the ascension of a technocratic class of "experts" to positions of power in relation to more and more questions which concern society as a whole— questions that concern education, the ecology, mental health, our economy, etc.—this political 'logocentrism' represents a grave threat to the ideals of a democratic society. For freedom is a matter of cultural autonomy and self-determination. The guided exchange of reason, by contrast, presupposes the cultural hegemony of one tradition over others and the disqualification of those forms of life that do not measure up to its particular standards.

From this perspective, Sartre's attempts to establish dialectical reason as the one universal method of the human sciences begins to look both theoretically and politically suspect. Politically, it would seem to paradigmatically embody Feyerabend's concept of a guided exchange, where the standards of legitimate discourse have been decided ahead of time and those who do not measure up are to be disqualified. As such, it would involve a play for power as much as anything else—an epistemic disenfranchisement of all bourgeois theoretical attitudes parallel to the political disenfranchisement of the bourgeoisie in the "dictatorship of the proletariat." Theoretically, it would embody an attempt to ground the theoretical practice of the human sciences in an epistemologically privileged theory of practice. It would, thus, represent another twist in the transcendental legacy of philosophy's attempts to legislate the limits and extent of its culture's epistemic practices. For Sartre, indeed, this project takes on an especially incoherent form since theory is itself supposed to be a moment of practice. As has been seen, Sartre's notion of evidence is relative to the pledge that constitutes the practical unity of a group.[32] What evidence can Sartre then offer for a theory of practice that would transcend the historical limitations of the social practices which produce it? Rorty and Feyerabend's case against method alert one to a range of questions that must be kept well in mind as we turn to an examination of the heart of Sartre's *critical* project. For if that project is to prove coherent, a way must be found of squaring his 'foundationalism' with his 'historicism' and of understanding, in short, how "the foundation of anthropology is man himself, not as the object of practical Knowledge, but as a practical organism producing Knowledge as a moment of its praxis."[33]

Chapter 7

Sartre's
Non-Theoretical Foundationalism

Sartre constructs his critical project on the ruins of the external dialectic. The empiricism of that approach, as has already been seen, entails a split at the heart of the dialectic between the irrational contingency of its appearance in the object and the unjustifiable rationality of its appearance in the subject. Remaining external to the object in an attempt to be empirically faithful to it, Marxism only succeeds in constituting itself as a dogmatic a priori. For the rationality of the dialectic is never accounted for, but merely presupposed, without warrant. Sartre's project must, then, offer an account of the dialectic which will allow it to "provide itself with its own reasons";[1] an account which does more than merely discover the dialectic as a contingent law of nature, but makes possible a critical justification of the dialectic as a rationally necessary form of thought.

The course left open for Sartre has, though, the appearance of an *aporia*. To avoid dogmatism, the dialectic "must be open to direct everyday investigation." To avoid empiricism, it "must be imposed *a priori* as a necessity."[2] The failure of the external dialectic marks the need to circumscribe a level or sense of experience that can support a critical investigation with more than empirical matters of fact; that can establish the dialectic with a sense of necessity proper to its bifurcated appearance as both a material process *and* form of rational inquiry. Sartre posits[3] such an experience in the *lived* experience (*le vécu*) we have of our own practical agency. And

111

this is, as we have already discussed, a matter of our practical "comprehension" of ourselves.

Comprehension and Anthropology

In the conclusion to *Search for a Method*, where Sartre deals at length with the question of the foundations of anthropology, he describes comprehension as a "human"[4] or "non-theoretical foundation"[5] of that theoretical enterprise. This conceptualization is crucial to Sartre's enterprise. For it designates a unique structure to his 'foundationalism', both in (1) the character of comprehension as a foundation—that it is not itself a theoretical knowing, but a praxis—and (2) the character of the relation between comprehension and the theoretical knowledge it grounds—that comprehension is not "prior" to the theory it grounds. Together these points constitute a decisive break with a traditional foundationalism which would attempt to secure a culture's epistemic practices in a form of knowledge more secure than that offered by those practices themselves. An understanding of Sartre's critical account of dialectical reason demands, therefore, an adequate grasp of the specificity of this "non-theoretical" foundationalism.

Beginning with the specific relation of comprehension to the theory it grounds, we find Sartre carefully distinguishing it from the way a science might be said to have a foundation in its axiomatic theoretical principles.

> We must beware here of a confusion heavy with consequences. In fact, in the order of Knowledge, what we know concerning the principle or the foundations of a scientific structure, even when it has come—as is ordinarily the case—later than the empirical determinations, is set forth first; and one deduces from it the determinations of Knowledge in the same way one constructs a building after having secured its foundations.[6]

Science is grounded by the theories in terms of which its empirical knowledge is systematically set forth. Empirical knowledge functions as a confirming or disconfirming consequence of theoretical hypotheses which provide a framework of explanation within which that knowledge may be evaluated. Even though the hypotheses themselves are usually generated on the basis of the empirical knowledge they explain, still, the very structure of the hypothetical-deductive model demands a logical priority for the theories in terms of which these empirical states of affairs are deduced *as* theoretical consequences. We know them first in that we only really know the facts we are confronted with on the basis of the theoretical knowledge that explains them. They are, thus, logically prior in the order of explanation.

No such priority can be granted to comprehension, however. As Sartre notes, "the foundation of Marxism, as a historical, structural anthropology, is man himself inasmuch as human existence and the comprehension of the human are inseparable. Historically Marxist Knowledge produces its foundation at a certain moment of its development. . . ."[7] As such, it is structurally dependent on the knowledge it grounds, and so incapable of grounding Marxism as a theory in a straightforward sense of offering it an explanatory or justificatory base that could be known prior to and independently of it. For if *that* were possible it would, Sartre argues, make it

> necessary to suppose that the freedom of the project could be recovered in its full reality *underneath* the alienations of our society and that one could move dialectically from the concrete existence which understands its freedom to the various alterations which distort it in present society. This hypothesis is absurd. To be sure, man can be enslaved only if he is free. But for the historical man who *knows* himself and *comprehends* himself, this practical freedom is grasped only as the permanent, concrete condition of his servitude; that is, across that servitude and by means of it as that which makes it possible, as its foundation.[8]

His point here seems to be that our comprehension of ourselves as free is not capable of being abstracted from our historical knowledge of ourselves as alienated. That comprehension only emerges in terms of our knowledge of the servitude that defines us historically; as both a condition of that servitude and, of course, a possibility of surpassing it. But it is for precisely this reason that we cannot treat it as logically prior to the knowledge of our alienation that Marxism, in particular, provides us with, and infer varieties of alienation from it in the way empirical consequences may be deduced from a theoretical principle. For that comprehension is embedded within and logically presupposes the knowledge of alienation in terms of which it appears as its "concrete condition." Far from entailing the anthropological knowledge provided by Marxism, it seems that it is entailed by it as a consequence of that theoretical system—a moment in its attempt to surpass the "dialectical opposition between knowing and being"[9] implicit in its theory, by grasping its own foundations in the praxis that produces it.

It is necessary, therefore, to reconsider our ingrained tendency to read Sartre's accounts of the freedom of individual action as an ontological recovery of a primordial sense of freedom which gets masked and distorted in particular strategies of personal self-deception or economic regimes of production. Sartre's insistence on the peripheral or ideological character of existential thought in *Search for a Method* underscores the extent to which, at least as far as his later work is concerned, such a reading is mistaken.[10] The comprehension of existence that existentialism embodies, its radical refusal to collapse our lived experience of ourselves into the structures of any theoretical knowing, is itself a consequence of the theoretical knowledge we have of ourselves—in particular, that provided by the theory of human labor elaborated by Marx. The theoretical framework of historical materialism and its implicit opposition between our knowledge of ourselves and the living material practice that gives rise to this knowledge, and is irreducible to it, is presupposed in Sartre's existentialism. "Comprehension—as a living movement of the practical organism—can only take place within a concrete situation, insofar as theoretical Knowledge illuminates and interprets this situation."[11] Comprehension grounds this theoretical knowledge internally, so to speak, as a non-theoretical limit of that theoretical system, whose position as limit is structurally made possible by that system itself.

These comments may seem paradoxical in the light of the characterization of comprehension in chapter 4 as an intuitive know-how identical to the movement of praxis itself. Is Sartre somehow arguing that the comprehensive, totalizing structures of praxis only emerge in the context of a nineteenth-century theory of political economy? Didn't people comprehend themselves as practical agents before this? Here it is necessary to draw a distinction between comprehension as the intuitive know-how materially embodied in every practical endeavor, and comprehension as the reflective grasp of one's praxis *as* a totalizing, comprehensive reality. "This comprehension," Sartre writes,

> which is not distinguished from *praxis*, is at once both immediate existence (since it is produced as the movement of action) and the foundation of an indirect knowing (*connaisance*) of existence (since it comprehends the ex-istence) of the other. By indirect knowing we mean the result of reflection on existence. This knowing is indirect in this sense—that it is presupposed by all the concepts of anthropology, whatever they may be, without being itself made the object of concepts.[12]

Neither sense of comprehension, as Sartre emphasizes, can be distinguished from the totalizing movement of praxis. But in its reflective sense, this totalization is focused on praxis *as totalization*—as a grasp of action in terms of "need, transcendence, and the project."[13] Just as praxis (as immediate existence) articulates its situation through a practical interpretation in the light of its specific aims and objectives, so reflective comprehension produces an interpretation of that process of practical interpretation, and in this way constitutes a *kind of knowledge* of it. But as an attempt to determine the sense of that which is itself productive of sense, to know that which is productive of knowledge, our reflective comprehension embodies a self-referential structure that prevents it from assuming a straightforward or "direct" form. It is limited, Sartre argues, to a use of language that is meant to invite a return from signified to signifier in such a way that the practical production of that signification is lived as a non-objectifiable process.[14] Concepts are transformed into what Sartre calls "notions," which introduce the time of their object into the thought of that object in such a way as to designate a temporalizing process that eludes fixation within a determinate signification. Sartre differentiates between these two uses of language primarily in terms of this temporal element. "A concept is a way of defining things from the outside, and it is atemporal. A notion, as I see it, is a way of defining things from the inside, and it includes not only the time of the object about which we have a notion, but also its own time of knowledge. In other words, it is a thought that carries time within itself."[15]

Sartre's enigmatic characterization of reflective comprehension in terms of "indirect knowing", "regressive" designations and "notions" that carry time within themselves reflects an inherent difficulty with the attempt to directly designate that which is the condition of all designation. It implies a use of language that self-consciously understands itself in terms of and restricts itself to a temporal or historical context which it attempts to specify or determine only inasmuch as it is specified or determined by it. To comprehend existence in terms of "need, transcendence and the project" does not, therefore, attempt to fix theoretically, once and for all, the essential univocal structures of praxis. It, rather, exploits a particular theoretical context in order to call attention to what amounts to a *problem*—that of the practical production of all theoretical knowing. It gains both its sense and interpretive power from the theoretical context that engenders it, and so could be said, in this way, to include within itself "its own time of knowledge" as it attempts to designate "the time of the object" of which it speaks. To employ language conceptually is to forget the historical production of those concepts by theoretically determining the object spoken of in terms of a univocal sense it must possess in any context whatsoever. The use of language as notion, on the other hand, embodies a recognition of language as a historical praxis that can only interpret the historicity of its situation in terms of the particular theoretical problematics that arise in particular attempts to know that historical situation. As such, the knowledge it embodies is "indirect in this sense—that it is presupposed by all the concepts of anthropology, whatever they may be, without being itself made the object of concepts"—an attempt to indirectly designate that which is presupposed in our historical knowledge of ourselves as the ultimate condition for the possibility of that knowledge, but that cannot itself be univocally determined as an object of theoretical knowledge, since it is the condition for the possibility of such knowledge.

Reflective comprehension is an attempt to designate the *lived* production of history in terms of the structural gaps that arise between any particular concept of history and history itself as a singular adventure. It is in this way that comprehension "can only take place within a concrete situation, insofar as theoretical Knowledge illuminates and interprets this situation." For it is only in terms of that theoretical interpretation, in its ability to account for all the facts of history *except* its own historical production as knowledge, that there arises the structural possibility of speaking, in a specific way, of the lived as the productive ground of the known. This mode of speaking does not, therefore, constitute a new theoretical attempt to know history. Insofar as theory connotes a direct conceptual knowledge of its subject matter, an external standpoint which univocally determines the essential identity of its object in a discourse which excludes the time of that object as well as that of its own knowledge, then the *comprehension* of history can only be a *non-theoretical* account of how both history-as-known and the knowledge-of-history are lived as practical determinations of the projects of the historical agents involved. As such, it constitutes a non-theoretical acknowledgment or recognition at the heart of historical knowledge that neither history itself nor the historical theory that knows it can be reduced to the structures of the known, but must be comprehended as products of a historical praxis that produces them as intelligible, and so rational, moments of its own development. "The true role of the ideologues of existence," Sartre writes, "is not to describe an abstract 'human reality' which has never existed, but constantly to remind anthropology of the existential dimension of the processes studied."[16]

Kierkegaard within Hegelianism; Sartre within Marxism

Sartre discusses this issue in relation to Kierkegaard, whose project of revealing the unsurpassable paradoxes and ambiguities of individual subjectivity is irrevocably situated in the context of Hegel's theoretical *aufhebung* of the individual on the way toward absolute knowledge. Kierkegaard's turn inward is foreseen, as it were, as a moment in the Hegelian system. "Soeren, whatever he did, acted within the limits of what Hegel had called the unhappy consciousness—that is to say he could only realize the complex dialectic of the finite and the infinite."[17] But in the way he plays it out, in his paradoxical use of language and, as Sartre emphasizes, the very way he *fails* at getting beyond Hegel, Kierkegaard manages to indirectly designate lived subjectivity as a "singular adventure" which eludes the incessant *aufhebung* of Hegel's dialectic. The designation itself, however, is only possible in terms of the conceptual problematics of the Hegelianism it opposes. For Kierkegaard's work is essentially an insistence of subjectivity as the nontheoretical necessity of *having to live* those dialectical contortions which Hegel claimed to know.[18] "Foreseen by the system, he disqualified its legitimacy by not appearing *in it* as a moment to be surpassed . . . [but as one who] had to live this foreseen life as if it were indeterminate at the outset. . . ."[19]

Sartre discusses his own existentialism after Kierkegaard's in part 1 of *Search for a Method* as an analogous response to the theoretical[20] developments of Marxism. It constitutes a renewed insistence of the individual as a "singular adventure," but now in terms of his or her theoretical designation as labor, productive of and exploited by historically

particular economic relations. The structures of "need, transcendence, and the project" arise as a way of indirectly designating the lived singularity of this theoretically demarcated reality—a dimension of labor otherwise forgotten
within Marxism's own positivistic misunderstanding of itself. The lived experience of praxis that Sartre attempts to
articulate arises in terms of the "dialectical opposition between knowing and being" internal to Marxism. His account
insinuates itself in the lacuna which arises between historical
materialism's analysis of labor as a positive historical reality
and its recognition (or lack thereof) of its own theoretical
apparatus as itself a form of labor. As seen in chapter 2,
Sartre's entire critical project is situated in terms of the contradiction between the being of knowledge and the knowledge of being—the inability, within a Marxist account, to
reduce the one to the other as well as the need to hold them
together in the unity of a single historical process. It is for
this reason that Sartre must emphatically reject, as he does,
the constraints of the phenomenological *epoché* in his approach to lived experience.

> Far from assuming, as certain philosophers have
> done, that we know nothing, we ought as far as pos-
> sible (though it is impossible) to assume we know
> everything. At any rate, we use the whole of knowl-
> edge in order to decipher the human ensembles
> which constitute the individual and which the indi-
> vidual totalises by the very style in which he lives
> them. We use this knowledge because the dream of
> an absolute ignorance which reveals pre-conceptual
> reality is a philosophical folly . . . the starting point
> of "supposing we know nothing" as a negation of
> culture, is only culture, at a certain moment of totalis-
> ing temporalisation, choosing to ignore itself *for its
> own sake*.[21]

Our reflective comprehension of the lived is no direct preconceptual grasp of the foundation of all concepts. It is an
indirect knowing, parasitic upon the direct conceptual
knowledge a culture has of itself at any given time.

The Dialectic as Theory and Praxis

"The experience of the dialectic," Sartre writes, "is itself dialectical. . . ."[22] It has nothing to do, therefore, with the sort of preconceptual givens that have traditionally been sought by empiricists and phenomenologists alike to ground theory in the certitudes of an indubitable experience. It forms, rather, a moment in the dialectic of theoretical practice where that practice turns back on itself in an attempt to critically account for itself. The reflective comprehension of praxis which Sartre presents us with constitutes a *regulative* moment in the dialectical thought developed in the theory of Marxism—a totalization of its ongoing totalization in which its status as a practical totalization is acknowledged. There is a peculiar self-referential structure to Sartre's non-theoretical foundationalism which corresponds directly to his insistence that dialectical reason must ground itself dialectically by "produc[ing] itself as [a] critical investigation of itself at a particular moment of its development."[23] By virtue of the opposition between knowing and being engendered within it theoretically, dialectical reason makes possible and necessary a critical, totalizing experience of itself as praxis. As a theory of historical existence, it comprehends itself as a theoretical moment of a historical totalization that is neither mute being nor lucid knowing, but is itself a lived comprehension of its practical situation. Dialectical reason grounds itself in a reflective comprehension of praxis by totalizing itself *as* a practical totalization. It overcomes the opposition between knowing and being, therefore, by understanding both its epistemic and historical reality as dialectically connected in the interiorizing/exteriorizing movement of praxis—as two moments of a historical movement which produces its own intelligibility in terms of both the practical intelligibility of its theoretical reflection as well as the theoretical intelligibility of its practical totalization.[24]

At this point the self-referential convolutions of Sartre's critical project may begin, if one is not careful, to resemble a play of mirrors where one is never sure what is being reflected where or to whom. To correct for this, it is helpful to

remember that, (1) as discussed in chapter 4, to act, to totalize and to comprehend are all one and the same; they refer to
a single movement which may be described as a practical or
productive interpretation—the determination of the sense of
a situation in terms of a practical context which is realized as
a correlate to every practical endeavor; and, (2) dialectical
reason has an equivocal sense, referring to "both a method
and a movement in the object."[25] In relation to the first point,
the *totalization* which dialectical reason effects on itself may
be thought of as an *interpretation* of itself. As Sartre's critical
investigation explores the structures of our reflective comprehension of praxis, disclosed within the parameters of
Marxism as a theory of historical existence, and uncovers its
dialectical intelligibility at every stage of possible complication (in its various relations to the collective and the group),
he produces an interpretation of the historical and epistemological status of dialectical reason as a praxis producing itself
as reflectively intelligible to itself. And inasmuch as it (the
critical investigation) interprets both itself and the theoretical
practice of Marxism as moments in that practical totalization
in process, it embodies the recognition of itself as an interpretation *of* an interpretation—a reflective moment in an
ongoing historical interpretation-totalization of social reality
which seeks to regulate itself (draw the limits and extent of
its validity) by comprehending itself as a practical interpretation. As a totalizing regulation of its own theoretical endeavors in terms of the lived experience of praxis, dialectical reason's attempt to ground itself is no more and no less than a
specific historical interpretation that attempts to account for
itself in an intelligible and coherent way. Rather than interpreting itself as blind product of a theoretically known de
facto law of historical development dogmatically asserting
itself as *the truth* (the external or dogmatic phase of dialectical
reason) it now interprets itself as an interpretation—a practical or lived attempt on the part of historical individuals to
articulate and make intelligible to themselves their own practical relations to their world and to each other. Dialectical
reason, in order to be coherent, must account for itself as
neither historical fact nor transcendent Truth, but as a practi-

cal totalization-interpretation of its situation. It must, in other words, comprehend itself as a praxis.

The structure of this comprehension demands, in turn, that dialectical reason *as a theory*, which grounds itself on the basis of our reflective comprehension, be distinguished from dialectical reason *as a praxis*, disclosed within the parameters of the reflective comprehension which grounds that theory. Neither sense may be completely abstracted from the other. But in the first case one refers to a constituted theoretical tradition, and in the second, to the constitutive or productive ground of all theoretical traditions. "It is, therefore," as Sartre writes, "both a type of rationality and the transcendence of all types of rationality."[26] As a type of rationality, Marxism offers a theoretical picture of the world within which our reasoning is situated and in terms of which it is evaluated.

> It *states* what a sector of the universe, or, perhaps, the whole universe is. . . . This particular rational system, however, is supposed to transcend and to integrate all models of rationality . . . it is Reason constituting itself in and through the world, dissolving in itself all constituted Reasons in order to constitute new ones which it transcends and dissolves in turn. . . . The certainty of always being able to transcend replaces the empty detachment of formal rationality.[27]

As a constituted system of rationality, Marxism grounds itself by interpreting itself as a praxis which *"in the course of its own accomplishment*, provides its own clarification."[28] It comprehends its knowledge, in other words, as the practical determinations of a historical project which aims to theoretically clarify its situation to itself. And it is this practical sense of dialectical reason, as it is disclosed within the reflective comprehension of historical knowledge *as* historical praxis, that proves to be primary, in the sense that it is grasped as the "concrete condition" of that knowledge—as the condition of its possibility as a form of knowledge. As a non-theoretical foundation it cannot be taken as logically or historically prior to the theory it grounds. Its articulation in reflective comprehension is, as has been seen, incapable of being abstracted from the theoretical context that engenders it. We can speak of dialectical reason as praxis only at the margins of dialectical reason as theory. But it constitutes, at the heart of theory, a non-theoretical recognition that it is but a moment in an ongoing practical interpretation-totalization of the world.

As opposed to the external dialectic, which was led by the logic of its own empiricism to an idealism which isolated the rational necessity of its procedures as a method of thought from the historical-material necessity of its object, Sartre's attempt to return Marxism to its foundations in praxis entails that, though we certainly may and even need to make such distinctions (between the dialectic as theory and as praxis), they must be grounded in an account of the dialectic sufficient to overcome the finality of such a distinction. It is necessary, therefore, to grasp that

> the dialectical method is indistinguishable from the dialectical movement; indistinguishable, that is to say, from both the relations which each person has with everyone through inorganic materiality, and from those which he has with his materiality and with his own organic material existence, through his relations with others.[29]

Through the problematics internal to its theory, especially that which Sartre has underscored as the opposition between knowing and being, dialectical reason is led to posit itself as a form of rationality constituting itself through the concrete practical relations established between individuals, their material milieu, and the social ensemble to which they belong. As a theoretical mode of thought, it must comprehend itself as a moment in the ongoing production of a practical rationality transcending the limitations of any formal theoretical system.

Chapter 8

Practical Reason
and Dialectical Intelligibility

As a non-theoretical foundation of dialectical reason, comprehension appears as a moment internal to the theoretical development of dialectical thought that marks a non-theoretical limit to those theoretical endeavors in a recognition that they are moments of an ongoing praxis. It is that reflective moment in the theoretical enterprise of anthropology when its own rationality as a social practice is posed as a problem. As such, it becomes necessary to expand our traditional conception of reason as a formal structure of theoretical judgements and inference to include the practice that envelops and conditions their formation—a non-theoretical form of rationality that produces, evaluates, and at times, overturns the formal structure in which those theoretical judgments and inferences are made, and which, consequently, establishes the practical conditions for their possibility as rational judgements and inferences.

Precedents: Practical Reason

Such an expansion of our understanding of reason is not, however, without precedent. Aristotle was perhaps the first to draw attention to a distinction between theoretical and practical reason. *Phronesis* or practical wisdom is, he argues, a mode of deliberation concerning the means of the good life irreducible to scientific reasoning. As opposed to scientific reasoning, which involves a demonstration of those things that follow with necessity from eternally valid first principles, practical reason concerns itself with that which is intrinsically variable; those practical contexts that raise a host of singular and unpredictable problems for the successful realization of a good life. *Phronesis* cannot, for this reason, be reduced to a set of principles concerning the formal constitution of the good life, but must involve a skill at applying such principles in a variety of contexts—a knowing-how to form prudent judgements in concrete situations that can only be learned through one's practical experience with a range of everyday situations. Aristotle emphasizes that *phronesis* must be concerned with the particulars of our experience. "This," he writes,

> is why some who do not know, and especially those who have experience, are more practical than others who know; for if a man knew that light meats are digestible and wholesome, but did not know which sorts of meat are light, he would not produce health, but the man who knows that chicken is wholesome is more likely to produce health.[1]

Aristotle's distinction between scientific and practical reason turns in large part on this question of the correct *application* of principles in prudent judgement. Learning a rule such as "light meats promote health" is insufficient for *phronesis*, for there is also the issue of how the rule is to be applied in particular contexts. And the correct application of a rule is not an issue that can itself be decided by an appeal to another rule inasmuch as the same issue must arise in relation to the application of *that* rule. This line of argument is most often attributed to Wittgenstein. But the essential point concerning the insufficiency of any theoretical understanding of a rule with respect to its own range of application goes back as far as Aristotle's concept of *phronesis*.

Kant's comments on judgement in the *Critique of Pure Reason* make this point as well. General logic, he argues, cannot dictate to judgement the way in which logical principles are to be employed, as it would generate the same regress of rules for the application of rules, demanding rules for their own application, etc.

If it sought to give general instructions how we are to subsume under these rules, that is, to distinguish whether something does or does not come under them, that could only be by means of another rule. This in turn, for the very reason that it is a rule, again demands guidance from judgement. And thus it appears that, though understanding is capable of being instructed, and of being equipped with rules, judgement is a peculiar talent which can be practiced only. . . .[2]

One can always question whether a rule has been correctly applied; whether a play has or has not gone out-of-bounds in football, whether we have correctly calculated a mathematical equation, or accurately designated an object's color. Availing oneself of meta-rules to determine correct ranges of application (say, by trying to spell out the precise conditions under which any play can be said to have gone out-of-bounds) only pushes the question back a step, as one must now determine *their* correct application (through questions that concern whether those precise conditions have been met; as concerns a pass, for instance, we would need to know whether the player was in control of the ball when he caught it to ascertain whether the play was completed in- or out-of-bounds). Somewhere along the line, the appeal to rules must end and some interpretation accepted as a matter of practice. To get on with things, we defer judgement to officials, expert consensus, tradition, or what have you.

There are no ultimate facts of the matter concerning a rule's *correct* interpretation. Even our intuitive grasp of its meaning cannot do the trick. As Wittgenstein's reflections on private language point out, the same concerns surface here in the form of whether we have taken the sense of the rule correctly.[3] Have I correctly understood the rule? Might I not be misinterpreting what is meant? My own indubitable certainty of the "sense of the rule as it appears to me" is irrelevant inasmuch as it only concerns *my* understanding of the rule, and not *the rule itself*. To collapse these is to identify following a rule with *thinking that* one is following a rule, which, if it were true, would make following it *incorrectly* (thinking one has got it right, but being mistaken) inconceivable. But what sense can we make of getting a rule right when we cannot in principle get it wrong?[4]

The moral here is, of course, that the very idea of following a rule makes no sense when it is abstracted from the public context of a custom or "form of life." At some level every rule demands an interpretation-in-practice involving a tradition of application accepted by the community as a kind of standard. The importance of such a practical interpretation can be seen in Thomas Kuhn's discussion of the non-rulelike character of scientific paradigms. Every paradigm involves a consensus on such things as exemplary symbolic generalizations—Newton's second law of motion (f=ma)—for example, and values such as the importance of prediction or theoretical simplicity. But such a consensus cannot be explicated in terms of formal rules, abstracted from the practices that interpret them. Exemplary symbolic expressions, for instance, are empirically empty outside of the context in which they are applied and systematically transformed to meet particular experimental needs.[5] And such applications are, to a great extent, a matter of skill—of knowing how to "see" such things as free fall and the motion of a pendulum in terms of the relevant forces, masses, and accelerations.[6] Values such as predictive ability and simplicity likewise resist translation in terms of "neutral algorithm[s] for theory-choice," by which we could specify precisely when any theory could be said to have lost its predictive value (What, for instance, are the permissible margins of error?) or have become cumbersome in its complexity. Consensus on values and symbolic expressions are always a matter of practice, of knowing how to apply them in ways the community at large can recognize as "its own."

The epistemic norms that characterize and regulate a theoretical tradition require, in this way, a practice that interprets them by applying them in particular historical contexts. Such applications demand prudent judgement in the sense that one must know how to successfully transform or modulate formal values and standards in keeping with the constraints and objectives of particular experimental situations or research programs. Only in this way do rules become more than empty principles of allegiance, attaining their normative force as a tradition's regulative ideals. And, finally, it is only by appeal to this level of prudent judgement that one is able to make sense of a traditions's ability to criticize itself. In just the way "normal science" requires a capacity for judgement in assessing a norm's applicability to particular situations, so criticism and revolutionary change presuppose a capacity to assess a norm's inapplicability. Every theory, for instance, has its share of anomalies. But in the context of a relatively vigorous and expanding research program, such anomalies are of little consequence whereas, for a research program in decline, they may be devastating. Forming a decision as to a norm's applicability to a set of problems requires, therefore, more than just calculating the degree to which it explains those problems. It requires assessing a whole range of practical issues revolving around the question of a tradition's expansion or decline.[7] This in turn, requires *phronesis*, formed in the light of extensive debate and acquaintance with the objectives and interests of the community in question.

We may understand Sartre's comments concerning the connection between dialectical reason and novelty in this light. In the introduction to the *Critique*, he writes, "if there is any such thing as dialectical Reason, it must be defined as the absolute intelligibility of the irreducibly new."[8] Sartre's comment here concerns his point that the primary intelligibility of dialectical reason must consist in the "transparency" of a practical totalization to itself: "the practical agent is transparent to himself as the unifying unity of himself and his environment. In this sense, the *new* is immediately intelligible to him in his activity (in so far as this activity *produces* it, not in so far as it comes from outside). . . ."[9] As praxis totalizes itself and its social and material field, it produces itself and that field as practically intelligible in terms of its ongoing totalization—as moments comprehensibly integrated into that totality in formation. As such, the intelligibility of its practical context need not be a matter of apprehending it as an instance of a rule or principle—a matter of "explaining new facts by reducing them to old ones."[10] It is rendered intelligible immediately, if only provisionally, in terms of the aims and objectives brought to bear within it. Praxis, in this way, constitutes a non–rule-governed or informal judgement which "defines its own practical understanding"[11] as it defines its own objectives with respect to the exigencies of the situation at hand. As such, the intelligibility produced and defined by our practical totalization of a context of action makes possible a prudent, rather than merely mechanical, application of formal rules and principle; an application which defines or interprets what principles it may apply as much by the novel and unpredictable features of the totalized context at hand as it defines or interprets the novel and unpredictable features of that context in terms of precedents set by the principle. It is the informal, dialectical intelligibility of a context which makes it possible for us to know how to prudently apply a rule to that which is new and undecidable in relation to the rule itself. Our practical understanding of a situation makes a practical intelligibility possible for formal rules and standards which they, otherwise, would not possess.

Dialectical Intelligibility and Analytical Reason

It is in this sense, as an informal, practical intelligibility produced in and through the totalizing movement of praxis itself, that dialectical reason comes to occupy its most apparently imperial role in Sartre's thought—that of "sustaining, controlling, and justifying all other forms of thought".[12] "Analytical reason", as Sartre elaborates this point,

> is really only the result of a synthetic transformation or, so to speak, a particular practical moment of dialectical Reason. . . . dialectical Reason sustains, controls and constantly recreates positivist Reason . . . [which] has its foundation and intelligibility only in dialectical Reason.[13]

Only the human sciences that explicitly take the practice of knowledge itself as one of their objects of study, and so owe an explicit account of the conditions of their own possibility, need explicitly integrate this "non-theoretical foundation" into their theoretical apparatus.[14] But any theoretical system, whatever its object, has its ultimate foundations in dialectical reason in the sense that it is a product of the totalizing movement of praxis and, to this extent, owes its prudent interpretation and application to the dialectical intelligibility that totalization affords. Sartre compares analytical reason to that of a machine[15] utilized by dialectical reason in its attempt to think the relations of exteriority which characterize its material environment and its own inert relations to that environment. By "transforming itself" into an inert system of formal rules and elements, it is able to make those external relations that are totalized in its practical organization of the environment intelligible to itself. Levi-Strauss's structuralist equations, for example, merely calculate the practically constructed rights and duties of organized groups in much the same way a train schedule calculates the inert coming and going of trains.[16] Both analytical systems capture the 'principle' behind a network of social relations in terms of a formalized set of rules which account for how those relations are organized. In the equations[17] they produce, both give one a handle on the predictable and rule-governed character of the practical systems they concern. They provide a map, as it were, for how to get around them.

In a long and rather dense footnote to chapter 2 of the *Critique*, Sartre extends this dialectical account of analytical reason to our knowledge of geometrical relations, specifically, the principle that a line that intersects a circle at one point must also intersect it at another.[18] One can, of course establish the truth of this principle through a formal geometrical proof. But prior to this, anyone can practically comprehend that since the line *enters* the circle it must also *come out*. We possess, Sartre argues, a *practical* certainty that any route which enters an enclosed area at one point (and continues on in the same direction) must leave it at another. The figure appears, thus, not as an abstract set of spatial coordinates requiring formal calculation, but as a lived space of flight and enclosure grasped immediately in terms of its significance for our totalizing practical concerns. Geometrical analysis transforms this practical certainty into a formal proof by abstracting from the 'flight and enclosure' which characterize our practical comprehension of the figure, leaving a set of idealized points and lines whose relations may be calculated according to strictly defined principles. One mode of certainty is, therefore, exchanged for another. For in putting out-of-play the totalization that produces its own practical understanding of the figure, one may no longer fall back on one's lived comprehension of how to get around an enclosed area, but must produce explicit chains of reasoning as to why certain relations are possible and others not. As with any analytical thought, geometry is a procedure in which we hold our practical comprehension of a situation in abeyance in order to formally articulate the relations of exteriority which are synthesized in that totalizing comprehension *as* relations of exteriority—dialectical reason deploying itself *as* a formal practice of analysis.

Beyond this rudimentary image of analytical reason as a kind of machine, deployed by dialectical reason as a moment in its comprehension of an inert milieu, it is difficult to specify the precise relations which hold between dialectical and analytical reason in Sartre's account. They are often couched in metaphors which only hint at how they are to be conceived. Certainly Sartre assumes that, in general, analysis presupposes synthesis. "In the process of labour, the practical field must already be unified before the worker can undertake an analysis of its problems."[19] The major thrust of his account of Levi-Strauss's structuralism is to argue that the analytical intelligibility of structural relations in a group presupposes the dialectical intelligibility of a group organizing itself in terms of reciprocal rights and duties. And in characterizing geometry as concerned with "relations of radical exteriority beneath the seal of interiority which is stamped on these figures when they are generated,"[20] he seems to be emphasizing that an analysis of a spatial figure presupposes the synthesis of that figure *as* a figure. The degree of an angle can, of course, only be calculated after the lines that form it have been synthetically connected. But, beyond this, it is not clear how this dependence is to be taken. Is a dialectical synthesis necessary for analysis simply because it must come first, as a field which is to be analyzed must be formed *as a field* prior to its analysis? Or is it that the very content of what is analyzed is to be explained in an account of its synthetic production? The first sense is true, but not very interesting. The second, on the other hand, commits the genetic fallacy of collapsing *what* is produced into *how* it is produced. Speaking of his account of Levi-Strauss, Thomas Flynn stresses just this point in reminding us that

> the fact that one can account for the socio-psychological genesis of structures does not suffice to dismiss them as *conceptually* derivative. Thus Sartre sees in respect for kinship relations, e.g., not a sign of some primitive logic, as Levi-Strauss has argued, but "a form of fidelity to the oath" which constitutes primitive society in the first place. But this confuses the practice of adhering to a structure with the structure adhered to. . . .[21]

There may, however, be a third way of viewing the relation. Sartre gets at this sense as one in which dialectical reason "must reveal certain structures, relations, and meanings which necessarily elude all positivism."[22] Here the idea seems to be not that one can explain the content of analytical relations by accounting for their production, but that a level of intelligibility can be circumscribed for those relations which necessarily eludes any analytical account. On this reading, analytical relations might still possess their own irreducible logic, which could only be adequately captured through formal analysis, and as such their own analytical intelligibility. But, as with a geometrical account of spatial relations, there is a level of practical intelligibility which is necessarily lost in any formal analysis. Our gain in formal intelligibility, one might say, is purchased only at the cost of a loss in practical intelligibility. This is, of course, sometimes a profitable exchange. Our practical certainty as to how to get around from place to place does us little good if we need to determine the flight trajectory of a rocket. A computer programmed only to manipulate formal elements according to strictly defined rules would do much better. But then *we* need not go through any formal steps to convince ourselves that a line which intersects a circle at one point must also intersect it at another. Lacking any practical comprehension of space, the computer must.

It need not be supposed, therefore, that Sartre intends to collapse the analytical intelligibility of a structure into the practice of adhering to it any more than he would collapse the analytical intelligibility of a formal geometrical proof into the practical intelligibility of the spatial relations articulated there. Analytical intelligibility, the rule-governed intelligibility of a set of formally defined elements and relations, is irreducible to dialectical intelligibility, the practical intelligibility that a totalization gives itself in the light of its own projected aims and concerns. But without the synthetic efforts of praxis, and the practical intelligibility it affords, that intelligibility is itself only a function of the necessity of a mechanical system set up to run one way rather than another. We can, for instance, program a computer to run a number of different analytical computations and it can run them mechanically without any practical comprehension of the situations those analyses concern. Hence, the structural autonomy of analytically defined relations. But there is a dialectical intelligibility to these formal analytical relations that eludes their analysis and sustains, in practice, the competence of those who know how to prudently apply them. For there is a difference, after all, between a computer that can mechanically generate geometrical proofs, and someone who possesses a practical comprehension of the lived space those proofs concern and can prudently apply them to the relevant situations, integrating their logic as a moment of his or her own practical totalization of a spatially dispersed milieu. It is this practical intelligibility of the analytical system, integrated as a moment in a developing praxis, that cannot be derived from any formal features of the analytical system itself, and which is necessarily lost if we take an analytical system only as it defines itself.

One need only imagine, for a moment, the loss that

would ensue if we could *only* relate to a geometrical proof as a matter of generating inferences on the basis of an axiomatically regulated set of formal propositions; as if we could never transcend the formal necessity of those inferences toward the intuitive grasp of how they clarify the relations inherent in our lived grasp of a concrete spatial figure, such as a line going through a circle. The intelligibility of the proof would be given completely in terms of having correctly followed a set of randomly generated rules and procedures, for which it would make no sense to ask *why* one was following *those* rules, as opposed to others. To this extent, it seems plausible to say that the analytical intelligibility of the system as a form of thought gives way to a mode of necessity which is, in the final analysis, utterly contingent and, as such, unintelligible[23]—at least to those bewildered souls who, without reason, must adapt themselves to the necessity of the system, in much the same way workers in a factory adapt themselves to the alien rhythms of a machine which defines and regulates, through the practico-inert exigencies of the relations of production, the character of their labor.[24]

The Rationality of Dialectical Reason

In an essay entitled "Why Reason Can't Be Naturalized," Hilary Putnam manages, I believe, to put his finger on the issue at stake here when he writes, "the 'standards' accepted by a culture or subculture, either explicitly or implicitly, cannot *define* what reason is, even in context, because they *presuppose* reason (reasonableness) for their interpretation."[25] Sartre's notion of dialectical reason as *praxis* is intended to capture just this sense of reasonableness which is presupposed in, but never exhausted by any formal rational system. For divorced from that dialectical intelligibility which would integrate it as an integral moment in its own totalization, analytical regimes and forms of thought become, in a sense, unreasonable. Without that intelligibility, conforming to their rules and procedures is analogous to adapting to a practico-inert order—a matter of adjusting one's conduct to a set of imperatives that do not offer themselves as justifiable, but as merely necessary. We ought, therefore, to examine in more detail the sense in which dialectical reason "justifies all other forms of thought."[26] How may dialectical reason justify other forms of thought, providing them with a rationality they would not otherwise possess? How may it constitute a *practical rationality*, irreducible to and demanded by the formal rationality of any analytically regulated form of thought?

"The basic intelligibility of dialectical Reason," Sartre reminds us, "if it exists, is that of a totalisation."[27] And, as we have seen, totalization is a practical synthesis that determines a context and the elements within that context with a significance for the aims and endeavors of that totalization. A totalization is always a movement of practical interpretation which, as Sartre also emphasizes, produces its own specific intelligibility for itself insofar as it "defines its own practical understanding (compréhénsion pratique) as the totalising grasp of a unified diversity."[28] In totalizing a context of practical action and interaction, a practical comprehension of that context is produced which establishes the intelligibility of that context in terms of its integration into the projected aims and concerns of that totalization. This practical comprehension of the situation constitutes what one could call a "horizon of intelligibility" for that totalization, a practical horizon which is the condition for the possibility of any particular understanding of ourselves or any given element in the situation undergoing totalization.

As we saw in chapter 4,[29] my companion's movement toward the window during a conversation in a room growing ever more stifling with heat is immediately comprehensible to me on the basis of my totalization of the room as a "place for our conversation." It is intelligible as an integral moment of that totalization—as a response to the heat threatening to render our project unfeasible ("it's simply too hot; we can't go on."). Now, the thing to note is that as integrated into that ongoing totalization the intelligibility of my companion's movement toward the window is secured as a *reasonable* moment of that project—as a relevant and defensible move to keep the conversation alive. Though no one will, in all probability, actually challenge my companion to defend his action as rational—since its rationality is readily apparent to anyone who comprehends our praxis; that is, to most anyone—a defense could, in principle, be produced that would be compelling to anyone who comprehended our ongoing totalization of the situation. Outside of this practical horizon of intelligibility—outside of the ongoing concerns and aims of the participants in the conversation—this is inconceivable, for none of the elements which go to make up this "situation" have any intrinsic relation to a standard against which they could be critically assessed. They simply are what they are in themselves, maintaining only contingent exterior relations with each other. As integral moments of the project of "having a conversation," however, they acquire a relation to an informal standard projected in the aims and concerns of that praxis. The dialectical intelligibility of the situation produced in and through our practical totalization and comprehension of it makes possible, in this way, a context-dependent rationality for our actions in terms of their contribution to or effective integration within our ongoing totalization and the practical intelligibility of the situation it defines.

In this way, every practical totalization establishes an informal sense of rationality which is able to secure what could be characterized as a *practical justification* of any action, discursive or otherwise, as an integral moment in its ongoing endeavors. The sort of analytical knowledge represented by Levi-Strauss's structural analysis of kinship relations may serve as a case in point. Just as the analytical relations captured in a geometrical proof possess their own irreducible intelligibility in terms of the necessity of the inferences prescribed by the formal axioms of the system, so the matrimonial relations captured in Levi-Strauss's analysis possess their own intelligibility in terms of the necessity of their combination, as prescribed by the formal rules of the structure that define the matrimonial possibilities of each element (each member in the kinship system), in terms of their position within the kinship system as a whole. The formal rules which define the structure will allow us to determine who may marry whom with the necessity of a mathematical proof, independently of any practical comprehension of what the structure concerns. A computer could do it as well as we could, if not better. And this analytical system of formally defined relations constitutes a form of rationality—an analytical form of intelligibility which the elements possess in relation to the rules that define the formal limits of their construction. We may justify certain statements as reasonable or criticize others as unreasonable, depending on whether or not they are implied by the rules and elements of the structure as we find them. The analytical intelligibility of the structural system is, thus, merely the inability to do or think otherwise, given the rules and state of the structure at any given moment.

What we will be unable to do, though, once we have divorced this analytical system of thought from the dialectical comprehension that sustains it in practice, is to account for the system itself as in some way reasonable. It becomes a contingent fact of the system as defined that it "behaves" in that way. Why it *ought* to behave that way, obeying just those principles, no one can say—indeed it really makes no sense even to ask. For the necessity of the system itself extends only to the manipulation of elements defined by the rules of the system and certainly not to the system as a whole. Only when integrated into the movement of practical comprehension that produces it does such a system as a whole become practically justifiable, precisely as an integral element in the development of the totalization of the situation at hand. For the group in question, an analysis of its kinship relations would be intelligible to it as a product allowing a reflective totalization of the functional distribution of roles that condition and go to form a part of their common praxis. In the case of a native attempting to explain his or her kinship relations to an anthropologist,[30] the rationality of such an analysis lies in the requirements posed by the task of having to explain the practical necessity of those roles to someone who does not possess a lived comprehension of them. For a hypothetical subgroup presented with the task of regulating and administering the group's kinship practices, such an analysis might have the same practical intelligibility that a train schedule has to an administrator of the railways—a useful tool for calculating relations and interactions (either of trains or marriages) that go beyond the immediate comprehension of any directly involved participant, and so of use in anticipating and, as such, regulating those relations and interactions. But in any case, the necessity of the analytical relations themselves would be comprehensible to the group as necessary moments of the group's own praxis, and so reasonable to the extent that it elaborates and explicates the horizon of intelligibility defined by the aims and concerns of the praxis—as a clarification to the group (or the anthropologist) of what they are doing.

Divorced from this relation to practice, an analytical system of thought is, as Sartre claims, less than a thought and more of an inert construction—a system of exterior relations fixed in matter by human hands. "It is obvious," Sartre writes,

> that this construction is not a thought. . . . It becomes one only through practice: the organiser creates analytical thought (and the rationalism which corresponds to it) with his hands; it is born within his hands because every *praxis* explains itself in terms of the objective and the object. . . . Practical knowledge unfolds simultaneously on two planes and according to two types of rationality . . . [and for this reason Sartre concludes] dialectical reason sustains, controls, and justifies all other forms of thought, because it explains them, puts them in their proper place and integrates them as non-dialectical moments which in it, regain a dialectical value.[31]

Dialectical Intelligibility and Reciprocity

It is in this light that we may better understand Sartre's comment concerning the production of Truth as the "elimination of all alterity"[32] in the group, as well. For one secures a truth about the world only in relation to a form of thought that allows that truth to be articulated and grasped. And a form of thought, in any concrete historical sense as the form of thought of a given historical period, community or research group, is necessarily a *social* product—it has a collective status as a discursive order that cannot be appropriated by any individual except insofar as they enter into it and allow their word and thought to be regulated by it. To this extent, as with any collective reality, the praxis of an isolated individual will be unable to practically transcend it except toward a future already fabricated by the norms and exigencies of that form of thought itself—a transcendence already anticipated and transcended by the possibilities of the system, and alienated toward the practico-inert end of the system's own repetitive maintenance.

It is only through the construction of a *common praxis* that any collective reality may be effectively transcended and integrated as a practically intelligible moment of an ongoing project. But the construction of a common praxis entails not only the totalization of a material field in the light of an end, but the totalization of a multiplicity of individual agents into a group altogether pursuing the same ends. And this is only secured through a practice of reciprocity which allows each individual to participate as both a regulated and regulating constituent of the group—as someone who is able to recognize the realization of their own aims in the realization of the group's objectives precisely to the degree that they have freely participated in constructing and realizing those ends themselves. If, as we have said, the practical rationality of a form of thought is only secured in terms of its integration within a practical horizon of intelligibility, then, insofar as that form of thought is common to a multiplicity of individuals, its dialectical rationality depends on the construction of a practical horizon of intelligibility which is itself, at least in principle, common to everyone who engages in that form of thought. And this common horizon of intelligibility is itself only defined by a common praxis, constructed through the reciprocal participation of a multiplicity of agents in the pursuit of a common set of aims.

Prior to this "elimination of all alterity," a multiplicity of individuals shares only a common necessity for each to conform their praxis to the set of practico-inert exigencies which define their possibilities for them. Since the necessity of their practico-inert relation to one another is defined not through a praxis they construct themselves, but through the counter-finalities of the material field, that necessity—be it the necessity of one's job, of belonging to a particular class, or of what one is able to think and say in a particular discursive regime—is not comprehended as an integral moment in the production of their own praxis, but as only an inert "limit within freedom."[33] And though the practico-inert field remains dialectically intelligible to those who inhabit it to the extent that they must actively adapt to that limit—it cannot merely be suffered by anyone but must be actively sustained by a multiplicity of isolated endeavors—this intelligibility is limited to the apprehension of and adaptation to the practical impossibility of acting or thinking otherwise;[34] to what is, in effect, one's impotence. It is not the constitution of a practical comprehension that would disclose one's relations to the others as practically intelligible. For this would involve the construction of alterity in the group according to a practical rule that would coordinate our differences in the light of a set of common, reciprocally supportive objectives. It would be a matter of everyone carrying out functionally differentiated tasks *"because it is necessary . . .* that this or that should be done, to allow the completion of some other task, which conditions the possibility of me carrying out mine." Lacking this, "as a member of a series, I do not understand [je ne comprends pas] why my neighbor is other; serial alteration reinforces accidental alterity (birth, organism) and renders it unintelligible."[35] Though individuals share a common destiny in the practico-inert field they inhabit, they lack a common praxis in relation to which that destiny could be totalized as an integral and intelligible condition of the pursuit of their own endeavors; as, in short, a practically reasonable moment in the construction of their own life together.

Returning to the example of the kinship relations dealt with by Levi-Strauss, the formal necessity of those functional relations will only appear as reasonable for the members of a group who transcend them toward the pursuit and maintenance of a praxis they share and determine in common—as a network of reciprocal relations determined by all through their mutual participation in the group. Should that praxis degenerate into the practico-inert necessity of merely having to behave in certain obligatory ways, regardless of the regulative concerns of its constituent members (as, for example, it must appear to an anthropologist who is situated external to the praxis of the group), then the necessity of those kinship relations can only appear as a practically unjustifiable limit to each of their individual endeavors—as merely "the way things are done in these parts, though for God knows what reason".

To this extent, the analytical intelligibility of those kinship relations becomes practically incomprehensible. The structural account that explains them, which grasps the formal necessity of kinship relations within the group, becomes merely a mute and frustrating index of the inability of each member of the collective to transcend their own practico-inert destinies. The formal intelligibility of the group's kinship relations will be identical to the sort of practically unintelligible necessity of a system of particularly pointless bureaucratic rules and regulations—"In these parts we fill the forms out in triplicate (even though the copies will be momentarily discarded), though for God knows what reason." Failing to be integrated as a necessary moment in the construction of a common praxis, such practico-inert imperatives maintain their necessity, and this necessity must be comprehended (if only as a "limit within freedom") by the praxis which adapts to it. But insofar as everyone's praxis is merely regulated by those imperatives, insofar as the necessity of those imperatives is not derived from everyone's ability to participate as a regulative member of a group which freely adopts them in the light of a commonly accepted set of aims, to this extent they lose their relation to a common horizon of practical intelligibility in terms of which they could appear as practically reasonable. Necessary for each, they are in effect reasonable for none.

This is why, as we examined in chapter 5, the practice of

knowledge may be understood as constructed on the alienated ground of belief through the subjection of those beliefs to a practice of critical reciprocity. For, as regards our epistemic practices, a claim is only secured as rational through its inherence in a practice of giving and asking for reasons open, in principle, to anyone's regulative or critical participation. It is that capacity to participate in the construction of their own set of beliefs which secures those beliefs as rational for a community. Foreclosing this dimension of reciprocal critical participation is precisely what constitutes a culture's epistemic regimes as more a matter of the maintenance of doctrinaire authority than the rational pursuit of knowledge.

Or, from a somewhat different vantage point, we might return to the case of Flaubert. His constitutional credulity or *maladie de la Vérité* was a function precisely of his inability to participate critically and reciprocally in the linguistic practices through which his community disclosed the world. This is not to say, of course, that he could not speak. It is not as if he could avoid speaking of the world in the ways prescribed by the linguistic culture of his time. To live in a world of others one must communicate with them and this is to adapt oneself to their language. But Flaubert's relation to language was not such as to allow him to appropriate it for himself. Unlike other children, he never took the initiative of forming playful conjectures about things and exploring them with his parents, establishing through this a rudimentary hold on his right to regulate, as well as be regulated by, the linguistic practices he must learn. "Flaubert," Sartre notes, "does not play at this game." His relation to language is, instead, that of one who "will serve the cult, a choirboy of language; he will even be required in certain circumstances to borrow this or that word and pronounce it—as he might be charged with sounding a gong or ringing the bells."[36] Excluded by his own constitutional passivity from making regulative claims on the linguistic practice to which he must otherwise submit, he is locked into a world thick with designations which do not unveil the world for him so much as they establish the world as belonging conclusively to others—as a world whose discursive truth must appear as an alien property to be put aside when the others have gone in favor of his own private reveries:

> Gustave engages in naming when he submits to the social world of communication; he names at the command of others, through them, for them. Returning to his solitude, he retrieves the semisecrecy of things and of himself; truth hovers about his head, and he doesn't even think to raise his eyes to see it.[37]

Subjecting the beliefs of others to a practice of reciprocity through which one is able to participate in the construction of those beliefs for oneself is a response to the sort of alienating lack of intelligibility highlighted in Sartre's discussion of Flaubert. Born into a world already worked over by others, with possibilities and imperatives inscribed in the very structure of the language to which one must adapt to be even minimally a part of a culture, the only option to slowly asserting one's regulative competence within the practices which sustain that culture is to live that culture as "other"; as obligatory but practically unintelligible. The construction of a culture as a common praxis is what it takes to establish its intelligibility for those who have no choice but to participate, if only as a "choirboy." To the degree that any part of a culture, such as its epistemic regime, is divorced from a practice of reciprocity and maintained through relations of authority, this is the degree to which it will lose its practical rationality, its dialectical intelligibility for those who must, nevertheless, submit to it. It is the degree to which its beliefs and forms of thought, no matter how pragmatically expedient (from some perspective), must appear as practically unjustifiable for those unable to integrate themselves into the praxis in terms of which that pragmatic expediency might be apparent.

"Truth," as Sartre writes in *The Family Idiot*, "is praxis itself, the double and complex relations among men through their work in the world, and between men and the world through the reciprocity (virtual or real) of human relations."[38] For this reason it is also "something which becomes . . . a totalization which is forever being totalized."[39] The dialectical or practical rationality of any form of thought is not, therefore, a matter of it conforming to any set of eternal norms or rules of thought that might constitute something analogous to a transcendental logic or canon. It is, rather, a rationality that is situated and can only be grasped as such through one's ability to participate in the practices through which it is constructed as a totalizing integration of its material and social milieu. As "the living logic of action . . . it is created anew in each action,"[40] and so can only be grasped from a perspective internal to its own development. This is, no doubt, why Sartre is careful to emphasize that every concept, including "the universals of the dialectic" are "individualised universals," valid only for the specific totalization in which they are engendered.[41]

But the historical specificity of the validity of every concept and, as such, every discursive regime or form of thought, need not entail their ultimate irrationality or unjustifiability. The dialectical rationality of a discursive regime will necessarily elude anyone who stands outside the praxis in which it is constructed. Unable to isolate a fixed and eternal canon of rationality in relation to which that regime's own rationality might be assessed, one is tempted to treat every form of thought as, at bottom, merely a product of the contingencies of history. We are set up for the traditionally unsatisfying options of either discovering "*the* method" for rightly conducting our thoughts or concluding with Feyerabend that "anything goes." And such an option is, indeed, warranted if our conception of rationality must be restricted to a formal or analytical conception of 'the rational' as "what necessarily follows on the basis of a set of formal rules and principles." But such a restriction and, therefore, such an option is entirely without warrant. For it overlooks the dialectical intelligibility which is secured for a form of thought from the vantage point of its participants, through its integration within a community's ongoing totalization of itself and its situation—an intelligibility not derived from the formal necessity of any rule-governed system which would then want justification in terms of another rule-governed system, and so forth, but produced within the movement of praxis itself. The practical rationality of a form of thought is, therefore, never a *given*. But for this very reason, its rationality may always be assessed in terms of the "double and complex" dimensions of the practical totalization in which it is engendered—that of the relations established between individuals and the particularities of their situation on the basis of the relations that obtain between individuals and other members of their community, and that of the relations of each member of the community to one another established in terms of their relation to the particularities of the situation they must deal with.

Chapter 9

Reciprocity and
Negotiation: Habermas and Lyotard

Sartre's understanding of dialectical reason concerns, as he puts it, "the constituent and constituted reason of practical multiplicities";[1] a form of rationality which emerges in and through the praxis by which social ensembles construct their own forms of life. Put in such a concise light, his thought invites comparison with the work of Jürgen Habermas. For Sartre's account of dialectical reason, like Habermas's work with his concept of communicative reason, underscores a mode of rationality that is bound up with the very construction of social forms of life—with a sense of reason that would not be peculiar to this or that community since its emergence would be part and parcel of the constitution of any community whatsoever. And yet, it is precisely this claim to universality that has proven most problematic in both their work. As Lyotard has pointed out in relation to Habermas, this very gesture toward universality seems to do "violence to the heterogeneity of language games"[2] by treating the incommensurability of our diverse forms of life as merely apparent—a suggestion Lyotard finds indefensible.

To the extent that Sartre's project seems complicit with Habermas's, it would also seem as if it must be vulnerable to this criticism as well. Or, at the very least, the same questions are bound to arise. As such, it may be useful to consider how these issues have been dealt with in the work of Habermas and Lyotard. For the debate between them sketches not only the usual options that define the parameters of the problem, but a way of approaching its resolution

147

as well, I believe, in and through their mutual emphasis on the significance of a practice of negotiation in the life of a community—of what, from a Sartrean vantage point we would describe as a practice of reciprocity. In coming to recognize the insistence of some account of reciprocity and negotiation in both their conflicting positions, it should be possible to more adequately appreciate the sense in which a *dialectical* understanding of reason is able to give voice to both the universality of reason as well as the "heterogeneity" of diverse forms of life precisely by articulating its claims entirely in terms of a practice of reciprocity which would place any and every form of life up for negotiation.

Habermas and Communicative Reason

Habermas's concept of communicative reason stems from the distinction he draws between instrumental and communicative action, and the distinct senses of rationality appropriate to each. With instrumental or teleological action, that is, action oriented exclusively toward the realization of a strategic goal, rationality is solely a matter of whether or not we are capable of technical success in meeting our objectives.[3] But with communicative action, that is, linguistic activity undertaken with communicative intent, rationality is a matter of what is involved in coming to an understanding concerning the issues at hand. For this is, after all, the intrinsic goal of communication: "to bring about an agreement that terminates in the intersubjective mutuality of reciprocal understanding, shared knowledge, mutual trust and accord with one another."[4]

Communicative action may be defined, then, as action oriented to reaching a common understanding or consensus among the participants of a linguistic interaction. But it is not just any form of consensus which is aimed at, but a consensus secured through, as Habermas puts it, "the intersubjective recognition of criticizable validity claims."[5] As such, the rationality of communicative action lies in the practice of 'giving and asking for reasons' for the claims we make; of instituting what Habermas describes as a process of "cooperative negotiation"[6] in which a community maintains its life-world—its forms of life and common understanding of the world—through its own discussions of the issues at hand. Linking back up with Sartre, one might say that communicative reason is that practice through which a community institutes reciprocity in the construction of its life-world; it is what is done to secure a common interpretation or understanding of the world as practically intelligible to every member of the community in terms of a communicative practice they cooperatively determine. By Habermas's lights, this is a matter of argumentation, of raising validity claims concerning the world that are, in principle, open to criticism and hence demand justification. Communicative rationality is, therefore, essentially defined by the forms that practice of argumentation may take in any concrete situation—whatever it takes to institute that "cooperative negotiation" in relation to the specific matters at hand.

Of course, as Habermas recognizes, this practice will vary considerably depending on the social and institutional contexts we emphasize. Our forms of argumentation will certainly differ, for instance, depending on whether we are discussing a legal decision, a scientific problem or the aesthetic value of a work of art. But this need not be taken to imply that the validity of an argument is constituted in relation to the goals of the practical enterprise in which it is embedded.[7] Concerned with the threat of relativism in such an account, Habermas argues that our various forms of argumentation are themselves only different ways of dealing with the different validity claims that are raised implicitly in any communicative endeavor. As he puts it, "forms of argument are differentiated according to universal validity claims, which are often *recognizable* only in connection with the context of an utterance, but which are not first constituted by contexts and domains of action."[8] The unity of communicative reason is not splintered into an incommensurable multiplicity of argumentative styles and strategies, for Habermas, since that very multiplicity is itself merely the explication of discursive possibilities inherent in speech, as such, defined in terms of the "universal rules and necessary presuppositions of speech actions oriented to reaching understanding."[9]

Drawing on Austin's theory of speech acts, Habermas attempts to account for the universality of communicative reason in terms of the pragmatic dimension of language designated by Austin as "illocution"—not what is said in speaking, but what is *done* in speaking.[10] For in addition to saying something when we speak we are also always doing something in what we say—promising, reporting, commanding, etc. And doing that is primarily a matter of making oneself understood; of securing, as Austin puts it, the "uptake" of one's illocution.[11] There are, of course, other things we can do with an utterance. We can attempt to influence our audience in certain ways through what Austin designates as a "perlocutionary" use of language. By reporting on the presence of a fire in the building I might manage to frighten an audience, or by promising that fire fighters will be coming quickly, calm them down. But since the perlocutionary influence we effect on an audience can only be achieved on the basis of the audience having understood our illocution *as* a report or a promise, Habermas argues that the latter is an *"original mode* of language use"[12] upon which the perlocutionary use of language is structurally parasitic. This analysis of the foundational status of illocution allows Habermas to claim, as he puts it, that "reaching understanding is the inherent telos of human speech."[13]

This being granted, the basis of communicative reason may be seen to lie not in any specific, pragmatically contingent contexts of action but in the very structure of speech itself, or as Habermas explicates it, in the conditions that are presupposed in realizing mutual understanding. For this, he claims, lies in grasping the *reasons* that could ground one's endorsement or acceptance[14] of the speech act in question. Making this point in connection with the hermeneutic attitude presupposed in textual interpretation, Habermas argues that the traditional dichotomy between understanding the *meaning* of an utterance and assessing the *validity* of a claim must be rejected. "Only to the extent," he argues, that the interpreter grasps the *reasons* that allow the author's utterances to appear as *rational* does he understand what the author could have *meant*. . . . the interpreter understands the meaning of a text only to the extent that he sees why the author felt himself entitled to put forward (as true) certain assertions, to recognize (as right) certain values and norms, to express (as sincere) certain experiences.[15]

The understanding aimed at in human speech depends essentially, for Habermas, on the ability to grasp and hence ask for and give reasons for one's entitlement to speak as one does. Every act of understanding presupposes a grasp of the specific validity claims raised by a linguistic utterance and a knowledge of how to argumentatively redeem or criticize them. In particular, Habermas claims that every linguistic agent who is oriented to communicative understanding must raise at least three validity claims for his or her speech act: truth for its propositional content or existential presuppositions, rightness or legitimacy with respect to the norms that govern its execution or for those norms themselves and truthfulness in its expressive relation to the subject who utters it.[16] These different validity claims, in turn, give rise to the different forms of argumentation we may observe in scientific, legal and aesthetic contexts where each specific context highlights or emphasizes one validity claim to the relative exclusion of the others. But any attempt to secure a communicative understanding must presuppose an implicit understanding of them all, insofar as every speech act implicitly raises all three simultaneously. And so any competent communicative endeavor must presuppose what Habermas describes as an "underlying agreement, which unites us before the fact"[17] on the terms of communicative rationality itself—an "underlying agreement" which functions as a regulative ground for any and every attempt to "cooperatively negotiate" a shared understanding of one's situation in terms of the argumentative criticism and redemption of claims to truth, rightness and sincerity.

Lyotard's Critique of the Universality of Communicative Reason

It is this idea—that the formal-pragmatic structure of language conceals an "underlying agreement, which unites us before the fact"—that seems especially indefensible to Lyotard. In *The Postmodern Condition*, he argues that this idea does "violence to the heterogeneity of language games." For though Habermas may not be accused of being blind to the social and historical diversity of life-worlds,[18] the essential thrust of his approach is to deny that there is, in the final analysis, any incommensurable diversity. "Particular forms of life, which only emerge in the plural," he emphasizes, "are certainly not connected with each other only through a web of family resemblances; they exhibit structures common to lifeworlds in general."[19] Lyotard, on the other hand, underscores in his work the dissemination of language and the impossibility of any meta-discourse which might encompass that dissemination or, above all, get to the bottom of it. Borrowing from Wittgenstein, he views discourse as a complex network of language games where each game may share much in common with one another and still be discontinuous, their respective rules and stakes incommensurable. "The social subject itself," he writes in *The Postmodern Condition*, "seems to dissolve in this dissemination of language games. The social bond is linguistic, but is not woven with a single thread. It is a fabric formed by the intersection of at least two (and in reality an indeterminate number) of language games, obeying different rules."[20] Carrying this perspective to its logical conclusion in *The Differend*, he writes, "There is no language in general, except as the object of an Idea,"[21] which is to say, as an object that can only be conceived, never presented or known as such.

Lyotard's arguments against Habermas center on the related ideas that, in the first place, there is or could be an "underlying agreement" on the terms of communicative reason as the *one* set of rules that would be applicable to any and every language game and, in the second place, that consensus itself is, as Habermas puts it, "the inherent telos of human speech."[22] The first idea, by Lyotard's lights, reflects a failure on the part of Habermas to recognize the incommensurable diversity of language games. For there are some language games in which the argumentative redemption of validity claims is appropriate and even necessary, such as that of science (or, generally, any denotative discourse), where an admissible statement may be defined in terms of whether or not it is argumentatively defensible.[23] But there are others, such as narrative, in which such a practice has no place. The narratives of the Cashinahua[24] of South America, he notes, have no need of argumentative legitimation. They produce their own legitimacy, he argues, through defining the rights of the Cashinahua entitled to tell them merely in terms of their having heard the narrative before. One does not argue about the validity of a narrative in order to understand it, Lyotard seems to be plausibly suggesting—one simply joins in the narration. To demand that those engaged to a narrative justify the worth of that discourse through an appeal to reasons which would make universal claims to its validity amounts to an unjustifiable demand that they play by a different set of rules; it demands, in effect, that they play by *our* rules. And this, Lyotard suggests, is at the heart of "the entire history of cultural imperialism from the dawn of Western Civilization."[25]

Lyotard takes issue with the second idea by arguing that the discernible aim of dialogue generally, and scientific dialogue in particular, is not consensus but dissension, or "paralogy"—the creative subversion of any established consensus in favor of experimental and novel forms of thought. His point here relates to what we have already discussed concerning paralogy in chapter 5. For Lyotard not only proposes the concept of paralogy as an alternative way of understanding the legitimation of scientific discourse, but argues that contemporary scientific practice is, in fact, already paralogical, already intrinsically antagonistic to the sort of stability sought in and through consensus. An intriguing claim, especially inasmuch as it seems to turn Habermas's own claim that "reaching understanding is the inherent telos of human speech" on its head (Is generating dissension the inherent telos of human speech?), it is probably indefensible as it stands. In arguing for his position, Lyotard seems to confuse contemporary scientific reservations regarding the self-sufficiency of stable systems in its *object* of study with a reflective insight into the unstable character of its own inquiry. He writes, "Postmodern science—by concerning itself with such things as undecidables, the limits of precise control, conflicts characterized by incomplete information, 'fracta', catastrophes, and pragmatic paradoxes—is theorizing its own evolution as discontinuous, catastrophic, nonrectifiable, and paradoxical."[26] Generalizing from statements that characterize the *object* of inquiry to a reflective characterization of the *subject* of inquiry, his characterization of paralogy as the *aim* of scientific discourse also seems to commit us to the empirically indefensible view that science is a completely revolutionary endeavor. As Rorty notes, "to say that 'science aims' at piling paralogy on paralogy is like saying that 'politics aims' at piling revolution on revolution. [But] No inspection of the concerns of contemporary science or contemporary politics could show anything of the sort."[27]

This being said, however, there remains a qualified plausibility to Lyotard's claim that cannot be dismissed so easily. For if we abstract from the idea that science *aims at* paralogy, Lyotard does seem to have a point concerning the indispensable role of paralogy in scientific discourse; a role that could be said, at a minimum, to call for rethinking the centrality of consensus, as posited by Habermas. "It is now," Lyotard writes,

> dissension that must be emphasized. Consensus is a horizon that is never reached. Research that takes place under the aegis of a paradigm tends to stabilize; it is like the exploitation of a technological, economic, or artistic "idea." It cannot be discounted. But what is striking is that someone always comes along to disturb the order of "reason." It is necessary to posit the existence of a power that destabilizes the capacity for explanation, manifested in the promulgation of new

norms for understanding. . . . it is a factor that generates blind spots and defers consensus.[28]

Certainly, we may claim to "aim at" consensus when we
raise an issue for argumentative examination. But, as
Lyotard reminds us, it is, by and large, dissension that is, in
fact, produced. And this surely cannot be relegated to the
role of an accident, as Habermas seems to do when he
characterizes argumentatively secured understanding as
"risky,"[29] for the dissension which is produced by argument
is, in and of itself, a spur not only to more argument, but to
the creative development of ideas (a goal which does not
seem external to argumentation) that would be otherwise
overlooked in the attempt to merely agree with one another.
One need not go to the extreme of claiming that "science
aims at piling revolution on revolution" to recognize the indispensable role which scientific revolutions have themselves played in the historical development of science. Similarly one need not go to such extremes to recognize the
indispensable role of dissension in scientific discussion itself.
But, granting this much is to grant with Lyotard that a 'defer-
ral of consensus' must play a crucial role in argumentative
discourse alongside the production of consensus. And this,
it seems, is not merely to grant with Habermas that consensus must remain a *regulative ideal* of discourse, counterfac-
tually possible in the sense that "if only the argumentation
could be conducted openly enough and long enough,"[30] we
must suppose that we'd eventually get there. It's rather to
admit that even if we had the time, it wouldn't be achieved
because if it were, something essential would be lost. If consensus is the *sole* aim of argumentative discourse, then surely it must be said to desire its own death.

And yet, as Lyotard himself readily admits, the consen-
sual moment of scientific discourse "cannot be discounted"
either. The development of scientific theories depends as
much on the periodic stability of a paradigm as it does on
periodic ruptures with paradigmatically stabilized research.
Though scientific revolutions are essential in allowing the

paralogical production of new theories, the stability of research conducted according to a commonly accepted paradigm is necessary for the exploration of a theory's implications and possibilities. And though it may be, as Lyotard has
it, that "consensus has become an outmoded and suspect
value," when he comes at the end of *The Postmodern Condition*
to sketch an approach to the idea and practice of justice ("a
value which," as he emphasizes, "is neither outmoded nor
suspect"), he is himself compelled to reemphasize its importance in stressing that a just language game is one whose
rules are a function of a "local" consensus, "agreed on by its
present players and subject to eventual cancellation."[31]

Negotiation and Reciprocity
in the Thought of Lyotard, Habermas and Sartre

It is especially with this idea that a just language game
must be formed through provisional agreements, always
subject to cancellation on the part of the players themselves,
that Lyotard begins, I believe, to recover a dimension of
Habermas's account of communicative reason that he otherwise rejects. For he effectively agrees with Habermas that a
community's forms of life ought to be the product of a process of "cooperative negotiation." To play any language
game in a manner that is just is to have the rules of that
language game on the table for discussion.

Paralogy itself seems to be subordinated to this idea. For
what is a paralogical move in a language game except an
occasion, even a "petition," to renegotiate the rules by which
the game is played?[32] Where Lyotard overlooks this point, as
in his discussion of the pragmatics of experimental art in *Just
Gaming*, the oversight draws attention to itself by virtue of
the inadequacy of the idiom to which he is forced to resort.
For example: "the experimental work will have as one of its
effects the constitution of a pragmatic situation that did not
exist before. . . . what is beyond doubt is the fact that if the
work is strong (and we don't really know what we are saying
by this) it will produce people to whom it is destined."[33]
Surely the mechanistic metaphor deployed here of the ex-

perimental work producing its own audience is a rather strained way of saying that the work invites a community to renegotiate the standard terms for its appraisal and potentially (though provisionally) define new terms. Lyotard's conception of the "pagan" character of our postmodern situation makes this point in a more direct way. Alluding to the agonistic and conflicted life of the gods, as presented in Greek mythology, he asks, "What does Greek mythology let us see? A society of gods that is constantly forced to redraw its code. . . . Here are people for whom prescriptions are subject to discussion. . . ."[34] Elsewhere he describes the *pagus* as "the place where one *compacts* with something else . . . a place of ceaseless negotiations. . . ."[35]

This idea of the indispensable role of negotiation, of being bound to negotiate and renegotiate the rules of a language game, provides a way of rethinking Habermas's concept of consensus which integrates the role of dissension underscored by Lyotard in a consensus that would be permanently unstable, precisely because it must be perpetually subject to negotiation. But, in addition, it may provide a way of rethinking the very concept of communicative reason in such a way as to free it of the limits of having to conform to the specific constraints of argumentatively redeeming claims to truth, rightness and sincerity. For there is certainly more than one way to negotiate the content and terms of a language game, and arguing about them may be merely one of them. The 'ruse of moderation' Lyotard isolates with respect to narrative may serve as the beginning of an example here. As he describes it, a good narrator among the Cashinahua will, at least with respect to their "profane" narratives, take liberties with the story and "ham it up."[36] Such liberties have their limits, of course. One may not go so far as to distort beyond all recognition the story being told. A good telling, Lyotard notes, "will not be a matter of conquering the narrative, that is, of putting oneself forward as the utterer, and imprinting one's name on it,"[37] if only because one has acquired one's name—one's identity—through being a referent in the ongoing set of narratives which are passed along and are definitive for the culture. In respecting the integrity of the narrative, the narrator recognizes a certain indebtedness to the culture he shares with his audience. And yet the liberties he takes are a way of negotiating, within these pragmatic limits, his own identity within the narrative life of the culture and, to that degree, the character of that narrative life itself. One negotiates one's identity as narrated by virtue of what one is able to get away with in one's position as narrator. And though no arguments may be forthcoming to justify one's version of the narrative as right or valid, one's negotiation of the narrative may be characterized as *reasonable* to the extent that it appeals to the uncoerced judgement of the community, and establishes itself in terms of a common horizon of intelligibility shared by the community at large. It attempts to integrate itself into what we could characterize as the common narrative praxis of the community—an ongoing story they tell themselves about themselves and the world around them.[38]

This can only be, in turn, a matter of the reciprocity between the narrator and his[39] audience. This reciprocity establishes the narrator in a regulative position in relation to his audience (and to himself, qua narrated) inasmuch as he controls the telling of the narrative, and each member of the audience in a regulative position for the narrator inasmuch as he must appeal to their judgement in the telling. Should his negotiation of the narrative be successful, each will be doing in his place (as member of the audience or narrator) what the other would be doing there, if only they were there. The significance of some idea of negotiation or "local consensus" in Lyotard's work, derives precisely, I would argue, from his need to refer, if only in a veiled way, to the practice of reciprocity. For without some appeal to this notion, it is impossible to distinguish between mutually regulative participants in a community and those who are only regulated by that community; between those who play a language game, and those who are only "played" or exploited by it. And though *our* need to make such distinctions may be conceptually alien to any particular language game, it is itself a function of our need to distinguish *not for, but with* any given community, the degrees of practical intelligibility its forms of life afford or deprive its participants; the degrees to which its forms of life foster or foreclose any meaningful sense of "participation."

Granted, this brings us a good deal of the way toward Habermas's position concerning the universality of a form of reason caught up in the communicative practices through which a community negotiates its own forms of life. But going this far, we should not go all the way and embrace Habermas's understanding of it as an "underlying agreement" on the "universal rules" that would organize our forms of negotiation ahead of time in terms of the argumentative redemption of validity claims. For it is this move which pins our conception of rationality far too heavily on *our* conception of rationality—on forms of reciprocity and negotiation that our own culture has emphasized, perhaps, to the exclusion of others—when what is needed is an understanding that will allow us to detect heterogeneous forms of rationality, reciprocity and negotiation as they are produced under social, historical and material conditions so numerous we could not possibly begin to anticipate them all with the aid of a theory produced under and tailored to meet the requirements of our own unique circumstances. What is needed is a conception of rationality that recognizes its dissemination, its permanently unfinished character.

As such it may be useful, and Habermas's work is extremely useful in this regard, to *begin* with an analysis of the pragmatics of our own modes of being reasonable with one another; where the rigors of the argumentative practice of giving and asking for reasons secures a kind of reciprocity for a community in which everyone is able, in principle at any rate, to negotiate the authority of particular claims to truth or normative legitimacy for themselves. But if we stop there and reify the conditions of that practice into a set of "universal rules" that define rationality as such, we are immediately put in a position in which those rules themselves become unreasonable, precisely to the degree in which they have been abstracted from the practical circumstances in which they can be comprehended *as* reasonable. For we must now ask *why* it is reasonable to expect a traditional culture founded on narratives to argue about those narratives in the way we do about truth claims. What relevance would such a practice have for them? Would it enhance the practices of reciprocity they may have instituted in their culture or would it simply destroy them? Would the particular sort of reflective distance that argument affords us necessarily be a progressive movement to a higher cognitive stage of development for them?[40] Or would it be more like providing an agrarian society with a nuclear power plant and then being aghast at their inability to make anything useful of it?

What is required, in short, is a dialectical conception of reason that would recognize the impossibility of reducing it to any specific analytical regime of rules and forms of argument. Though Habermas at times seems to recognize something like a dialectical character to communicative reason by emphasizing its inability to provide us with a conception of a rational life in any substantial sense,[41] he undercuts this sketchy recognition by attempting to theoretically fix the formal rules that any communicative rationality must presuppose. From a Sartrean perspective this amounts to an attempt to ground the dialectical intelligibility afforded by praxis on the analytical intelligibility of a rule-governed system. It amounts to yet another version of the empiricism that infects Engels's "external dialectic." For in basing his account of reason on a theory of the formal-pragmatic structure of speech acts, he looks to discover rationality, if not in precisely the same way one would discover "some area of the earth," then in the way one would discover a principle of cognitive development or the grammar of a language.[42] In a peculiar complicity, it would appear that Habermas and Lyotard fundamentally agree at this level—on the need to find or discover 'the laws of reason' or abandon the search for reason altogether. But whereas Lyotard is, at times at least, content to abandon the search and "gaze in wonderment at the diversity of discursive species, just as we do at the diversity of plant or animal species,"[43] Habermas feels certain that the search has reached its goal in the rational reconstruction of the formal presuppositions of speech acts.[44] Both steadfastly avoid the possibility that reason might not be found, but made, and that the production of reason itself might be assessable on its own terms as an informally rational process.[45]

If rationality is, as Habermas argues, a matter of the "cooperative negotiation" of a community's life-world, then the rules that govern that cooperative negotiation cannot themselves be excluded from the process of negotiation that would constitute them as reasonable. If rationality is ideally a matter of being able to place anything on the table for discussion, then the rules that regulate that negotiation must themselves be negotiable. And to grant this is to recognize the rationality of a process of cooperative negotiation that would not be regulated by any one, theoretically determinable, set of rules, but that would be adrift, in the sense of a process that is set adrift[46] to perpetually renegotiate its terms and conditions as circumstances demand. It is, indeed, the very attempt to fix, once and for all, what could count as a rational negotiation that is the distinguishing mark of dogmatism and the death of thought. Thought gives way to police action as the defenders of Reason seek to defend its Canon against those who would propose to think differently. If it is unreasonable to suppose that we might uncover that one discursive order that would never draw any unreasonable limits to what may be reasonably discussed, then being reasonable must consist in putting everything on the table—making everything, including the rules that regulate our practices of negotiation themselves, negotiable.

Dialectical Reason and the Heterogeneity of Language Games

The suspicion is bound to remain, however, that in attempting to discern a mode of intelligibility and rationality that would be presupposed in any practical endeavor, Sartre's understanding of dialectical reason harbors an unjustifiable nostalgia for a lost sense of totality which is inconsistent with a recognition of the incommensurable diversity of language games and forms of life. Our own emphasis on dialectical reason as the construction of a common horizon of intelligibility, necessarily based on a practice of reciprocity, can only exacerbate this suspicion. For does not the production of commonality entail the repression of difference? And is not our emphasis on the indispensable role of reciprocity in that project only a backhanded way of once again attempting to stipulate "universal rules" which any and every form of life must share?

In responding to these suspicions, it is important to note Sartre's own emphasis on the role detotalization plays in the totalization effected in any common praxis. This is a point which differentiates Sartre's understanding of totalization from that implied in most post-structuralist denunciations of the idea.[47] For the totalization effected through the construction of a common praxis *could* consolidate itself as a completed totality only through the *"real* integration" of the individuals who form it, that is, if the group managed to form itself as a kind of hyperorganism of which the individual members would be no more than functionally regulated organs. This, however, is simply impossible. As Sartre succinctly puts it, "a group *is not*,"[48] but can only be perpetually made and remade.

The reciprocities which integrate each individual into the group, by virtue of establishing each as a regulative "third" in relation to the group itself, guarantees that no one will ever simply be a regulated organ of the group's hyperorganic purposes. Though, *as regulated* by the common aims of the group, each individual is immanent to the group, *as regulative*, they establish a relation of transcendence to the group which is always detotalizing the totalization under way there. Sartre discusses this as a form of tension between immanence and transcendence which effects a "shifting dislocation" in the 'life' of the group—a dislocation that permanently establishes the group within "a possible dimension of escape or of tyranny": "escape," as the possibility of individuals pursuing their own ends irrespective of the group threatens the fragmentation of the group, or "tyranny," as the possibility of individuals or subgroups pursuing their own ends *through* the actions of the rest of the group, though without allowing themselves to be regulated by the others, threatens the reemergence of a practico-inert unity for those who have lost their regulative hold on the group.[49] For this reason, the integration of any individual within the group must always remain "a *task to be done.*"[50]

As such, the constitution of a common praxis must be a matter of negotiating differences and conceiving strategies and modes of practical combination that can support what amounts to the individual's differential input into the group. The "group in fusion" which Sartre describes as constituted in the streets of Paris before the Storming of the Bastille, for example, was not formed through the repression of hetero-geneous individual aims, but "was created *on the basis of a number of objectives* which gradually became more definite and converged into a single one: the defense of Paris."[51] The defense of Paris, as the common aim of the group, was not an aim that obliterated those individual objectives, but a practical strategy that supported the aims of the individuals involved through an action which, though indispensable to each, could not have been undertaken separately.

In his discussion of the attempts of an organizational subgroup to formulate a plan of action resolving the emer-gence of contradictory interests in the group as a whole— resolving traffic problems in Paris in the light of the con-tradictory interests of car owners, traffic police, garage own-ers, shop owners, etc.—Sartre is careful to emphasize that though there is always a temptation to merely eliminate mi-nority positions, this option is never one of *thought*. It is not, as I would phrase it, the production of a common horizon of intelligibility in terms of which each faction in the group can integrate the solution as a reasonable moment in the pursuit of aims they share in common with the others, now re-defined in terms of the plan itself. It is, to this extent, not a matter of renegotiating a common praxis in which all partici-pants play a regulative role, but simply a matter of terroriz-ing a minority unable to muster the strength to resist. A plan of action will never appear as practically reasonable to that minority inasmuch as they were never integrated *as* regulative participants into the aims of the plan through a practice of reciprocity. It can only appear as an inert necessity they must adapt to, because they are unable to do otherwise.

"If thought does take place . . . ," Sartre insists, "what is important is that everyone . . . produces it as a free dialectical movement of his own thought." A solution in which thought is realized, in which a common praxis is negotiated, will be one in which "the contradictory terms are preserved as indissoluble elements of a new arrangement, and their mediated contradiction becomes an adopted heterogeneity."[52] This is, of course, dialectics, but not a dialectics that cancels heterogeneity in favor of a speculatively assumed unity of purpose concealed beneath it, but a dialectics that respects and fosters heterogeneity through a unity of purpose which can only be constructed through negotiation and reciprocity among antagonistic parties. It is not a matter of attaining a theoretical perspective which might one day ideally embrace every possible language game as moments in an all encompassing totality, but of creating the practical conditions that make it possible for a community's traditions and forms of life to be genuinely, as Lyotard puts it, "subject to discussion."

Finally, Sartre's understanding of dialectical reason precludes any theoretical determination of dialectical reason that would provide us with a knowledge capable of prescribing the "universal rules" of any rational discourse or practice. Such is the import of Sartre's emphasis on the "nontheoretical" character of comprehension and his characterization of his own discursive strategy as a matter of "try[ing] to be rigorous with *notions*,"[53] not concepts. The indispensable notion of reciprocity may serve as a case in point. For it may not be justifiably reified into a concept which would provide us with a theoretical knowledge of the criteria definitive for its referent. This would be a matter of excluding from the notion of reciprocity "not only the time of the object about which we have a notion, but also its [the notion's] own time of knowledge."[54] It would, in effect, abstract the notion of reciprocity from the discursive context that engenders it and fail to allow the kind of dialectical openness to the notion that would allow it to define itself anew in terms of the historical specificity of the various contexts to which it must, if it is to prove useful, apply. Sartre alludes to this point himself in connection with his characterization of reciprocity as an "individualised universal." He writes,

> it must be recognized that a friendship in Socrates' time has neither the same meaning nor the same functions as a friendship today. But this differentiation, which completely rules out any belief in "human nature", only throws more light on the synthetic bond of *reciprocity* . . . an individualised universal, and the very foundation of human relations.[55]

Sartre's formal understanding of reciprocity in the *Critique* does not attempt to analytically fix a theoretically determinable essence of reciprocity which would function as a new sense of human nature for us. The multiplicity of unforeseeable historical contexts in which reciprocity might institute itself—now as an ancient sense of friendship and now in a peculiarly modern sense—forecloses any attempt to theoretically determine its content. But, deployed as a notion designed to include "the time of the object about which we have a notion," this need not constitute a problem. For the historical heterogeneity of reciprocity may serve to enrich and amplify our understanding of it as a *practical*, non-theoretical foundation of any social interaction; as a foundation we comprehend more than know.

Reciprocity, as a notion, is indispensable insofar as it attempts to "chart" an appeal inherent in the construction of any common praxis, and so in the construction of any form of practical intelligibility and rationality. But it is not an appeal to a formal set of rules that could be specified and followed in the production of common forms of life—as a kind of dialectical blueprint to revolutionary rationality—but is only an appeal to the "unconditioned possibility of making man";[56] to the possibility of making something out of what has been made of one. It is not a concept that can authorize a meta-discourse that would stand over and above the historical multiplicity of every practical totalization of a collective situation that has ever been attempted and place them on a continuous scale of more-or-less successful approximations to a norm. It cannot allow us to determine what the nature of dialectical reason might ultimately and persistingly consist in, but is more like an ideal that projects the possibility of a sense of rationality which is always, more or less, compromised and violated; an ideal that allows us to make provisional distinctions between practically reasonable and unreasonable forms of thought and life, but always relative to the specific contexts and pragmatics of the situation in which they are engendered. It is, therefore, an appeal to an ideal that cannot legitimate the attainment of any formal and universal standard of rationality, because it does not provide us with any theoretical knowledge of what the rationality of any specific discourse or action must consist in,[57] but only legitimates our ability to make reasonable (because negotiable) distinctions in the midst of the fray, as it were; not for, but with the participants of any given community. Neither completely determined nor completely indeterminate, dialectical reason can only be thought as a task, unconditionally posed in every practical endeavor—the enormously difficult task of constructing and negotiating with others a measure of practical intelligibility for one's situation capable of sustaining common forms of life.

Chapter 10

The Practical
Foundations of Rational Necessity

What sense of rational necessity can Sartre preserve within his account of dialectical reason? In part 1, this question was raised in terms of the need to recognize both the contingency of the being of knowledge as well as the necessity of our knowledge of being. It was, I argued there, the failure of empiricism to adequately account for rational necessity within the terms of that contradiction that motivated and framed Sartre's own epistemological concerns. But it was unclear what sense of rational necessity, if any, he could endorse given his commitments to both the historically situated character of knowledge, as well as the need for an a priori, apodictic foundation for our knowledge of those historical situations. In part 2, it was argued that Sartre could account for the normative sense of necessity emphasized by Sellars. The rational necessity of the social practice of knowledge may be understood as a way in which that practice lives the exigencies of its historical situation in terms of epistemic norms or imperatives which define the limits and conditions of its discursive possibilities. Our epistemic practices give themselves their own sense of necessity as they regulate themselves in terms of norms and standards to which they either passively adapt or actively construct in a milieu of group reciprocity.

This, however, only raised the further question as to whether those epistemic norms are themselves historically contingent or rationally necessary. Could they be, as Husserl argues, the "apodictic consequences" of a sense of eidetic necessity that transcends history? Or are they, as Rorty argues, historically contingent conventions grounded upon nothing other than their own pragmatic expediency for the goals of the practice in question? And what of the politics inherent in the very attempt to ground a *universal* sense of rational necessity? Must it be, as Feyerabend supposes, a politically oppressive attempt to "guide" the exchanges between competing traditions? Or, to the contrary, is our comprehension of the dialectical foundations of rationality the condition for the possibility of an exchange that would be both politically open and rationally coherent?

Eidetic Necessity and Apodicticity: Husserl

As noted in part 1, Sartre's emphasis on the a priori and apodictic character of his own critique of reason suggests, on the face of it, a Husserlian account of rational necessity. Epistemic norms, for Husserl, define a sense of rational necessity for a community's epistemic practices only insofar as they technically prescribe how to conform our thoughts and deliberations to eidetic judgements and intuitions which are not themselves of a practical or normative character at all. They prescribe how we should technically form our judgements if we want to preserve truth or validity in them. But they make such prescriptions only in relation to a theoretical knowledge of the essential constituents of truth and validity in their own right. Every epistemic norm could, in this way, be said to presuppose a form of theoretical knowledge that grounds its epistemic authority in relation to an eidetic insight concerning truth and validity. Or, as Husserl generalizes this idea, every norm implies a theoretical proposition from which it can be deduced as an apodictic consequence.

> Every normative proposition of, e.g., the form "An A should be B" implies the theoretical proposition "Only an A which is B has the properties C", in which "C" serves to indicate the constitutive content of the standard-setting predicate "good" (e.g. pleasure, knowledge, whatever, in short, is marked down as good by the valuation fundamental to our given sphere). The new proposition is purely theoretical: it

contains no trace of the thought of normativity. If, conversely, a proposition of the latter form is true, and thereupon a novel valuation of C as such emerges, and makes a normative relation to the proposition seem requisite, the theoretical proposition assumes the normative form "Only an A which is B is a good A", i.e. "An A should be B." . . . [1]

The first part of Husserl's claim, that every norm implies a theoretical proposition, is quite true. It is impossible to evaluate any state of affairs, be it empirical or ideal, without a grasp of the empirical or eidetic relations involved. And these relations may be formulated in expressions that exclude entirely any allusion to their evaluation. The law of noncontradiction, for example, need not be formulated in a prescriptive way, concerning judgements that one ought or ought not to make. One need only note that there is nothing which is both itself and its opposite: $-(P \& -P)$. Anyone who grasps this theoretical principle will, assuming they wish to remain logical, constrain their judgement to a prescriptive form of it: "No P should be judged not P." There is a sense, then, in which Husserl's point is perfectly clear and without objection.

The rub comes only when one tries to clarify the status of the judgement that grasps that theoretical proposition. For Husserl, its validity is a function of "inner evidence." *"Truth,"* he writes, *"is an idea whose particular case is an actual experience in the inwardly evident judgement.* The inwardly evident judgement is, however, an experience of primal givenness. . . ."[2] Truth is ideal. It concerns eidetic relations such as, with logic, that between any possible object of judgement. These eidetic relations are realized in the particular case, however, only in terms of the eidetic judgement in which they are given. Such judgements constitute, for Husserl, a form of experience in which the "primal givenness" of truth is "inwardly evident." They are apodictically evident, constituting an immediate and indubitable possession of the truth they present. It is for this reason that they may serve as a theoretical foundation for our epistemic norms. For they do not themselves need any further justification, which would call for a normative evaluation of the worth of their claims. They are *self*-evident—forms of judgement about which we cannot be mistaken; forms of judgement we cannot, in principle, get wrong.

But, as seen with Wittgenstein, if we cannot get something wrong, it cannot make sense to speak of getting it right either. Every theoretical judgement, no matter how apodictic, makes a claim for its own validity which places it, in principle, in an arena in which its own normative evaluation as valid or invalid, correct or incorrect, is essential. Even an apodictic judgement must appeal, minimally, to the epistemic appropriateness of primal givenness as an indubitable form of evidence. And this appeal, this *evaluation* of the status of primal givenness as a form of evidence is, as is known all too well these days, itself far from apodictic. It brings with it a history of problems and debates in which the epistemic authority of the given has been itself put up for question. The theoretical judgement that grounds the norm is, therefore, itself embedded in a field of questions and concerns that constitute a normative evaluation of its particular claims to validity. For this reason it cannot serve as a sufficient *theoretical* foundation for that norm.

We could sensibly speak of a theoretical foundation for our epistemic norms only if our theoretical understanding of the world were independent of our practical totalization of it; if we could circumscribe an epistemologically privileged set of givens which had no dependence on our evaluative attitudes toward them. But every theoretical judgement presupposes an interpretation or totalization of its object which constitutes a practical assessment as to how the object ought to be construed, given a particular array of aims and concerns. In an eidetic grasp of the principle of noncontradiction, I have presupposed that "any object of judgement" *ought* to be construed in terms of a determinate significance that would define it in opposition to other determinate objects. This rests, in turn, on a practical concern with objects *as* determinate to the exclusion of any ambiguity which might haunt their appearance in our everyday life-world.[3]

My totalization of the world in the light of this concern provides a normative standard against which the law of non-contradiction cannot but appear obligatory. But this means that the theoretical judgement in which the law of non-contradiction is given can only ground an epistemic norm which would regulate my judgement *because* it presupposes a totalization that has already prescribed how objects ought to be understood in the first place. To this extent, it must remain insufficient as a theoretical foundation. For it must presuppose a practical totalization of the world in the light of which it may itself appear as a normatively appropriate, and hence, justifiable judgement to make.

Sartre's own paradoxical demand for an a priori foundation for dialectical reason which would have "nothing to do with any sort of constitutive principles which are prior to experience," and an apodictic experience contained "in the concrete world of History"[4] must be understood in this light. In insisting that we uncover a priori, apodictic foundations for dialectical reason within history, Sartre is attempting to chart his own distinctive path for the overcoming of empiricism. Though Sartre follows Husserl in rejecting an empirical understanding of reason, he does not attempt to overcome the historically contingent character of rationality by grounding 'the laws of reason' in an eidetic experience beyond history. The sense we have of the historical contingency of our attempts to rationally understand ourselves and our situation is not mistaken. But that sense needs to be deepened to include the sense of necessity that is engendered in the way the contingencies of history are lived as we attempt to make something of what history has made of us.

Apodicticity, for instance, only emerges in Sartre's account as a moment within the practical totalization of history. It constitutes a "formal inertia of intelligibility" as "the intelligibility of *praxis* comes to depend on the *result* of the *praxis*, both as it was projected and yet *always different*."[5] For praxis is always both a production of its own sense of intelligibility through its synthetic organization of exterior conditions in the light of its own aims and objectives, as well as the interiorization of that exteriority, not only as it was projected, but as distorted and altered by counter-finality. It is for this reason that Sartre describes the sort of alienation presupposed in our lived experience of the practico-inert as "the first structure of apodicticity."[6] It is *only the first* because it will demand significant complication in the forms of necessity instituted in and through the common praxis of the group. But *it is the first* in that all necessity is only a complication of this structure of praxis having to reinteriorize its exteriorized product as a normative structure of its endeavors—as the necessity of having, or of being obligated, to act in a certain manner. It is precisely this unsurpassable dependence of praxis on its altered product—"the indissoluble unity . . . of the organic on the inorganic"—that is "the absolute requirement *that there must be* a necessity at the very heart of intelligibility—and perpetually dissolved in the movement of practical understanding (*l'intellection pratique*)."[7]

Apodicticity, in Sartre's account, must be construed as a *practical* form of apodicticity. It is not the intuitive grasp of a theoretically indisputable eidetic relation, but only refers to our practical experience of necessity under specific social-historical conditions. Sartre's sense of apodicticity is irretrievably historical. The apodicticity of his own critical investigations does not reflect the indubitability of any timeless self-evidence, but only the necessity, under *our* particular circumstances, of having to cross the way of the dialectic when dealing with our knowledge of historical reality; of requiring precisely this form of thought, at this point in time, as an integral moment in our own attempts to rationally understand how our knowledge of history could be inextricably embedded in the history it attempts to know.[8]

Sartre's insistence that dialectical reason be grounded a priori, but not in terms of "any constitutive principles which are prior to experience" is, in much the same way, a mark of his own distinctively dialectical rejection of empiricism. Since the lived comprehension of praxis which grounds dialectical reason gives itself as a totalizing production of the practical contexts in terms of which the determination of empirical facts is first made possible, it resists characterization as an *a posteriori* foundation. Praxis is comprehended as a totalizing dimension of experience which is constitutively prior both to any theory as well as the range of empirical facts for which any theory must account. This comprehension may be said to ground dialectical reason (as a theory of history) a priori, because it gives itself not *as given*, but *as productive* of the given; as a practical realization of our historical situations with which any theory of history must come to terms. Sartre's critique of dialectical reason is, therefore, a priori and apodictic only insofar as the practical comprehension of history it articulates is historically and theoretically unsurpassable; not a theoretical foundation for our attempts to know history, but a non-theoretical limit of those theoretical endeavors.

Dialectical Reason and the Human Sciences: Rorty

To this extent, it is a mistake to seek theoretical foundations for the epistemic norms which define a sense of rational necessity for our epistemic practices. But this is not to deny any foundation whatsoever to those norms. Norms, as we have seen, demand interpretation that must ultimately be a matter of practice. And this interpretation-in-practice constitutes a practical foundation for our sense of rational necessity that cannot be overlooked in any adequate account of knowledge. For if we remain only with the denial of theoretical foundations, if we follow Rorty in reading the lesson of Sellars's critique of the myth of the given simply in terms of a need to give up our Cartesian desire for an Archimedean foundation for knowledge, we risk losing a dimension of our epistemic practices that is crucial to any coherent account of them *as epistemic* practices. We lose that totalizing, evaluative and interpretive dimension that "sustains, controls, and justifies" their formal structure. We lose, in other words, any comprehension of the practice itself *as rational*.

A symptom of that loss may be discerned from an examination of Rorty's rejection of the idea of an epistemological distinction between the natural and human sciences. Extrapolating from the demise of foundationalism, Rorty argues that all science is equally hermeneutic, equally attempts at "muddling through, rather than conforming to canons of rationality—coping with people and things rather than corresponding to reality by discovering essences."⁹ With this point, Rorty correctly grasps the impossibility of specifying *a* definitive methodology for the human sciences, given the absence of any theoretical foundations for our epistemic practices. But he fails to grasp the specific pragmatic constraints that are placed on the human sciences by virtue of their need to account not only for their objects of study, but for their own knowledge of those objects inasmuch as that knowledge is, as one social practice among others, one of those very objects. For despite his pragmatism, Rorty fails to recognize the need to account for the practical foundations of our attempts to know the world in a way which can appreciate not only their historical contingency, but their rational necessity as well.

In an article addressed to Rorty on just this issue, Hubert Dreyfus has focused on the specific sorts of non-theoretical constraints the social sciences face in terms of their inability to form, in Kuhn's sense, a normal or paradigmatic discourse. He argues there, that inasmuch as every theoretical account is itself made possible by a range of background skills or practices which form the specific historical-pragmatic context in which it is deployed; and inasmuch as the constitution of normality in a science is made possible by placing such pragmatic contexts of inquiry out of legitimate scientific consideration (embodying, as they do, an entire range of pretheoretical assumptions about the mode and object of inquiry); then the rise of normality in the human sciences must take on a very different significance from its counterpart in the sciences of nature. For in the natural sciences, there is no loss. The pragmatic background of their inquiry is not, per se, an object of their study. Placing it out of consideration is only a matter of taking for granted the practical or technical conditions that make their study *of other things* possible. In the human sciences, however, it constitutes an internal blind spot—an ability to account for every facet of social reality except its own historical genesis as a theoretical practice. Normality, therefore, spells the end of the critical/reflective character of the human sciences in favor of a naive discourse which dogmatically limits the range of its questions in just such a way that it does not raise the question of its own conditions of possibility.

> Thus, while in the natural sciences it is always possible and generally desirable that an unchallenged normal science which defines and resolves problems concerning the structure of the physical universe establish itself, in the social sciences such an unchallenged normal science would only indicate that an orthodoxy had gained control. It would mean that the basic job of exploring the background of practices and their meaning had been forgotten, and that the unique feature of human behavior, the human self-interpretation embodied in our everyday know-how (*Vorhabe*), was not being investigated but simply ignored.[10]

There are, though, two quite different ways in which this ignorance might be avoided. On the one hand, Rorty counsels a strategy of simply deferring the honors of "science" and "objectivity" to the objectifying tendencies within the social sciences, and letting it go at that.[11] One need not worry that their growing hegemony, their push toward normality, will end in the ignorance of our ongoing practical self-interpretation.

> Given leisure and libraries, the conversation which Plato began will not end in self-objectification—not because aspects of the world, or of human beings escape objects of scientific inquiry, but simply because free and leisured conversation generates abnormal discourse as the sparks fly upward.[12]

Rorty imagines a place for a nonobjectifying self-interpretation outside the fortified boundaries of normal discourse, segregated, if you will, from its "serious" epistemic domain—a sort of "conversational" homeland for critical, philosophical discourse. Such a segregated homeland would in practice, though, only constitute a discursive ghetto. As Dreyfus points out, this strategy reduces abnormal nonobjectifying discourse to the status of subjective opinion or preference; nothing which need, in short, be taken too seriously.[13] Serious scientific endeavor would be on one side of the fence, quietly uncovering the laws or contingencies of human behavior. On the other side, there would only remain an irrational squabbling over what to do with or make of such knowledge. And this would, no doubt, be impotent as well, as such issues would already be decided objectively by trained economists or political scientists.

If this bleak prospect is to be avoided, one must insist that the investigation of our practical interpretation of ourselves, the exploration of the sense and direction of the practices that form the background of our theoretical endeavors, be integrated into the theoretical projects of the human sciences themselves. The idea of integrating these endeavors never occurs to Rorty precisely because he assumes that an account of practice internal to theory would constitute a foundation of the *practice* of theorizing in a *theory* of practice. And, as he emphasizes,

> The last thing I want is what Dreyfus says theoretical holists want, namely a theory of practice. It is precisely Habermas' mistake to think that everything will be fine once we bring theory and practice together by having, of all things, a theory of practice. It would make as much sense to say, lets have a practice of theorizing. We've already got one, and if you have a practice of theorizing, you don't need a theory of practice.[14]

Limiting himself to a rejection of all theoretical foundations for knowledge, Rorty embraces the very discursive options presupposed by Habermas and fails to imagine the possibility of a non-theoretical account that would disclose, internal to theory itself, its own foundations in practice. This is, of course, the strategy Sartre offers. For Sartre, the self-referential character of the human sciences need not entail that they construct a theory of practice which would itself presuppose an unexamined pragmatic background of pre-theoretical assumptions and interests, making yet another theory of practice necessary, and so on. The exploration of our ongoing practical interpretation-totalization of ourselves, our common practical sense of who we are and what we are about, must constitute a non-theoretical moment of our theoretical knowledge. It constitutes a recognition on the part of those theories that take human beings as their object, that their theoretical endeavors are only a moment of that practical self-interpretation which envelops them and that, consequently, their object of study cannot be both coherently and exhaustively explained *as an object*.

It is difficult to imagine what precise theoretical effects this non-theoretical foundationalism might have. Analytical models of human action, such as those which have proliferated with such abundance in this century—behavioral, structural or cognitive approaches—could not integrate a practical comprehension of their endeavors without a significant modification of their understanding of the meaning of behavior, structure or cognition. It would, minimally, entail a recognition of the provisional status of those conceptualizations—an insight into their nongeneralizability outside a limited range of pragmatically defined parameters. It is useful, at times, to think of human beings as a set of behaviors or formal computations. It is necessary to comprehend, however, that these objects of knowledge are themselves productive of that knowledge, and so cannot be exhaustively objectified in any theoretical system without undercutting our own claims to know. As Sartre notes,

> This perpetual dissolution of intellection in comprehension and, conversely, the perpetual redescent which introduces comprehension into intellection as a dimension of *rational non-knowledge* at the heart of knowledge is the very ambiguity of a discipline in which the questioner, the question, and the questioned are one.[15]

Sartre's dialectical vision of the human sciences does not entail the elimination of analytical models of understanding. To the contrary, it demands a multiplication of them. In *Search For a Method*, Sartre recommends the integration of various analytical disciplines—psychoanalysis and American sociology, in particular—within Marxism as a way of overcoming its abstract dogmatic[16] status through the concrete mediations those disciplines offer. In doing so he, therefore, recognizes the importance of a diversity of analytical accounts in bringing to light aspects of our social-historical situation which might otherwise go unnoticed. But it is equally important to ground that methodological pluralism in a non-theoretical comprehension (a "rational non-knowledge") of the historical practices they are meant to illuminate. This is, after all, the heart and soul of Sartre's progressive-regressive "method"—a theoretically unfettered use of whatever facts may lie at our disposal, disclosed from whatever theoretical perspective, followed by a comprehensive integration of those facts in an attempt to recapitulate the totalization which must live them as the conditions of some practical endeavor. This "dissolution of intellection in comprehension" does not establish any formal methodological or theoretical constraints within the human sciences. Sartre's efforts to establish "the dialectic as the universal method and universal law of anthropology"[17] would only entail a set of formal methodological or theoretical constraints if the dialectic could itself be reduced to a formal system of rationality or a formal theory of history. But it does place definite non-theoretical constraints on their practice as it conditions the pragmatic way in which their project may be pursued—as an ongoing practice of self-interpretation which cannot, as Dreyfus notes, end in a stable theoretical knowledge of their object.

Incommensurability and the Politics of Dialectical Reason: Feyerabend and Lyotard

Sartre's non-theoretical foundationalism differs from the antifoundationalism of Rorty or Feyerabend only in its insistence on the need to recognize a sense of rational necessity which can, at bottom, only be lived or comprehended, never theoretically determined or known. In failing to recognize this specifically dialectical sense of rationality, both Rorty and Feyerabend wind up painting an implicit picture of our epistemic practices which is inadequate to their own pragmatic need to comprehend themselves as historically situated, yet rational endeavors. For Rorty, this inadequacy is apparent in his inability to appreciate the non-theoretical distinctiveness of the human sciences. For Feyerabend, it emerges in the way he overlooks the role of practical comprehension in the very idea of incommensurable theoretical traditions.

His point concerning incommensurability is, of course, well taken. If theory is itself a form of praxis which forms its experience of the world in line with its own theoretical and practical presuppositions, then there is no reason to suppose that the same set of facts will hold across all cultures and at all times. But the possibility of grasping this point presupposes an ability to experience this incongruity. It takes for granted a capacity to be taught other ways of seeing the world and to comprehend these ways as divergent forms of life. And since this cannot be a form of translation from one theory into another (as this would only be completely possible with commensurable theories), it can only be a function of our ability to *practically* appropriate other theoretical practices, to learn other languages—to comprehend other practices *as*, like our own, historically particular totalizations-interpretations of their material and social environments. Sartre clearly has something like this in mind when he writes,

> It would be impossible to find a "human nature" which is common to Murians, for example, and to the historical man of our contemporary societies. But, conversely, a real communication and in certain situations a reciprocal comprehension are established or can be established between existents thus distinct (for example, between the ethnologist and the young Murians who speak of their *gothul*). It is in order to take into account these opposed characteristics (no common *nature* but an always possible communication) that the movement of anthropology once again

and in a new form gives rise to the "ideology of existence."[18]

Theoretical incommensurability implies practical comprehension. For otherwise communication between incommensurable cultures would be impossible and incommensurable theoretical practices would appear to each other not as alien systems of thought and action, but as merely bizarre phenomena, utterly lacking in any coherent sense. Our need to appreciate incommensurable forms of rationality presupposes that we are able to practically comprehend a sense of rational necessity that cannot, in principle, be defined in terms of "our own" particular epistemic norms. It presupposes that we are able to comprehend the rational necessity of other modes of life and thought in terms of the practical totalizations which engender them.

Feyerabend's discussion of an open exchange between theories suffers from the same limitation. As long as rational necessity is only understood theoretically, as a formal system of rules of correct inference and assertion, Feyerabend is accurate in describing a rational exchange as guided. With such hegemony, reason translates as the oppression of imagination and dissent. Feyerabend's critique joins here with Lyotard's defense of the heterogeneity of language games. For knowledge under such a guided regime could only be a function of the domination of one language game over others. But without at least a degree of comprehension on the part of the traditions involved that their various positions are practical interpretations, formed in terms of individualized universals whose validity is limited by their respective social and pragmatic contexts, an open exchange must inevitably degenerate into a babble of mutually incomprehensible tongues, in which, in the best case, all leave each other to "do their own thing," or, in the worst case, each jockies for power over the others. In the case of competing theoretical traditions this would be a matter of each dogmatically asserting the truth of *their own* position to the exclusion of the others, with a best case in which everyone ignores the claims of the others, and a worst case in which everyone attempts to bring the others to some version of their own inquisition. In neither case, however, is anything like an "exchange" possible.

Grounding the exchange in a practical comprehension of the positions of the participants, on the other hand, does not legitimate some voices to the exclusion of others. It, rather, makes possible the self-conscious production of an exchange *as open*, where all parties recognize their positions as pragmatically limited, and so without any absolute claim to epistemic authority over the others. And for that reason, they may enter the exchange with a sense of their reciprocity in relation to one another and a need to keep their positions negotiable. The possibility of "reciprocal comprehension" which Sartre notes between ethnologists and the communities they study, is an example of this. Such reciprocity is only possible on the basis of each recognizing the provisional and limited character of their own traditions, if only at a level which is lived and for the most part unthematized. For theoretical traditions, a truly open exchange is only possible to the extent that such a lived reciprocal comprehension can be replicated in terms of a recognition of the need to develop, evaluate, and in time, discard any formal canon of rationality in line with the various problems and interests that motivate their specific inquiries.

If Sartre's thesis involved grounding all social-theoretic discourse on the theory of historical materialism, his foundationalism would be open to Feyerabend's criticism. Dialectical reason cannot, however, be reduced to any specific theoretical system, but is, in the primary instance, the practical rationality that "sustains, controls, and justifies" every formal sense of rationality. The comprehension of this nonformalizable rationality is not only *not* inconsistent with the values of an open exchange, it is presupposed by them. It is what it takes to keep the exchange open. For dialectical reason is, as Sartre and Marx before him knew, a political rationality bound up with the practical transcendence of alienated forms of existence. It is the comprehension of one's freedom on the basis of the denial of that freedom in the midst of concrete historical circumstances,[19] and so remains, as Sartre puts it in the *Critique,* one with "the practical consciousness of an oppressed class struggling against its oppressor."[20] Though an open exchange cannot, if it is to remain open, presuppose any formal set of rules that would guide and define it, it must, nevertheless, presuppose a political practice capable of resisting the potential hegemony of any particular discursive regime; a politics that would resist the practico-inert repetition of traditional standards and forms of life through the inability of the community to act or think differently in favor of the cultivation of a milieu of reciprocity and negotiation in which their standards may be, as Feyerabend describes it, "determined, improved, refined, [and] eliminated by the traditions themselves. . . . "[21] For the exchange to be open, it must rest on the comprehension, both practical and political, of resisting the practico-inert authority of any received form of life on the basis of, as Sartre puts it, "the unconditioned possibility of making man."[22]

The political dimension of Feyerabend's critique of reason, understood as a guided exchange, is motivated, I believe, by an awareness of the same sort of radical injustice that Lyotard describes in his discussion of "the differend." "As distinguished from a litigation," Lyotard stipulates, "a differend (différend) would be a case of conflict, between (at least) two parties, that cannot be equitably resolved for lack of a rule of judgment applicable to both arguments."[23] A differend is, as such, a dispute between traditions or forms of life with incommensurable standards. Resolving the dispute in terms of either set of standards must, then, wrong one of the parties by forcing them, illegitimately, to accept the standards of the other. Lyotard gives as an example of such a wrong the case of bourgeois economic contracts that require employees to resolve any dispute with their employer in terms of a frame of reference in which they may only speak of their work as a service or commodity they own and freely sell. Imposing this rule on both disputants, of course, allows both parties to "have a say," but only on terms that prevent employees, in principle, from being able to speak of the damages done to them by virtue of having to treat their labor as a commodity.[24] They are effectively silenced in that regard by the rules that guide the exchange or, in this case, the resolution of the conflict between them. To the extent that no set of discursive rules or standards is applicable to any and every culture, tradition or situation, every *guided* exchange must, therefore, harbor the threat of a differend and a form of injustice it can only sustain in silence.

The politics that would resist that silence, that would construct the practices and idioms necessary for differends to be expressed and respected, cannot take the form of a *single* form of life or discursive order, as that would only renew the problem to be addressed. This is why Lyotard insists that politics, or the politics that would be adequate to the conflict between incommensurable forms of life and discourse, may not take the form of one discursive genre among others, but must be a "deliberative concatenation of genres" in which differends are capable of being exposed as such.[25] Echoing Feyerabend's emphasis that a genuinely open exchange between traditions cannot take place in terms of the standards of a single tradition, Lyotard projects a vision of politics that would be constituted only in an arena of deliberation between traditions and discursive genres—a deliberative arena "where the multiplicity of genres and their respective ends can in principle be expressed . . . which is sensitive to the heterogeneous ends implied in the various known and unknown genres of discourse, and capable of pursuing them as much as possible. . . ."[26]

This would be impossible, however, without some form of "reciprocal comprehension" between the participants of the deliberation. Lyotard and Feyerabend are correct in emphasizing the need for a politics that would not be grounded in any one tradition. But a politics capable of sustaining an open exchange in which differends are exposed rather than silenced must foster a dialectical comprehension of the positions of the participants of the exchange *as* historically limited practices, totalizing the world from formally incommensurable, but reciprocally comprehensible perspectives. The exchange swims, so to speak, in this comprehension, which allows a recognition of the potentially multiple legitimacy of the claims raised there. Far from limiting the exchange, it is what opens it up. The deliberative arena which Lyotard describes is part and parcel of the constitution and elaboration of that reciprocal comprehension. For it is only in and through such open and unconstrained deliberations that one can hope to comprehend both the heterogeneity of the participants as well as the possibility of common practices which might foster and support that heterogeneity in a milieu of mutual cooperation.

Dialectical reason resists formal definition precisely because it is a praxis through which any and every formal sense of rationality is constructed and, in time, subverted. This implies, in turn, a politics that resists theoretical closure to the degree that it is constituted in a praxis that can only define itself through its own project. But in that very gesture of self-determination, it projects itself as unconditionally possible, as the unconditional possibility of making itself anew through opening up the material and discursive traditions which condition it to an open-ended practice of reciprocity and negotiation. This practice *is* dialectical reason as a simultaneously rational and political endeavor. Though it is beyond the scope of this essay to deal with this point in any really adequate way, it is not difficult to discern the beginnings of a convergence here between Sartre's epistemological and political concerns. For both ultimately rest on the affirmation of the "unconditioned possibility of making man" inherent in the totalizing movement of praxis itself, in which rationality and freedom are posed as a single task.

This "task" of dialectical reason, if one may speak this way, is that of securing common horizons of intelligibility in terms of which communities may construct their forms of life for themselves, through what Feyerabend describes as an open exchange or through what Lyotard describes as a form of politics in which the rules of our language games and forms of life are "subject to discussion."[27] In emphasizing a convergence between rationality and political emancipation, Sartre's work seemingly joins with Habermas's, as well. Though, as we have seen, Habermas's project of determining the formal rules and principles that would regulate rational forms of life must be abandoned, the idea of a convergence between rationality and "democratic decision-making"[28] is not alien to Sartre's thought. As discussed in chapter 5, the practice of giving and asking for reasons in our epistemic practices is itself a democratization of the power relations that condition the social practice of knowledge and, as discussed in chapter 8, the rational intelligibility of a form of life is ultimately contingent on the relations of reciprocity that allow a community to actively participate in its formation. If it were not for their failure to discern the seeds of a practical form of rationality implicit in their critiques of the limitations of formal rationality, the same convergence might be apparent in the work of Feyerabend and Lyotard. For both correctly sense the political issues posed by the recognition of incommensurable forms of rationality, and succeed in grasping the outline of a politics that would respect that incommensurability. But they fail to discern the dialectical rationality inherent in that politics; a rationality capable of sustaining, in a coherent way, the rationality of their own politically informed critiques of reason.

The idea of a common praxis, formed and maintained through the reciprocity and cooperative negotiation of its participants, is, therefore, a simultaneously political and epistemological ideal. It makes possible an epistemological distinction between rationality and irrationality in terms of the difference between the rational necessity of a form of thought that is practically intelligible to those engaged to it as an integral moment of their own common praxis and the practico-inert necessity of a system of beliefs that maintains its hegemony through the practical inability of anyone to think otherwise. And it makes possible a political distinction between freedom and oppression in terms of the difference between the sort of libertarian[29] or democratic socialism that would foster the social and economic conditions for the transcendence of alienated forms of life and any of the bourgeois or collectivist forms of oppression that deprive individuals of their ability to become participants in the negotiation of their own forms of life. It is important to remember, though it is all too easy to forget, the lesson of Foucault's account of power and knowledge: that politics and epistemology are essentially two sides of the same coin. The dialectical production of rationality implies the free participation of the community in the common practices through which it is produced and the freedom of the community to negotiate its own future is, in that very gesture, the production of a form of rationality appropriate to its aims and concerns. To this extent, the practical foundations of rational necessity are also political foundations. They sketch not merely the "always-to-be-determined" horizon of multiple and formally incommensurable modes of rational intelligibility, but the "never-to-be-foreclosed" horizon of multiple and formally incommensurable modes of political self-determination.

Chapter 11

The Transhistorical
Conditions of Historical Knowledge

Our knowledge of history is, in the final analysis, inextricably historical. There is no Archimedean point outside the flux of history upon which that knowledge might be secured or anchored. But in recognizing this, one is not forced back to the sort of empiricism that can only chart the contingent links between knowledge and its historical conditions. For there is a sense of necessity, of rational necessity, preserved in the way praxis must appropriate the contingencies of its historical situation and comprehend them as the intelligible conditions of its own endeavors. The dialectical rationality of history appears there—in the lived comprehension of our own practical production of history which gives itself within history, paradoxically, as the absolute condition for the possibility of history; which gives itself, as Sartre puts it, as "transhistorical."[1]

Comprehension, Historicity, and Transhistoricity

In characterizing our lived comprehension of history as transhistorical, Sartre intends, I believe, to draw attention to the inadequacy of accounting for our lived experience of history as merely another empirically discernible moment in the contingent unfolding of history itself. For history *as lived* is, in fact, the condition for the possibility of there being *historical facts*, in that, (1) it gives itself as the productive-interpretive ground for anyone being able to take something as a *fact* (the totalizing context within which determinate significance is formed), and (2) it gives itself as the form our

187

historical knowledge must take if it is to coherently grasp any situation *as historical* (as, that is, the specific product of the labor of individuals who are themselves the product of the labor of others). It is, therefore, the absolute foundation for any contingent historical event not by virtue of its transcendence of history, but by virtue of its transcendence of *specific histories*, as the productive ground of history itself; a *trans*historical condition of historical knowledge.

Sartre grapples with this point extensively in his essay on Kierkegaard, where he writes,

> To seek the beginning of knowledge is to affirm that the foundation of temporality is, precisely, timeless, and that the historical individual can wrench himself free of History, de-situate himself and relocate his fundamental timelessness by a direct vision of being. . . . To avoid this, Kierkegaard took as his point of departure the *person* envisaged as non-knowledge, that is to say in as much as he both produces and discovers, at a given moment in the temporal unfolding of his life, his relation to an absolute which is itself inserted in History. In short, far from denying the beginning, Kierkegaard testified to a beginning that is lived.[2]

To endorse a "beginning which is lived" is not, however, to surreptitiously return to a "direct vision of being" that could constitute a *pre*theoretical insight into history as it is in itself. There is no experience (with any even *indirectly* epistemic status) that is not theory laden. Sartre's explicit recognition that "comprehension . . . can take place only within a concrete situation, insofar as theoretical knowledge illuminates this situation,"[3] reflects just this point. As has already been seen, he regarded both Kierkegaard's thought, as well as his own, as theoretically parasitic attempts to indirectly designate "the lived" within the contexts of Hegelianism and Marxism, respectively. Our comprehension of the lived is, as any concrete praxis must be, historically determined in terms of the theoretical and practical possibilities which envelop it.

> The paradox . . . is the fact that we discover the absolute in the relative. . . . the experience which turns back upon itself, after the leap, comprehends itself more than it knows itself. In other words, it sustains itself in the milieu of the presuppositions that are its foundation, without succeeding in elucidating them. Hence a beginning that is a dogma.[4]

Our reflective comprehension of ourselves can only articulate itself in terms of the theoretical and non-theoretical discursive possibilities at its disposal. It is in the very attempt to know ourselves historically as a product of social, political and material conditions, that there arises the structural possibility of speaking, in particular ways, of having to live those conditions as the historical presuppositions of our practical endeavors. The paradox remains, though, in that the historical knowledge which makes possible such comprehension also makes it necessary that one grasp this living of history as itself irreducible to the array of historical facts in terms of which it is designated. If our knowledge of ourselves as historical determines, by its theoretical exclusion of it, a comprehension of that history as lived, then

> each of us, in our very historicity, escapes History to the extent that we make it. I myself am historical to the extent that others also make history and make me, but I am a transhistorical absolute by virtue of what I make of what they make of me, have made of me and will make of me in the future—that is by virtue of my historiality (*historiality*).[5]

The paradox of escaping history through one's historicity, of affirming the absolute in the relative, the transhistorical at the heart of the historical; these dialectical twists where the conditioned (history) is understood as, at bottom, unconditional (transhistorical), and the unconditional as itself subject to conditions (our comprehension of the transhistorical dimensions of praxis as a theoretically parasitic or "indirect" designation), resolve themselves ultimately into an epistemological circle. Our knowledge of history is conditioned by our transhistorical comprehension of history, which in turn is conditioned by the knowledge of history it makes possible. Such is the price one pays for Sartre's non-theoretical foundationalism. If it were possible to remain content with either no beginnings or a beginning that is known, such circularity could be avoided. A "beginning which is lived," on the other hand, appears as if it involves a hopelessly vicious form of circularity. And indeed it *is* vicious *if* one still asks of it what is asked of theoretical foundationalism, i.e., a formal ground in relation to which the validity of other theoretical knowledge may be derived. For here the ground presupposes the validity of the knowledge it would establish, and so begs the question. But if it is taken for what it is—an interpretive account of our knowledge of ourselves that seeks to render its historicity coherent with its rationality—then it ceases to be vicious, and becomes a more-or-less adequate formalization of how such practical self-interpretation is possible. It resembles a materialist version of the hermeneutic circle, where every interpretation presupposes a prior interpretation which functions as the horizon of meaning within which it takes place. Only here, the horizon of meaning is a material totalization involving, among other things, a discursive totalization of that totalization.

The circularity of dialectical reason is the residue of the contradiction of the knowledge of being and the being of knowledge, dialectically overcome. In the first chapter of the *Critique,* Sartre had characterized the epistemological challenge of the materialist dialectic as that of the coherent elaboration of a material interdependence between thought and its object where

> thought must discover its own necessity in its material object, at the same time as discovering in itself, *in so far as it is itself a material being,* the necessity of its object. This could be done within Hegelian idealism, and either the dialectic is a dream or it can be done in the real material world of Marxism. This inevitably refers us from thought to action.[6]

How can the knowledge of being know itself as a being conditioned by other beings and still assert its rationality? The key lies in Sartre's linking of material and rational necessity in his dialectical account of praxis. Thought discovers its necessity in its object as a function of its recognition of itself as a material praxis, conditioned historically by its situation. And yet, it also discovers the necessity of its object in itself as a materially productive totalization of its situation. Once it comprehends itself as praxis, thought is able to recognize both its material contingency and its rational necessity as complementary modes of the deployment of a practical rationality that is irreducible to either. As practical reason, thought "legislates" the epistemic contours of the world[7] through the production of a practical horizon of intelligibility in terms of which anything can be known as such. But in giving up its claim to a transcendental status, thought must also recognize its epistemological access to itself as conditioned by the historical situation that envelops it, including among other things, the theoretical discourse it comprehends itself as productively or constitutively prior to.

Hilary Putnam's argument for the irreducibility of reason to whatever set of epistemic standards happen to be currently accepted by the community[8] needs, therefore, to be balanced by his other claim: that our conception of this transcultural sense of reason cannot exist apart from the cultures in which we happen to find ourselves.

> On the one hand, there is no notion of reasonableness at all *without* cultures, practices, procedures; on the other hand, the cultures, practices, procedures we inherit are not an algorithm to be slavishly followed. . . . Reason is, in this sense, both immanent (not to be found outside of concrete language games and institutions) and transcendent (a regulative idea we use to criticize the conduct of all activities and institutions).[9]

It is important to grasp both aspects of this "reasonableness" in their interdependence—reason as immanent *and* transcendent; dialectical reason as historical knowledge (a constituted theoretical tradition) *and* transhistorical comprehension (constitutive practical reason). For in losing sight of its transcendence, one loses sight of the practical, interpretive and evaluative dimension of reason. And in overlooking its immanence, one implicitly idealizes one's own cultural interpretation of reason as the vantage point of eternity.

The Historical Conditions of Transhistorical Comprehension

If our indirect knowledge of this transhistorical dimension of reason is indeed immanent to a specific historical tradition; if, as Sartre emphasizes, "the universals of the dialectic—principles and laws of intelligibility—are individualised universals; attempts at abstraction and universalisation . . . valid *for that process*,"[10] then the question that immediately follows concerns the *historical* limits of the validity of these very claims. Sartre's *Critique* is an attempt to establish the limits and extent of the validity of dialectical reason. But what of the limits and extent of the validity of that very project? Sartre himself provides an implicit answer to this question by situating his thought in terms of the opposition between knowing and being, as this arises as a theoretical problem within Marxism. The notion of praxis as comprehension, as a nonformalizable, transhistorical rationality, is a specific response to a specific problem. Its validity is, therefore, limited to the extent of this problem. In traditions for which the historicity of knowledge is not a problem,[11] a dialectical conception of praxis is not so much invalid, as it is neither valid nor invalid, but simply irrelevant, addressing itself to nothing at all. Are Sartre's ideas, then, valid only for Marxists? Is the idea of integrating comprehension into the human sciences as their non-theoretical foundation only compelling to the theoretical "vanguard" of the proletariat? Surely not. As illustrated by our dialogues with Foucault, Rorty, Feyerabend, Habermas, and Lyotard, the relevance and validity of Sartre's thought is not restricted to the specific context in which it was engendered. Though the problem of the opposition of knowing and being, of the relation between theory and practice is, perhaps, most explicit for historical materialism, it is not limited to this tradition. It extends, in principle, to any attempt to account for knowledge as a finite, historical or material state of affairs, realized by individuals or communities under specific conditions. It is, therefore, valid for any of the self-referential disciplines which, in a rather motley fashion, go to make up the human or social sciences.

Michel Foucault's account of the structure and historical genesis of these disciplines in *The Order of Things* is of particular relevance here. For he sketches there a picture of the historical singularity of the human sciences. "Man," he claims rather dramatically, "is only a recent invention, a figure not yet two centuries old. . . ."[12] Far from supposing, as most do, that the figure of "man" has been an object of knowledge since antiquity, Foucault sets out to show that the human sciences emerged in terms of a historically particular understanding of human reality. Specifically, "man . . . is a strange empirico-transcendental doublet, since he is a being such that knowledge will be attained in him of what renders all knowledge possible."[13] Emerging in the light of developments in the sciences of life, labor and language which disclosed our relation to the world in terms of organic, economic and linguistic mechanisms that could not be understood as transparent mediums in which the truth of the world might be represented,[14] it was impossible for the human sciences to remain content with a Cartesian understanding of knowledge as a matter of "clear and distinct" representations of the world. For those representations were now understood as conditioned by historically contingent forces which called into question their uncritical claim to provide a cognitively adequate representation of the world. The figure of man was born as the seat of such problematic representations. In organizing themselves around the study of man, therefore, the human sciences found themselves with an empirical object that could no longer be studied uncritically as one object of nature among others because it was that particular object which made possible (or impossible) the very knowledge that would account for it. The problem of the conditions of the possibility of knowledge emerge here, for the first time, as a unique problem to be addressed either in terms of the empirical givens of the human condition or the transcendental presuppositions which make the knowledge of such givens possible. The "sciences of man" as we know them today were born, according to Foucault, at the heart of this historically singular problematic.

It is in terms of this split between the empirical and transcendental aspects of man that Foucault outlines a number of strategies by which the human sciences have attempted to overcome the structural instability of their object. Vacillating between conflicting tendencies toward understanding the empirical or positive appearance of its object in the light of a transcendental or foundational reflection, or those transcendental reflections in the light of its empirical knowledge, Foucault's account of the necessary ambivalence of the human sciences mirrors their own historical failure to form a single coherent theoretical discourse.

> It is the status of this true discourse that remains ambiguous. . . . either this true discourse finds its foundation and model in the empirical truth whose genesis in nature and in history it retraces, so that one has an analysis of the positivist type (the truth of the object determines the truth of the discourse that describes its formation); or the true discourse anticipates the truth whose nature and history it defines; it sketches it out in advance and forments it from a distance, so that one has a discourse of the eschatological type (the truth of the philosophical discourse constitutes the truth in formation).[15]

And since neither position is ultimately tenable, with positivism always contesting the transcendental status of any philosophical discourse and the epistemological inadequacy of positivism always calling forth a philosophical reflection on the foundations of its knowledge, the attempt to know man as an empirico-transcendental doublet is formed as an essentially unstable enterprise, forever ambivalent between its positivist and transcendental tendencies.

Clearly, it is in just this sort of discursive context, where there is an inherent instability and tension between man as knowing subject and as known object, that Sartre's critical reflections are situated. The opposition between knowing and being, between labor as an enveloping ground of theory and theory as a valid account of labor, is the particular form in which the empirico-transcendental doublet is sketched as a theoretical issue within Marxism. Of course, Sartre himself would *and did* balk at the suggestion that he was a philosopher of man. As he noted in an interview concerning Foucault himself, " 'Man' does not exist, and Marx had rejected it long before Foucault or Lacan when he said: 'I do not see man, I see only workers, bourgeoisie, intellectuals.' "[16] This misses the point, however, as far as Foucault is concerned. It is, no doubt, true that Sartre, as Marx before him, had turned away from an abstract analysis of human nature toward an account of the praxis which produces 'human nature' under concrete historical circumstances. But insofar as Sartre continues to think of human praxis as the condition for the possibility of any knowledge one might have of it, the instability of the empirico-transcendental doublet is maintained in his thought as a conceptual frame of reference in terms of which "the human condition" may be understood.

The relevance of Foucault's analysis lies, then, in his circumscription of what might be the discursive and historical limits of the validity of Sartre's account, and in his further unsettling claim that this context is itself drawing to a close; that the "true contestation of positivism and eschatology" lies not in attempts to question after the unity of the transcendental and empirical dimensions of the human condition, but in being done with the whole anthropological enterprise by raising the more radical question, "Does man really exist?"[17] From this perspective, Sartre's project appears already dated; a final variation on an anthropological theme whose theoretical potential has been exhausted. To challenge the instability of the empirico-transcendental doublet one must be rid of the anthropological obsession which links every question concerning knowledge with a question concerning its "human" foundations. One must follow Foucault in seeking a mode of thought that no longer presupposes that anthropological frame of reference. And yet, as Dreyfus and Rabinow argue, Foucault's own attempt to overcome the epistemological instability of the emprico-transcendental doublet remains inscribed in the instability of that frame of reference despite his critique of our "anthropological sleep."[18] Their comments suggest a need to rethink the significance of Foucault's analysis. For it is not the *anthropology* that is unstable in anthropological theory so much as it is the *theory*—the attempt on the part of the human sciences to theoretically objectify the background conditions of their own discourse. "As Foucault has shown us, all such theories of human beings must fail because the attempt to grasp the total picture requires theories to objectify the conditions which make objectification possible."[19] And Foucault remains committed, in his own way, to that unstable theoretical project.

As emphasized in chapter 3, Foucault attempts to adopt a perspective of strict exteriority in relation to the practices he describes. "My aim was to analyze this history in a discontinuity that no teleology would reduce in advance; to map it in a dispersion that no pre-established horizon would embrace . . . to cleanse it of all transcendental narcissism."[20] His analysis consequently rejects taking discourse as it is lived by the individuals who engage in it. His aim is to account for the appearance of discourse in terms of the rules of formation that explain the particular dispersions it assumes when analyzed in its inert silence as a series of historical "monuments."[21] This attempt to stand outside any "pre-established horizon" of meaning or truth, as it is lived by those engaged in the discursive practices in question, commits Foucault, however, to an inherently ambivalent discursive position. On the one hand, he must understand the horizon of meanings lived by the participants of the discourse he analyzes, if he is to be able to distinguish different statements. For identical discursive events may differ in their function as statements, depending on their significance. On the other hand, he must stand outside this horizon if he is to grasp the rules of formation that govern, exterior to that lived significance, the discourse as a set of inert events. He, therefore, replicates the empirico-transcendental split, placing his own discourse in the position of a detached spectator, unable to account for its own detachment.[22]

Foucault may have been aware of this difficulty. As he playfully admitted in the conclusion to *The Archeology of Knowledge*, "as far ahead as I can see, my discourse, far from determining the locus in which it speaks, is avoiding the ground on which it could find support."[23] Unable to account for its own detachment or, in that detachment, to involve itself in the lived horizon of meaning which animates the discourse it studies, Foucault's archeology must vacillate between the two, rendering both untenable. For the horizon of meaning which animates the discourse of the community is illusory in relation to the rules of formation that underlie it, as judged from Foucault's position of detachment. But the detachment that uncovers this is unable to determine the status of its own perspective in relation to that community. Rejecting the "transcendental narcissism" of anthropology is, therefore, no guarantee of freeing oneself from the structural instability of the empirico-transcendental doublet, inasmuch as it is the attempt to theoretically objectify that which is taken as the condition of objectification that generates the instability of "man" as a theoretical object of knowledge, not an emphasis on 'the human' as such.

Sartre's position could be best described, then, as a different sort of response to this instability. Instead of rejecting the anthropological dimension of thought, he challenges our understanding of the role of theory by integrating it into the unknowable, yet comprehensible movement of praxis. The *Critique of Dialectical Reason* is, therefore, a critique undertaken at the heart of the empirico-transcendental doublet which attempts to defuse its instability by abandoning the *theoretical* project that generates it. Taking seriously this received interpretation of ourselves instead of trying to step outside it, Sartre constructs an interpretation of this interpretation which renders it *practically* coherent, in terms of reinterpreting the human foundations of knowledge as nonobjectifiable and non-theoretical. The theoretical project of *knowing* the identity of the empirical and the transcendental is replaced by an interpretive project which practically *comprehends* their identity in terms of the mutual envelopment of the historical and transhistorical dimensions of history as lived. The 'doublet' remains, then, in terms of the epistemological circle which animates dialectical reason. But its ambivalence and instability are overcome as both the empirical and foundational dimensions of the human condition are comprehended as moments of an ongoing practical self-interpretation which can never be arrested in theory, but only further interpreted in terms of the social practices and commitments which determine it.

Dialectical Reason and Historical Relativism

The historical limits and extent of the validity of Sartre's interpretation of dialectical reason are clearly bound up with the self-referential project of the human sciences, both as this has emerged theoretically in terms of the empirico-transcendental doublet, and as it might be continued in terms of a practical self-interpretation that comprehends its own epistemic status as such. It is, therefore, a historically relative account of the historical relativity of knowledge. Everything leads one to the conclusion that Sartre's thought stays consistently within the limits of what might be called his first premise—that knowledge is a moment of praxis. All knowledge, including the indirect knowledge of praxis itself, must be relativized to the historical developments of praxis. But in insisting on the irreducibility of a practical, dialectical sense of reason to a formal, analytical sense of reason; in emphasizing that the apprehension of our own historicity must include the recognition of this historicity as irreducible to any set of historical facts—as, in short, transhistorical; Sartre underscores a fine line which must be preserved if *relativism* is not to collapse into *scepticism*.

To be coherent, historical relativism cannot, as it so often does, limit itself to pointing out the relativity of all theoretical reason to its historical contexts. This limitation of historical reason to the theoretical regimes that define a particular sense of rationality for any given time and place fails in its inability to account for the rationality of those theoretical systems and, as such, for the rationality of the claims (its own, for instance) that are made within them. Such a position is only an apparent advance over the empiricism that reduces epistemic practices to contingent historical events. Though the necessity of any specific claim may be salvaged in relation to the epistemic norms that prescribe valid modes of inference and assertion, the empiricism that is avoided here is encountered again at the level of the norms that undercut the empiricism of the first level. The norms that guide rational inquiry are taken as de facto states of affairs, with no inherent rationality to them. Any assertion is, therefore, as reasonable as any other, so long as it accords with the culturally relevant norms that govern its production, and the very idea of assessing the rationality of those norms themselves gets dismissed as either a matter of politics[24] (if it is an internal or revolutionary attempt to move beyond a specific paradigm of thought) or cultural imperialism (if it attempts to judge one set of standards in terms of another). Reason, in this limited sense of formal, theoretical reason, is unable to "provide itself with its own reasons."[25] And so we are left with many different varieties of what is reasonable-for-us or reasonable-for-them, all of which are ultimately as unreasonable as the others.

Affirming the transhistoricity of dialectical reason does not, however, provide an objective sense of rationality which could substitute for all these various senses of what is reasonable-for-us or -them a sense of what is reasonable, period. As emphasized in connection with Lyotard's critique of Habermas, Sartre's understanding of dialectical reason does not provide a point of view "above it all," from which one might survey the vast array of discursive regimes and make theoretical judgements concerning their rationality or lack thereof. It no more provides a theoretical knowledge of 'what reason is' than it provides a theoretical knowledge of 'what praxis is'. It does, however, make possible a less ambitious, though interminable project—that of a situated comprehension of how specific forms of thought may be themselves reasonable or unreasonable, relative to their own specific circumstances. For one can understand how any given discursive or epistemic regime allows a community to construct a practical response to their situation which, in the broadest possible terms, "comes to terms" with their situation in a way that is practically intelligible to them, given the specific discursive and practical possibilities at their disposal. Conversely, one is also able to assess how specific discursive or epistemic regimes become unreasonable when they stifle a community's capacity to construct such an intelligible response; when their epistemic authority is, for example, maintained not through a practice of reciprocity which would establish their 'rights' in terms of their practical intelligibility for the community, but through relations of authority which are themselves beyond question.

Rorty, for instance, is right to claim that there is no *formal* way of deciding the issue between Galileo and Bellarmine concerning the validity of the Copernican theory of the universe, except by appeal to standards of what is and is not scientific that were only in the process of being formed at the time.[26] Bellarmine's appeals to scriptural authority were still theoretically acceptable in terms of the epistemic norms of that period. To rule out, on the front end, his arguments as unreasonable, because unscientific, is simply to impose contemporary standards for scientific argumentation onto a discursive situation in which different standards were accepted. Or, to be more precise, since the question of which standards to accept was precisely the issue beginning to surface in those arguments, assuming one set of standards as the basis for deciding between Bellarmine and Galileo simply begs the question. But does this mean, as Rorty advises, that we are limited to merely noting "that Galileo was *creating* the notion of 'scientific values' as he went along" and then applauding his feat as "splendid"? Does the fact that Galileo was making the standards up imply, as Rorty concludes, "that the question of whether he was 'rational' in doing so is out of place"?[27] Or can there be, as Sartre's understanding of dialectical reason suggests, a kind of practical rationality to the process of making the standards up that is irreducible to the rationality that may be defined by any particular set of standards that might be made up in that process?

To answer this last question affirmatively, to hold that "the question of whether he was 'rational'" is *not* out of place, is not necessarily to imply that there is no "room for rational disagreement"[28] between Galileo and Bellarmine. It is not even, I would think, necessarily to decide the issue between them, for it is not a matter of deciding the issue *for* them, but of judging *with* them[29] in terms of the web of issues and stakes between them. To this extent, assessing the practical rationality of the debate is not a matter of conclusively resolving the issue one way or another, but of leaving "the question of whether [Galileo] was 'rational'" *in place*. Leaving the question "in place" is what may allow us, if only with the reckoning of hindsight, to reconstruct those issues and stakes with greater clarity than they could themselves; enabling us to see how Bellarmine's attempts to limit the scope of Copernicus's theories to that of "an ingenious heuristic device"[30] was, in all probability, a gesture whose pragmatic effect was merely to subordinate the emergent stakes of Copernicus's discourse to the authoritative hegemony of the Church. It is what allows us, at a minimum, to recognize that when the reciprocity of argument has completely given way to the authority of inquisition, then reason must also be said to have given way to unreason. For, in this case, a 'resolution' of the dispute through the Church's ability to reestablish its own position *as reasonable for the participants* of the debate, through its practical intelligibility for everyone involved,[31] gives way to an 'extermination' of the dispute which no longer even has the pretensions of an appeal to the reciprocity of the other's judgement. But even this minimal recognition seems impossible if we are content, as Rorty seems to be, to stand outside the perspective of the participants, noting the course of history as it unfolds, and merely applauding the performance of the winner as "splendid."

In raising the question of the rationality of Galileo's production of new scientific standards we are, in effect, evaluating them as individualized universals, whose validity may

202 QUESTIONS OF METHOD

only be assessed in terms of how they function in relation to the totalization in which they were engendered. To a great extent, it is a matter of asking to what extent they were able, or perhaps ought to have been able, to have established themselves as reasonable for the social ensemble involved with and enveloped by that totalization. The inability to maintain Bellarmine and the Church's position, for example, except through relations of authority which exclude reciprocity, suggests that the epistemic norms endorsed and defended in those arguments were themselves simply unable to serve any longer as integral moments in the development of scientific practice, especially as it was beginning to be pursued by the likes of Copernicus and Galileo. Such a judgement is, of course, informed by hindsight. But it is *not* a matter of applying our norms of inquiry onto theirs, which would beg the question as to which was most reasonable, but of assessing the practical rationality of those norms, in the light of what we know, in terms of their own historical situation.

The point that should be emphasized, at any rate, is not that such judgements as I have only begun to hastily sketch here are easily made or capable of being brought to a conclusion that would command everyone's assent. Properly carried out, they need to be informed by a good deal more sensitivity to the particulars of the historical situation than I can muster here. And there are no guarantees that further investigation will not overturn the provisional assessments made at an earlier phase nor that, as is quite probably the case, this process would not repeat itself indefinitely. But the question itself—of the practical rationality of any formal theory or set of epistemic standards; of whether Galileo was 'rational' in making up the particular standards that he did— *the question itself* is not out of place. Indeed, the question as to whether a specific model of rationality is itself reasonable or has been reasonably produced and secured, is never out of place, and is the basis for the critical appraisal and reevaluation of our epistemic traditions. Keeping the question in place on the grounds of the transhistoricity of dialectical reason does not automatically rule any form of thought out of court. But it does make the court itself possible, inasmuch as it makes sense of raising the question.

In the *Critique of Pure Reason*, Kant described his work as a kind of tribunal in which reason is called to establish its "lawful claims." The value of Sartre's dialectical account of reason is that it preserves this critical tribunal as a coherent possibility. Not that it is preserved in the way Kant imagined, as a tribunal in which reason may establish its claims "according to its own eternal and unalterable laws."[32] The idea of formally defining the "eternal and unalterable" laws of reason is lost in Sartre's account. The dream of a conclusive verdict in which the claims of reason would be decided once and for all, the fantasy of a judgement which would bring the tribunal to a close, is and ought to be abandoned. But the idea of a tribunal in which the question of the rationality of our epistemic standards may be raised and discussed, even if never conclusively decided to everyone's satisfaction, must be preserved if we are to continue to speak critically of the rationality (or irrationality) of our own epistemic practices. For the idea of a critique of reason is part and parcel of the life of reason itself. It is not an extraneous idea that might merely serve to provide reason with transcendental foundations. It is that critical moment in which the claims of reason are first established *as reasonable*, through being put up for question and discussion, their authority limited to what may be decided in and through a practice of reciprocity and negotiation.

In preserving this critical possibility in the life of reason, Sartre's *Critique* accomplishes its goal of "providing Reason with its own reasons." For the point is not to justify this or that formal sense of rationality, but to account for an informal sense of rationality in terms of which a reasoned critique of the claims of reason becomes possible. And the reasons which make a dialectical account of reason compelling are just that it can make sense of that possibility—that it can critically account for the possibility of a critical account of reason itself. Sartre's understanding of dialectical reason is, therefore, inextricably connected with the idea of a critique of dialectical reason. But the idea of a critique of dialectical reason is not that of a tribunal in which the claims of reason will be conclusively decided according to eternal and unalterable laws, but of a tribunal that is interminable precisely because there are no eternal and unalterable laws which might regulate it. It is the idea of a tribunal every tradition must make for itself, in terms of the historical possibilities at its disposal, as a constitutive moment in the production of a practical totalization of its historical circumstances that would be intelligible to all concerned—the idea of a practical arena of reciprocity and negotiation in which any epistemic tradition may, in principle, be comprehended as a practically reasonable totalization of history; as historically limited, though not for that reason, lacking in reason itself.

Notes

Preface

1. Allan Bloom, *The Closing of the American Mind* (New York: Simon & Schuster, 1987), p. 25.

2. Ibid., p. 39.

3. Ibid., p. 31.

4. Edmund Husserl, "Philosophy and the Crisis of European Man," in *Phenomenology and the Crisis of Philosophy*, trans. Quentin Lauer (New York: Harper and Row, 1965), p. 156. Also, see p. 175 where he describes this task as a "special vocation in life correlative to the attainment of a new culture."

5. Jonathan Culler notes the melodramatic shortcomings of the "crisis narrative" with respect to recent debates over the role and status of the humanities in the university in "The Humanities Tomorrow," in *Framing the Sign* (Norman, OK; University of Oklahoma Press, 1989), pp. 41–56.

6. See Plato, *Theaetetus*, in *The Collected Dialogues of Plato*, ed. Edith Hamilton and Huntington Cairns (Princeton: Princeton University Press, 1961), especially 161–71.

7. See Friedrich Nietzsche, *The Will to Power*, trans. Walter Kaufmann and R.J. Hollingdale, ed. Walter Kaufmann (New York: Vintage Books, 1968), in particular, n. 5, p. 10.

8. Jean-Paul Sartre, *Critique of Dialectical Reason*, trans. Alan Sheridan-Smith (London: NLB, 1976), p. 40.

9. With the notable exception of two articles by Thomas R. Flynn which have served as a basis for much of what I continue to explore here: "An End to Authority: Epistemology and Politics in the Later Sartre," in *Man and World* 10 (1977), pp. 448–465, and "Praxis and Vision: Elements of a Sartrean Epistemology" in *Philosophical Forum* (Boston) 8 (1976), pp. 21–43.

10. See, in particular, Richard Rorty's "Solidarity or Objectivity," in *Relativism: Interpretation and Confrontation*, ed., Michael

Krausz (Notre Dame, Indiana: University of Notre Dame Press, 1989), especially p. 44.

Chapter 1

1. Jean-Paul Sartre, *Critique of Dialectical Reason*, trans. Alan Sheridan-Smith (London: NLB, 1976), p. 19.

2. Ibid., p. 40.

3. See Leszek Kolakowski's *Main Currents of Marxism*, Vol. 2, *The Golden Age*, trans. P.S. Falla (Oxford: Oxford University Press, 1978), p. 3.

4. Jean-Paul Sartre, "Materialism and Revolution," in *Literary and Philosophical Essays*, trans. Annette Michelson (New York: Collier Books, 1955), p. 205.

5. Sartre, *Critique*, p. 25.

6. See ibid., p. 27.

7. Ibid.

8. Ibid., p. 30.

9. Ibid., p. 34.

10. Ibid., p. 31.

11. Ibid., p. 32.

12. These objections to analytically deriving dialectical reason, although clearly an important part of Sartre's arguments in the *Critique* against Engels, have still been overlooked by some commentaries on that work. See, for example, Wilfred Desan's *The Marxism of Jean-Paul Sartre*, where he interprets Sartre's rejection of Gurvitch's hyper-empiricism as merely involving a practical inclination on Sartre's part to found the dialectic a priori. He writes, "The grounds for this dialectical approach could eventually be demonstrated by induction, but in Sartre's view this would be an endless task, and for all practical purposes it need only be stated *a priori*" (Wilfred Desan, *The Marxism of Jean-Paul Sartre* [New York: Anchor Books, 1966], p. 70). Sartre's point, however, is *not* that one could ground dialectical reason inductively, but it would take forever. It is, rather, that even if one had the time, one could do no more than establish the generality of an empirical fact and *this* is, as we shall see, epistemologically untenable, in principle.

13. Sartre, *Critique*, p. 17.

14. Ibid., p. 20.

15. Ibid., p. 22.

16. Ibid., p. 24.

17. Ibid.

18. Ibid.

19. Ibid., p. 31.

20. Wilfred Sellars, "Empiricism and the Philosophy of Mind," in *Science, Perception, and Reality*, (New York: The Humanities Press, 1963), p. 169.

21. Ibid.

22. Sartre, *Critique*, p. 25.

23. Ibid., p. 32.

24. Edmund Husserl, *Logical Investigations*, trans. J.N. Findley, (New York: The Humanities Press, 1970), p. 135.

25. Ibid., p. 144.

26. Ibid., p. 169.

27. Ibid., p. 104.

28. Ibid., pp. 148, 149.

29. I do not mean to imply that Sartre's notion of rational necessity must exactly correspond to either Sellars's or Husserl's. I refer to these *two* only to establish the outside parameters of the problem.

30. Actually, it is unclear whether Husserl believes that normativity eludes a psychologistic understanding of logic. In number 19 of volume 1 of *Logical Investigations*, he seems to argue that the psychologistic position could deal with the normative dimension of logic as a merely technological extension of its proper theoretical domain of study. But, given his later assertion that psychologism "ignores the fundamental distinction between normative and causal regulation," it is questionable whether he actually accepts the validity of this response. Clearly, he views the normative line of argument as insufficient, but this turns more on its inability to capture the *ideality* which Husserl believes to be essential to the

laws of logic. And, since it shares this inability with psychologism, the real dividing line in the battle for the status of logic falls, for Husserl, between ideal vs. normative or causal regulation. For Sartre, it falls between empiricism and a proper dialectical account of necessity.

31. Sartre, *Critique*, p. 18.

32. Ibid., p. 49.

33. For a more extended discussion of these two epistemological tendencies in Sartre's work, see chapter 2, "The Knowledge of Being and the Being of Knowledge."

34. See chapter 10, "The Practical Foundations of Rational Necessity."

Chapter 2

1. Sartre, *Critique*, p. 15.

2. Ibid., p. 24.

3. I will discuss Sartre's understanding of "totalization" in more detail in chapter 4. In the meantime, let it suffice to say that by that term Sartre refers to the synthetic efforts of an individual or group in working over their environment in the light of a projected end. The efforts of the citizens of Paris in seizing the Bastille could serve as an example of an historical totalization. So could the efforts of a research group to produce a theory adequate to its theoretical needs. Indeed any praxis, for Sartre, is necessarily a synthetic effort to totalize some practical field in the light of some end.

4. Sartre, *Critique*, p. 49.

5. I take the concept of "epistemic regime" from Foucault's discussion of the "regime of truth" peculiar to each society. He writes, "Each society has its own regime of truth, its "general politics" of truth: that is, the types of discourse which it accepts and makes function as true; the mechanisms and instances which enable one to distinguish true and false statements . . . " (Michel Foucault, *Power/Knowledge: Selected Interviews and Other Writings 1972–1977*, ed. Colin Gordon, trans. Colin Gordon, Leo Marshall, and Kate Soper (New York: Pantheon Books, 1980), p. 131). The concept is, thus, intended to refer to knowledge as a material practice of a community, operating under and producing relations of

power specific to that community as a whole—the "political economy of truth."

6. See especially, Michel Foucault, *The Order of Things* (New York: Vintage Books, 1973).

7. See especially, Paul Feyerabend, *Against Method* (London: Verso, 1978).

8. Jean-Paul Sartre, *Search for a Method*, trans. Hazel Barnes (New York: Vintage Books, 1963), p. 33.

9. Ibid., p. 32.

10. Ibid.

11. Sartre, *Critique*, p. 18.

12. Ibid., p. 35.

13. Ibid.

14. I take my characterization of the bifurcation within Sartre's epistemology as one of "praxis and vision," as well as a good deal of my overall approach to the issues raised in this chapter from Thomas R. Flynn, "Praxis and Vision: Elements of a Sartrean Epistemology," *Philosophical Forum* (Boston) 8 (1976), pp. 21–43.

15. Jean-Paul Sartre, *Being and Nothingness*, trans. Hazel Barnes (New York: Philosophical Library, 1956), p. 240.

16. Jean-Paul Sartre, *Psychology of the Imagination*, trans. Bernard Frechtman (U.S.A.: Philosophical Library, 1948), p. 3.

17. Flynn, "Praxis and Vision," pp. 30–34.

18. Jean-Paul Sartre, "Consciousness of Self and Knowledge of Self," trans. Mary Ellen and N. Lawrence, in *Readings in Existential Phenomenology*, ed. Nathaniel Lawrence and Daniel O'Connor (Englewood Cliffs, N.J.: Prentice-Hall, 1967), p. 20. Quoted in Flynn, "Praxis and Vision," p. 25.

19. Flynn, for one, seems to opt for their incoherence. At the beginning of "Praxis and Vision," he writes of Sartre's full theory of knowledge, "The theory may be complete; it is not, however, fully coherent." Flynn, "Praxis and Vision," p. 21.

20. Sartre, *Critique*, p. 28.

21. Karl Marx, *Preface to a Critique of Political Economy*, in *Karl Marx: Selected Writings*, ed. David McLellan (Oxford: Oxford University Press, 1977), p. 389.

22. Ibid.

23. As Franz Jakubowski points out, this identification fails to hold up. "Base and superstructure should not be identified with that other contrasting pair, being and consciousness. Social being is certainly founded in the economy, but it is not restricted to it; social relationships, though essentially they are determined economically, reappear in the various forms of the superstructure, for example, in legal, political, or religious relations" (*Ideology and Superstructure in Historical Materialism*, trans. Anne Booth [London: Allison and Busby, 1976], p. 38).

24. See Karl Marx and Frederick Engels, *Selected Works* (New York: International Publishers, 1968), p. 692.

25. Michel Foucault, *Discipline and Punish: The Birth of the Prison*, trans. Alan Sheridan (New York: Vintage Books, 1979), p. 27.

26. Richard Rorty, *Philosophy and the Mirror of Nature* (Princeton: Princeton University Press, 1979), p. 9.

27. Richard Rorty, "A Reply to Dreyfus and Taylor," *Review of Metaphysics* 34 (1980), p. 44.

28. Jean-François Lyotard, *The Postmodern Condition: A Report on Knowledge*, trans. Geoff Bennington and Brian Massumi (Minneapolis: University of Minnesota Press, 1984), p. xxv.

Chapter 3

1. Michel Foucault, *The History of Sexuality*, vol. 1,: An Introduction, trans. Robert Hurley (New York: Vintage Books, 1980), p. 92 (hereafter cited as *History of Sexuality*).

2. Foucault, *Power/Knowledge*, p. 89.

3. Foucault, *History of Sexuality*, p. 94.

4. See Jacques Derrida, "Structure, Sign and Play in the Discourse of the Human Sciences," in *Writing and Difference*, trans. Alan Bass (Chicago: The University of Chicago Press, 1978), p. 279.

5. Foucault, *History of Sexuality*, p. 93.

6. Ibid., pp. 94–95.

7. See, for example, Charles Taylor's criticism in his article, "Foucault on Freedom and Truth," *Political Theory* 12 (1984), pp. 168–72.

8. See Foucault, *Discipline and Punish*.

9. See Foucault, *History of Sexuality*.

10. In Hubert Dreyfus and Paul Rabinow, *Michel Foucault: Beyond Structuralism and Hermeneutics* (Chicago: The University of Chicago Press, 1983), p. 187. What Foucault says here could also be applied, without qualification, to Sartre's concept of counterfinality. More on this in chapter 4.

11. Michel Foucault, "The Subject and Power," in Dreyfus and Rabinow, *Michel Foucault*, p. 221.

12. See Foucault, *Discipline and Punish*, p. 300.

13. Foucault, "The Subject and Power," p. 208.

14. Foucault, *History of Sexuality*, p. 136.

15. See Foucault, *Discipline and Punish*, pt 1, ch. 2, especially p. 48.

16. Foucault, *History of Sexuality*, p. 139.

17. Foucault, *Discipline and Punish*, p. 137.

18. Ibid., pp. 170–71.

19. See ibid., pt. 3, ch. 3.

20. See ibid., pp. 187–92.

21. Ibid., p. 189.

22. Ibid., p. 191.

23. Ibid.

24. See ibid., p. 170—"Discipline 'makes' individuals"—and p. 194, "The individual is no doubt the fictitious atom of an 'ideological' representation of society; but he is also a reality fabricated by this specific technology of power that I have called 'discipline'."

25. I take this distinction between a genealogy of objectifying and subjectifying human sciences from Dreyfus and Rabinow, *Michel Foucault*.

26. Foucault, *History of Sexuality*, p. 116.

27. Ibid., p. 63.

28. Ibid., p. 65.

29. The historical function of the "psy" disciplines in the administration of the sexual life of the population is too complex a matter to be adequately treated here. Foucault's *History of Sexuality* sketches a few of these functions in a somewhat summary fashion (see especially, pp. 127–30). Jacques Donzelot's *The Policing of Families* goes into much more detail concerning psychiatry's "colonization" of the welfare agencies (see Donzelot, *The Policing of Families*, trans. Robert Hurley [New York: Pantheon Books, 1979], especially ch. 6, "The Regulation of Images").

30. Foucault, *Power/Knowledge*, p. 112.

31. Ibid., p. 113.

32. Michel Foucault, *The Order of Things: An Archeology of the Human Sciences* (New York: Vintage Books, 1973), p. xi.

33. Michel Foucault, *The Archeology of Knowledge*, trans. A.M. Sheridan-Smith (London: Tavistock Publications, Ltd., 1979), p. 38.

34. Ibid., p. 74.

35. Ibid., p. 115.

36. Ibid., p. 46. Without pressing the analogy too far, it could be said that Foucault's rules of formation concern discourse as a set of "speech acts"—of statements conceived at the level of what they do or accomplish and the conditions of that accomplishment. For more on this point, see Dreyfus and Rabinow, *Michel Foucault*, pp. 45–46, especially n. 1.

37. Foucault, *Power/Knowledge*, p. 131.

38. See Thomas Kuhn, *The Structure of Scientific Revolutions* (Chicago: The University of Chicago Press, 1962), p. 8, where he writes, "I may even seem to have violated the very influential contemporary distinction between 'the context of discovery' and 'the context of justification'. . . . Rather than being elementary logical or methodological distinctions, which would thus be prior to the analysis of scientific knowledge, they now seem integral parts of a traditional set of substantive answers to the very question upon which they have been deployed."

39. Ibid., p. 183.

40. See Ibid., pp. 121–24.

41. See Ibid., p. 69.

42. Foucault, *Power/Knowledge*, p. 131.

43. Foucault, *Archeology*, p. 168.

44. Foucault, *Power/Knowledge*, p. 118.

45. Friedrich Nietzsche, "On Truth and Lie in an Extra-Moral Sense," in *The Portable Nietzsche*, ed. and trans. Walter Kaufmann (New York: The Viking Press, 1968), p. 47.

46. My reference to this reading as "Nietzschean" is only meant to capture a sceptical tendency that is often *associated* with Nietzsche's own genealogies. It is not, however, meant to attribute by implication such a scepticism to Nietzsche's own work. I am not in a position to discuss Nietzsche except in the most general way as a theoretical predecessor of Foucault's project. I only borrow the name of Nietzsche as a way of designating a particular line of thought that has, rightly or wrongly, grown up around him.

47. Michel Foucault, *Language, Counter-Memory, Practice: Selected Essays and Interviews*, ed. Donald Bouchard, trans. Donald Bouchard and Sherry Simon (Ithaca, New York: Cornell University Press, 1977), p. 144.

48. Michel Foucault, "The Discourse on Language," in *Archeology*, p. 219.

49. Foucault, *Power/Knowledge*, p. 132.

50. Gilles Deleuze, "Nomad Thought," in *The New Nietzsche*, ed. David Allison (London: MIT Press, 1985), p. 145.

51. Gilles Deleuze and Felix Guattari, *Anti-Oedipus: Capitalism and Schizophrenia*, trans. Robert Hurley, Mark Seem, and Helen Lane (Minneapolis: University of Minnesota Press, 1983), p. 133.

52. If I seem to be pushing this reading in a rather unrealistic direction, one should turn to Larry Shiner's account of *The Archeology of Knowledge* as an extended *parody* of methodological inquiry ("Reading Foucault: Anti-Method and the Genealogy of Power/Knowledge," in *History and Theory* 21 (1982), p. 386), or perhaps to Jean Baudrillard's article, "Forgetting Foucault," where he writes, "Foucault's is not therefore a discourse of truth but a mythic discourse in the strong sense of the word, and I secretly believe that it has no illusions about the effect of truth it produces" (in *Humanities and Society* 3 (1982), p. 87).

53. Michel Foucault, "La Souci de la Vérité," in *Magazine Littéraire* 207 (1984), p. 22.

54. Dominique LeCourt, *Marxism and Epistemology: Bachelard, Canguilhem, and Foucault*, trans. Ben Brewster (London: NLB, 1975), p. 204.

55. See Foucault, *Archeology*, p. 33; "The unity of the discourses on madness would be the interplay of the rules that define the transformations of these different objects. . . ."

56. See Dreyfus and Rabinow, *Michel Foucault*, pp. 81–85, where they discuss this problem in terms of how such rules could function as more than mere descriptions of discursive systematicity in Foucault's account, and possess the sort of causal efficacy in governing the material formation of discursive practices which he seemed to need.

57. LeCourt also emphasizes, in his *Marxism and Epistemology*, the inadequacy of Foucault's conception of practice. But he derives his criticism from an Althusserian perspective somewhat alien to the Sartrean approach I will be taking.

58. Foucault, *Power/Knowledge*, p. 96.

59. See Foucault, *Archeology*, p. 125. Although Foucault's admission is largely rhetorical, it is not for all that inaccurate.

60. See Hector Mario Cavallari, "*Savoir* and *Pouvoir*: Michel Foucault's Theory of Discursive Practice," in *Humanities in Society* 3 (1980), pp. 69–70 on Foucault's need of a notion of productive subjectivity as a mediating element between the historical conditions of discourse and discourse as a finished product.

61. Foucault, "The Subject and Power," p. 221.

62. Ibid.

63. Michel Foucault, *The History of Sexuality, vol. 2, The Use of Pleasure* trans. Robert Hurley (New York: Pantheon Books, 1985), p. 6 (hereafter cited as *The Use of Pleasure*).

64. Charles Taylor, "Foucault on Freedom and Truth," in *Political Theory* 12 (1984), p. 172.

65. From the Greek, meaning "combat," Dreyfus and Rabinow note that it implies "a physical contest in which the opponents develop a strategy of reaction and of mutual taunting, as in a wrestling match." (*Michel Foucault*, p. 222n.)

Chapter 4

1. Sartre, *Being and Nothingness*, p. 20.

2. Karl Marx, *Capital,* vol. 1, trans. Ben Fowkes (New York: Vintage Books, 1977), p. 283.

3. Sartre, *Critique,* p. 46.

4. Sartre, *Search for a Method,* p. 91.

5. Ibid., p. 97.

6. Jean-Paul Sartre, *Life/Situations,* trans. Paul Auster and Lydis Davis (New York: Pantheon Books, 1977), pp. 127–28.

7. Sartre, *Critique,* p. 558.

8. This example is taken from Sartre, *Search for a Method,* pp. 152–155.

9. Sartre, *Critique,* p. 74.

10. See Gilbert Ryle, *The Concept of Mind* (New York: Harper and Row, 1949), ch. 2, especially pp. 25–27.

11. See Hubert Dreyfus, *What Computers Can't Do* (New York: Harper Colophon Books, 1979), pp. 100–107.

12. Jean-Paul Sartre, *The Family Idiot,* vol. 1, trans. Carol Cosman (Chicago: The University of Chicago Press, 1981), p. 37.

13. Sartre, *Critique,* p. 807.

14. "What becomes of *matter,* that is to say, Being totally without meaning? The answer is simple: it does not appear *anywhere* in human experience. At any moment of History things are human precisely to the extent that men are things" (Sartre, *Critique,* p. 180).

15. Jean-Paul Sartre, "Kierkegaard: The Singular Universal," in *Between Existentialism and Marxism,* trans. John Matthews (New York: William Morrow and Company, 1976), p. 120.

16. Sartre, *Critique,* p. 178.

17. Ferdinand de Saussure, *Course in General Linguistics,* trans. Wade Baskin (New York: The Philosophical Library, 1959), p. 120.

18. Jean-Paul Sartre, "Replies to Structuralism," *Telos* 9 (Fall, 1971), p. 118.

19. Martin Heidegger, *Being and Time,* trans. John Macquarrie and Edward Robinson (New York: Harper and Row, 1962), p. 189.

20. Friedrich Nietzsche, *The Will to Power,* trans. Walter Kaufmann and R.J. Hollingdale, ed. Walter Kaufmann (New York: Vintage Books, 1968), p. 267.

21. Sartre, *Search for a Method*, p. 88.

22. Sartre, *Critique*, p. 124.

23. "Although exploitation as alienation is inscribed in materiality with its own characteristics and mingles there indissolubly with alienation through recurrence (counter-finality), the latter cannot be reduced to the former. The former defines the relation of forms of production to productive forces in a concrete historical society; the latter, although it appears in the relevant aspect only at a certain technical level, is a permanent type of separation *against* *which* men unite, but which attacks them even when united" (Sartre, *Critique*, p. 164n). Counter-finality is a more or less untranscendable mode of alienation which always erodes one's praxis to some degree. But Sartre's pessimism (which might also be described as 'realism') with regard to overcoming this primitive alienation cannot be extended to alienation in its properly Marxist sense as exploitation. There is no reason to presume, as Pietro Chiodi (see *Sartre and Marxism*, trans. Kate Soper [Sussex: The Harvester Press, 1978], ch. 6, "Alienation") seems to, that Sartre has contradicted the essential Marxist vision of a non-alienated existence, or equivocates between Hegelian and Marxist concepts of alienation (see Chiodi, *Sartre and Marxism*, p. 100). Sartre's focus in the *Critique* is on primitive alienation as the overlooked condition for the possibility of exploitation, and so the tone there is a necessarily pessimistic one, involving the inevitable reemergence of alienation at the heart of the group praxis struggling for its dissolution. It is nowhere implied that exploitation is a permanent feature of social existence, though linking its emergence with material scarcity does force one to be more realistic about the difficulties involved in overcoming it.

24. Sartre, *Critique*, pp. 161–63.

25. Ibid., pp. 166–79.

26. Ibid., p. 223.

27. Ibid., p. 165.

28. Ibid., p. 233.

29. See ibid., pp. 310, 489.

30. Ibid., p. 230.

31. Foucault, "Subject and Power," p. 221.

32. See Sartre, *Critique*, pp. 175–76.

33. See Sartre, *Critique*, pp. 607–35, "Institutionalisation and Sovereignty."

34. Foucault, *History of Sexuality*, p. 92.

35. Ibid., p. 93.

36. In Dreyfus and Rabinow, *Michel Foucault*, p. 92.

37. See Sartre, *Search for a Method*, p. 91, and Jean-Paul Sartre, *Saint Genet: Actor and Martyr* (New York: George Braziller Inc., 1963), p. 49.

38. Sartre, *Critique*, p. 326.

39. Ibid., p. 191.

40. That is, on the *serial* individual whose only practical connection to others is as a member of a series of anonymous interchangeable 'others', formed on the basis of the particular exigencies of the practico-inert field. Clearly such duties are not untranscendable for a group which is formed against their practico-inert destinies.

41. Though it is possible to view things this way from a perspective which abstracts, to a degree, from one's lived practical engagement to the situation.

42. Sartre, *Critique*, p. 190.

43. Sartre, *Family Idiot*, p. 425.

44. Jean-Paul Sartre, *L'Idiot de la famille*, vol. 3 (Paris: Éditions Gallimard, 1971), p. 1477.

45. Sartre, "Kierkegaard: The Singular Universal," p. 160.

46. Sartre, *Search for a Method*, p. 101.

47. Sartre, *Critique*, p. 71.

48. "The first practical experience of necessity occurs in the unconstrained activity of the individual to the extent that the final result, through conforming to the one anticipated, also appears as radically Other, in that it has never been the object of an intention on the part of the agent" (Sartre, *Critique*, p. 273).

49. See Sartre, *Critique*, p. 247n.

50. See ibid., p. 340.

51. "All these manipulations, which make freedom into a curse, presuppose that the relation of men to matter and to other men resides above all in *doing*, as synthetic creative work" (Sartre, *Critique*, p. 327).

52. Sartre, *Critique*, p. 563.

53. Foucault, *Archeology*, p. 12.

54. I am thinking here not only of the counter-finalities of the practico-inert, but of the detotalization which occurs within the group as a function of its totalization from a multiplicity of directions. See Sartre, *Critique*, p. 443.

Chapter 5

1. Sartre, *Critique*, p. 340.

2. Robert Stone and Elizabeth Bowman, "Dialectical Ethics: A First Look at Sartre's Unpublished 1964 Rome Lecture Notes" in *Social Text* 13/14 (1986), pp. 195–215. A short selection of these notes has been published in Jean-Paul Sartre, *Sartre*, ed. Francis Jeanson (Paris: Desclée de Brouwer, 1966), pp. 137–38, under the heading "Notes sur les rapports entre la morale et l'histoire."

3. Stone and Bowman, "Dialectical Ethics," pp. 197–98. See also, Sartre, "Notes," where he writes, "La praxis naît de la nécessité de la fin . . . elle procède de l'avenir: pusique'elle affirme inconditionnellement la nécessité que son object soit possible, et qu'elle l'affirme *par-delà toute* impossibilité de fait" (p. 138).

4. See Stone and Bowman, "Dialectical Ethics," p. 197. Their use of these terms to denote exclusively practico-inert norms is congruent with Sartre's discussions of imperatives and values in the *Critique*. See especially his long footnote on values beginning on p. 247 of the *Critique*.

5. See Sartre, "Notes," p. 138, where he writes, "La racine de la morale est dans le besoin. . . . "

6. Ibid., p. 137.

7. Stone and Bowman conclude on the basis of their review of the entire unpublished 1964 manuscript that "we will look in vain among Sartre's dialectical ethics for general rules or principles of right action" ("Dialectical Ethics," p. 209.).

8. Counter-finality was "the first practical experience of necessity" (Sartre, *Critique*, p. 345.).

9. Sartre, *Critique*, pp. 345, 357.

10. That is, the individual as a member of a practico-inert series.

11. I am using "collective" in this passage as synonymous with "social," not in Sartre's more limited sense of a practico-inert gathering.

12. Sartre, *Critique*, p. 422.

13. See ibid., pp. 428–45.

14. Ibid., p. 426.

15. See ibid., pp. 450–51.

16. "In this sense, reciprocity is no longer the living creation of bonds; it is on the contrary, reciprocal inertia . . . the heterogeneity of functions (even in a hierarchy) is simply a determination of inert reciprocity" (Sartre, *Critique*, pp. 470–71.)

17. Ibid., pp. 424–25.

18. Sartre, "Notes," p. 137.

19. Even the apocalyptic situation of the fused group shares a formal sense of alterity in the tension of "immanence-transcendence"—see Sartre, *Critique*, p. 381.

20. Ibid., p. 465.

21. Ibid., p. 453.

22. Ibid., p. 489.

23. This is not, of course, to imply that counter-finality is ever completely overcome. The inertia of the functionally determined reciprocities of the group always threatens to establish connections of exteriority between common individuals which are not anticipated by the practical rule which regulates the distribution of tasks (See Sartre, *Critique*, pp. 474–78). Counter-finality always eats away at praxis, whatever form it takes, and can transform the functional empowerment of the individual back into serial impotence. Even at the artificially abstract moment of the group-in-fusion, the formal alterity of the "immanence-transcendence" tension threatens constantly to restore the seriality of the practico-inert. Autonomy is still realizable, however, as a *struggle* against alienation taking the form

of a revolutionary praxis which rebels against the practico-inert and maintains a vigilance against its reemergence in its own ranks. In the same vein, I believe, it is also necessary to take the *unconditional* character of non-alienating norms, whose problematic status is briefly discussed by Stone and Bowman (see "Dialectical Ethics," p. 212), as denoting *not* the overcoming of all inert conditions, but a way of living those conditions which subordinates their determination of praxis to objectives projected by the group, subject to everyone's critical appraisal.

24. "Collective" is Sartre's technical term for the social gathering produced on the basis of the practico-inert.

25. My discussion of this distinction draws much from and stays generally close to Thomas Flynn's discussion of it in "An End to Authority: Epistemology and Politics in the Later Sartre," in *Man and World* 10 (1977), pp. 448–65. The only significant divergence is that I treat the practice of knowledge (as opposed to belief) primarily in terms of the active passivity of the organized group, whereas Flynn seems to limit his discussion of it to the apocalyptic situation of the group-in-fusion and the exclusion of all inert exigency. The distinction between the non-alienating inertia of the group (active passivity) and the alienating inertia of the practico-inert (passive activity) is invaluable, however, in allowing one to see how a non-alienating sense of rule following (and, even, authority) is possible for Sartre. For surely any sense of "knowledge" must be able to distinguish correct from incorrect, true from false, and these are, at the pragmatic level at least, normative affairs. But the inertia of the epistemic norms or rules of the group need not imply alienation as long as, as we shall see, they are practiced in *reciprocity*. This is what Flynn gets at, I believe, when he writes, "A form of 'oath' preserves the autonomy of free, reciprocal praxis. As long as the object of the oath remains the other Freedom[s] and only indirectly the rule itself; the latter can function as a 'vehicle of sovereignty' . . ." (Flynn, "End to Authority," p. 461). So perhaps even this divergence is less substantive, and more a matter of style or exposition.

26. See Sartre, *Family Idiot*, p. 155.

27. Ibid., p. 158. "Truth rigorously excludes belief." In the discussion of belief and its relation to knowledge and truth on pages 151 to 170 of *Family Idiot*, Sartre does not appear to distinguish between knowledge and truth. He speaks of them both there as practical enterprises.

28. Sartre, *L'Idiot de la Famille* vol. 1, p. 164.

29. See Sartre, *Family Idiot*, p. 152. "Tasting is not knowledge. . . ."

30. *Ibid.*, pp. 152–54 and Sartre, *L'Idiot de la Famille*, vol. 1, p. 161. Cosman translates *dévoile* as *discover*. *Unveil* is a more accurate translation, however, which has the virtue of conveying no "scientific" or "experimental" overtones.

31. Sartre, *Family Idiot*, p. 133.

32. Ibid., p. 154.

33. Ibid., p. 157.

34. Ibid., p. 159 and Sartre *L'Idiot de la Famille* vol. 1, p. 167. Cosman leaves out the phrase *"c'est-à-dire."*

35. Sartre, *Critique*, p. 608.

36. Ibid., p. 663.

37. Ibid., p. 579.

38. Ibid. Although Sartre is here describing the group-in-fusion, his point still holds in the pledged and organized groups insofar as sovereignty is not yet institutionalized as authority.

39. To borrow Flynn's phrase from the title of his essay, "An End to Authority."

40. Sartre, *Critique*, p. 298.

41. Sartre goes further than this and says of the serial idea, *"It is not a thought at all"* (Sartre, *Critique*, p. 300).

42. Ibid.

43. See ibid., pp. 300–303n.

44. For a less morally loaded, more epistemologically interesting example of serial ideas, we might turn to what I would call the 'methodological fetishism' of the contemporary behavioral sciences. Nearly a century of arguments against the value of transporting methods which work quite well in one sphere of endeavor (the natural sciences) into another quite different sphere (the social/human sciences) have not been rejected as fallacious, so much as they have simply been ignored as irrelevant. The critical importance of defining the object of study (behaviors) in ways that (supposedly) do not admit of "subjective" interpretation, of measuring

lengths of social interaction down to fractions of a second, of isolating dependent and independent variables for experimental manipulation—none of these methodological norms are ever intended as theoretical claims which might merit questioning. They are just the "behavioralist's" (behavioral scientists need not and probably are not, for the most part, behaviorists in anything like a Skinnerian sense) tools of the trade. As with all serial ideas, the epistemic value of their methodological norms is equivalent to their exchange value—the degree to which all the others in the field take them for granted. Methodological rigor is measured by what the others take as methodologically rigorous, and what they take as such is determined by what still others believe. Methodological norms have the status of inert exigencies which realize a unity in exteriority for the ensemble of researchers (as, say, a serialized audience for particular journals). At this point, of course, it is possible to isolate any number of groups (in Sartre's sense of the term) formed around the genuinely critical examination of various isolated topics. But at the fundamental level of method, there is still a fetishistic inversion where various procedures are taken as justified in themselves (because of their quantitative rigor or reliability) and not in relation to the degree in which they 'unveil' their object in ways one might consider significant. (This is, of course, akin to Marx's commodity fetishism where a commodity's value is thought of as inhering in it as a natural attribute outside of the process of production which creates that value and the exchange which expresses it.) These reflections, moreover, raise the question of whether every "normal" science, in Kuhn's sense, that has set enough fundamental issues outside the range of appropriate scientific questioning (and so has formed for itself a paradigm) has relegated a vital dimension of its practice to the practico-inert of belief. Is all knowledge, in its proper sense for Sartre, what Kuhn would call revolutionary?

45. Sartre, *Critique*, p. 535; "The truth in its original sense, therefore, as sociality and within an integrated group, is the elimination of all alterity."

46. Sartre, *Family Idiot*, p. 155 and Sartre, *L'Idiot de la Famille*, vol. 1, p. 163. *I have modified Cosman's translation of this passage to include an important qualifying passage she leaves out: "- en principe sinon dans chaque cas—." Evidence need not be actual in every case, but only at one's disposal *in principle*.

47. Sartre, *L'Idiot de la Famille*, p. 622. He says of Flaubert, there "Faute d'intuition—c'est-à-dire d'un dévoilement pratique—il joue à juger."

48. Ibid., p. 159.

49. See Sartre, *Family Idiot*, p. 154.

50. Sartre, *Being and Nothingness*, p. 240.

51. Edmund Husserl, *Cartesian Meditations*, trans. Dorian Cairnes (The Hague; Martinus Nijhoff, 1973), p. 12.

52. For a discussion of Sellars's point here, see above, chapter 1.

53. Sartre, *Critique*, p. 502.

54. Ibid., p. 533.

55. See Foucault, *The Use of Pleasure*, p. 6.

56. Lyotard, *Postmodern*, pp. 44–45.

57. Ibid., p. 64.

58. Ibid., p. 65.

59. See Foucault, *History of Sexuality*.

60. Indeed, Lyotard goes so far as to characterize it as a form of "terror": "The application of this criterion (performativity) to all of our games necessarily entails a certain level of terror, whether soft or hard: be operational (that is, commensurable) or disappear" (*Postmodern*, p. xxiv).

61. Lyotard, *Postmodern*, p. 67.

62. Sartre, *Family Idiot*, p. 151.

63. Truth probably ought to be distinguished, though, in a way in which Sartre does not, from the social practice of knowledge itself. Truth, as an epistemic value of certain propositions, is that which we claim for our assertions within a given epistemic practice. It is, moreover, a *justified* claim when it accords with the epistemic norms which regulate that practice and, in this way, comes to command the assent of those pledged to the group in question. But a group will often come to regard a claim which they justifiably held at one time, or which a momentarily isolated subgroup justifiably holds now, as nevertheless false. After all, it is always possible to gain new or more complete information about some state of

affairs which compels one to change one's mind without admitting the earlier claim as unjustified. In this light, truth emerges as a regulative ideal, in Kant's sense, of a given epistemic practice—as an *ens imaginarium* at which that practice is aimed, where all questions are resolved and nothing relevant is left outstanding. One needs to distinguish, then (1) truth as a finite achievement of our epistemic practices—as those assertions which emerge as justified according to a set of epistemic norms and condition the practical integration of the group, and (2) truth as a regulative ideal of our epistemic practices. Truth, in both these senses needs further to be distinguished from the social *practice* of knowledge, of which it is the effect, condition, and regulative ideal. None of this, however, contradicts Sartre's basic point of truth as the elimination of alterity and knowledge as a practice of group reciprocity.

64. Husserl, *Logical Investigations*, p. 149.

65. Sartre, *Search for a Method*, p. 179.

Chapter 6

1. Feyerabend, *Against Method*, p. 28.

2. Ibid., p. 23.

3. Richard Rorty, "Pragmatism, Relativism, and Irrationalism," *Proceedings and Addresses of the American Philosophical Association* (August, 1980), p. 737.

4. Ibid.

5. "As long as we see James or Dewey as having 'theories of truth' or 'theories of knowledge' or 'theories of morality' we shall get them wrong. We shall ignore their criticisms of the assumption that there ought to *be* theories about such matters." (Ibid., p. 719).

6. Ibid., p. 721.

7. Sellars, "Empiricism and the Philosophy of Mind," p. 169.

8. Ibid., p. 167

9. Rorty, *Philosophy and the Mirror of Nature*, p. 177.

10. For an historical account of this debate see, Richard Bernstein, *Praxis and Action* (Philadelphia: University of Pennsylvania Press, 1971), Ch. 4, especially p. 282.

11. See Richard Rorty, "In Defense of Eliminative Materialism," *The Review of Metaphysics* 24 (1970), pp. 113–15.

12. See ibid., p. 115.

13. Ibid., p. 119.

14. Rorty, "A Reply to Dreyfus and Taylor," p. 44.

15. Ibid.

16. Feyerabend, *Against Method*, p. 73.

17. Ibid., p. 71.

18. Ibid., pp. 82–84.

19. Actually Feyerabend is not quite convinced of this (Ibid., p. 72), though his reservations in favor of some sort of Whorfian interpretation are, as was noted in relation to Sellars and Rorty, epistemologically irrelevant. And so I will proceed, as does Feyerabend himself, to assume the identity of the *perception* throughout its different interpretations.

20. Ibid., pp. 85–87.

21. Kuhn, *Structure of Scientific Revolutions*, p. 121.

22. Ibid., p. 150.

23. See Kuhn, *Structure of Scientific Revolutions*, p. 150, and Feyerabend, *Against Method*, pp. 225–27.

24. Feyerabend, *Against Method*, pp. 230–66. Feyerabend's analysis, though carefully done, is probably too cursory to be anything more than a historically *suggestive* account of the conceptual framework of Homeric thought. It ought to be taken, therefore, as a historically plausible thought-experiment designed to illustrate the idea of incommensurability rather than establish the historical reality of incommensurable world-views.

25. Ibid., p. 233.

26. Ibid., p. 241.

27. Ibid., p. 264

28. Ibid.

29. Ibid., p. 271

30. Feyerabend, *Science in a Free Society*, p. 28.

31. Ibid., p. 85.

32. See below, chapter 5.

33. Sartre, *Search for a Method*, p. 179.

Chapter 7

1. See Sartre, *Critique*, p. 31, and above, chapter 1.

2. Sartre, *Critique*, p. 35.

3. The structure of Sartre's critical investigation is, as he himself says, analogous to a scientific experiment (*Critique*, p. 42). Initially, the dialectical intelligibility of praxis is *posited* as an hypothesis which still needs to be born out. "It is possible that, on some plane, individual *praxis* is transparent to itself and that, in this transparency, it provides the model and the rules of full intelligibility; but this still has to be proved" (*Critique*, p. 61). Thus, the *critical* impetus of the project preserves, in its formal structure, some of the elements of empirical thought. But to argue from this, as Marjorie Greene does, that Sartre operates even provisionally in terms of a hypothetical-deductive model of explanation (*Sartre* [New York: New Viewpoints, 1973], pp. 190–96) misses Sartre's warning that one must "let it not be imagined that this experience is comparable to the 'intuitions' of the empiricists" (*Critique*, p. 390). There is an appeal to experience in Sartre's work, but neither the appeal nor the status of the experience appealed to will bear an empirical interpretation.

4. Sartre, *Search for a Method*, p. 176.

5. Ibid., p. 179.

6. Ibid., p. 176.

7. Ibid.

8. Ibid., p. 180.

9. Ibid., p. 177. "Marx's own Marxism, while indicating the dialectical opposition between knowing and being, contained implicitly the demand for an existential foundation for the theory."

10. It has been brought to my attention that Sartre seems to contradict this point in his 1974 discussion with Ph. Gavi and P. Victor (a.k.a., Benny Lévy), *On a raison de se revolter* (Paris; Gal-

limard, 1974), where he rejects Victor's (Lévy's) suggestion that his idea of freedom could be the product of a particular class. "La notion de liberté," Sartre argues, "implique des structures qu'une seule classe est incapable de donner. . . . je pense qu'il s'agit d'une de ces notions rares mais importantes qui existent chez toutes les classes, et qui ne sont pas tout la fait les mêmes d'une classe à une auntre, mais quie contiennent des éléments communs . . . " (pp. 340–41) Though there does seem to be a suggestion here of a sense of freedom that "could be recovered in its full reality *underneath* the alienations of our society . . . " it may be read, I believe, in a way that preserves Sartre's claim in *Search for a Method* that such a recovery is absurd. For the point is not that freedom is a class-bound idea, but that it can only be grasped in terms of our knowledge of the conditions which alienate us, as a specific presupposition of our specific misery. But no concept, forged in terms of the experience of a single class, could ever be adequate to that experience inasmuch as it adumbrates the possibility of going beyond the conditions which form the practical horizon of that experience. This is why it can only be a "notion" and not a "concept." For a further discussion of this distinction, see below as well as the end of chapter 9. For a further discussion of this issue, see Thomas R. Flynn, *Sartre and Marxist Existentialism* (Chicago; The University of Chicago Press, 1984), especially, pp. 130–132 and Thomas W. Busch, *The Power of Consciousness and the Force of Circumstances in Sartre's Philosophy* (Indianapolis; Indiana University Press, 1990), especially, pp. 71–73, & 85.

11. Ibid., pp. 180–81.

12. Ibid., pp. 170–71.

13. Ibid.

14. See ibid., pp. 171–73, and Sartre, "Kierkegaard: The Singular Universal," pp. 163–65.

15. Jean-Paul Sartre, "On *The Idiot of the Family*," in *Life/Situations* (New York: Pantheon Books, 1977), p. 113.

16. Sartre, *Search for a Method*, p. 174.

17. Sartre, "Kierkegaard: The Singular Universal," pp. 143–44.

18. In a similar way, Walker Percy has succeeded at designating the irreducibly lived character of psychiatric and neurological "pathology" precisely in terms of the success of that knowledge to encompass everything but the singular adventure which is lived in

that pathology. In *The Second Coming*, Will Barrett's troubles with his life are successfully diagnosed in the end as symptoms of an underlying neurological dysfunction. Percy places the gap between lived experience and symptomatology in sharp relief, however, in the way he presents Barrett coming to terms with the lived reality of those symptoms. "Did it all come down to chemistry after all? Had he fallen down in a bunker, pounded the sand with his fist in a rage of longing for Ethel Rosenblum because his pH was 7.6? . . . Had his longing for her been a hydrogen-ion deficiency. . . . No, hydrogen or no hydrogen, he wanted to see her face" (Walker Percy, *The Second Coming* (New York: Pocket Books, 1980), p. 350).

19. Sartre, "Kierkegaard: The Singular Universal," p. 144.

20. . . . and *practical* development. By emphasizing the embeddedness of reflective comprehension in a theoretical context, I only mean to draw attention to and articulate its "indirect" status as knowledge. I do not mean to sever its ties with practical history.

21. Sartre, *Critique*, p. 55.

22. Ibid., p. 39.

23. Ibid., p. 49.

24. See Sartre, *Critique*, p. 503, where he writes, "Practical knowledge unfolds itself simultaneously on two planes and according to two types of rationality."

25. Ibid., p. 20.

26. Ibid., p. 21.

27. Ibid., pp. 20–21.

28. Sartre, *Search for a Method*, p. 32.

29. Sartre, *Critique*, p. 36.

Chapter 8

1. Aristotle, *Nichomachean Ethics*, Book 6, Chapter 7, 1141b in *The Basic Works of Aristotle*, ed. Richard McKeon (New York: Random House, 1941).

2. Immanuel Kant, *Critique of Pure Reason*, trans. Norman Kemp Smith (New York: St. Martin Press, 1965), A133, B172.

3. See Simon Blackburn, *Spreading the Word: Groundings in the Philosophy of Language* (New York: Oxford University Press, 1984), p. 72. For a more detailed discussion, see Saul Kripke, *Wittgenstein on Rules and Private Language* (Cambridge: Harvard University Press, 1982), pp. 7–75.

4. "To *think* one is obeying a rule is not to obey a rule. Hence it is not possible to obey a rule 'privately' otherwise thinking one was obeying a rule would be the same thing as obeying it" (Ludwig Wittgenstein, *Philosophical Investigations*, trans. G.E.M. Anscombe [New York: The MacMillian Company, 1953], para. 202).

5. Kuhn, *Structure of Scientific Revolutions*, pp. 188–191.

6. Indeed, such applications often involve complex transformations of the original equation which could not be anticipated on the basis of the original. See Kuhn, *Structures of Scientific Revolutions*, pp. 180–89.

7. For more on this specific point, see Imre Lakatos, "Falsification and Methodology of Research Programmes," in *Criticism and the Growth of Knowledge*, ed. Imre Lakatos and Alan Musgrave (Cambridge, 1970), and Feyerabend, *Against Method*, pp. 184–86.

8. Sartre, *Critique*, p. 58.

9. Ibid., p. 61.

10. Ibid., p. 58.

11. Ibid.

12. Ibid., p. 504.

13. Ibid., p. 59.

14. See Ibid., p. 20, where Sartre endorses this epistemological distinction between the natural and human sciences: "Scientific research can in fact be unaware of its own principal features. Dialectical knowledge, in contrast, is knowledge of the dialectic."

15. See, ibid., p. 60.

16. Ibid., p. 480.

17. . . . . if we might, for a moment, treat a train schedule as an equation of sorts, showing in a schematic way, the relation of various elements in terms of a set of spatiotemporal coordinates.

18. Ibid., p. 61n.

19. Ibid., p. 93.

20. Ibid., p. 64n.

21. Flynn, "Praxis and Vision," p. 42, n. 56.

22. Sartre, *Critique*, p. 58.

23. See ibid., p. 75, and *Critique de la raison dialectique*, p. 161, where Sartre asserts this lack of intelligibility even more emphatically. "There is no such thing as *intelligibility* in the sciences of Nature. . . . Necessity as succession in exteriority (the moments are *exterior* to each other and they cannot occur in a different order) is only the mind producing and discovering its own limit, that is to say, producing and discovering *the impossibility of thinking in exteriority*. The discovery of thought as impossibility is the complete opposite of understanding (intellection), for understanding can only be the recognition of the accessibility (perméabilité) of the real to a rational praxis . . . *praxis* producing itself along with its own elucidation."

24. See Sartre, *Critique*, p. 233.

25. "Why Reason Can't Be Naturalized," in *Realism and Reason* (Cambridge: Cambridge University Press, 1983), p. 234.

26. Sartre, *Critique*, p. 504.

27. Ibid., p. 44.

28. Ibid, p. 60, and *Critique de la raison dialectique*, p. 149. See also, *Critique*, p. 61, where he writes, "all the activities of a practical agent are to be understood *through the future* as a perpetual re-totalisation of the provisional totality. And the ensemble of these moments, themselves re-totalised by the temporalisation, is in fact original intelligibility, for the practical agent is transparent to himself as the unifying unity of himself and his environment."

29. See also, Sartre, *Search for a Method*, pp. 152–55.

30. See Sartre, *Critique*, pp. 502–503.

31. Ibid., p. 503.

32. See ibid., p. 535, and the discussion of this point above, in chapter 5.

33. Ibid., p. 339.

34. See Ibid., pp. 328–30.

35. Ibid. p. 465.

36. Sartre, *Family Idiot*, p. 153.

37. Ibid.

38. Sartre, *Family Idiot*, p. 158.

39. Sartre, *Search for a Method*, p. 30.

40. Sartre, *Critique*, p. 38.

41. See ibid., p. 49.

Chapter 9

1. Sartre, *Critique*, p. 69.

2. Lyotard, *Postmodern*, p. xxv.

3. Jürgen Habermas, *The Theory of Communicative Action*, vol. 1, *Reason and the Rationalization of Society* (Boston: Beacon Press, 1981), pp. 10–11.

4. Jürgen Habermas, "What is Universal Pragmatics," in *Communication and the Evolution of Society* (Boston: Beacon Press, 1979), p. 3.

5. Habermas, *Communicative Action*, p. 17.

6. "*kooperativen Aushandelns*," ibid., p. 69 and Jürgen Habermas, *Theorie des kommunikativen Handlens; Band I, Handlungsrationalitat und gesellschaftliche Rationalisierung* (Frankfurt am Main: Suhrkamp Verlag, 1981), p. 106.

7. See Habermas, *Communicative Action*, in particular, pp. 31–38.

8. Ibid., p. 38.

9. Ibid., p. 138.

10. See J.L. Austin, *How to do Things with Words* (Cambridge: Harvard University Press, 1962) p. 99–100 where he defines *illocution* as the "performance of an act *in* saying something as opposed to [the] performance of an act *of* saying something. . . ."

11. Ibid., p. 117.

12. Habermas, *Communicative Action*, p. 288. For a critical rejoinder to Habermas's argument for the "original" status of illocu-

tionary acts relevant to the issue under discussion here—
Habermas' attempt to secure the rationality of communicative action independently of any context of particular purposes or aims—
see Jonathan Culler's "Habermas and the Norms of Language" in
his *Framing the Sign* (Norman, OK; University of Oklahoma Press,
1989), especially pp. 188–90.

13. Habermas, *Communicative Action*, p. 287.

14. *"We understand a speech act when we know what makes it acceptable"* (Habermas, *Communicative Action*, p. 297).

15. Ibid., p. 132.

16. See, for instance, Ibid., pp. 98–99.

17. Ibid., p. 134.

18. See *Communicative Action*, pp. 73–74, where, in a closing
remark to a discussion whose primary moral is otherwise to
ground our sense that for all their cognitive and social sophistication, mythologically based cultures are, indeed, fundamentally irrational, he comes as close as any place to recognizing the dangers
of hastily generalizing from modernity's own "formal concept of
reason" any substantial sense of an ideal for any and every culture.

19. Jürgen Habermas, *The Philosophical Discourse of Modernity*
(Boston: Beacon Press, 1987) p. 326.

20. Lyotard, *Postmodern*, p. 40.

21. Jean-François Lyotard, *The Differend* (Minneapolis: University of Minnesota Press, 1988), p. xii.

22. See Lyotard, *Postmodern*, pp. 65–66.

23. See ibid., p. 23, for Lyotard's analysis of the pragmatics of
scientific discourse.

24. Lyotard's primary example of narratives in traditional cultures from *The Postmodern Condition* through *Just Gaming* and *The
Differend* are those of the Cashinahua Indians of South America
documented by André M. d'Ans in his *Le Dit des vrais hommes*
(Paris: Union Générale d'Edition, 1978).

25. Lyotard, *Postmodern*, p. 27.

26. Ibid., p. 60.

27. Richard Rorty, "Habermas and Lyotard on Post-Modernity," *Praxis International* 4, 1 April 1984, p. 33.

28. Lyotard, *Postmodern*, p. 61.

29. Habermas, *Communicative Action*, p. 70.

30. Ibid., p. 42.

31. Lyotard, *Postmodern*, p. 66.

32. See ibid., p. 65, where he emphasizes that the point of paralogical activity is to point out the norms presupposed in scientific activity and "petition the player to accept different ones."

33. Jean-François Lyotard, *Just Gaming*, trans. Samuel Weber (Minneapolis: University of Minnesota Press, 1985), p. 10.

34. Ibid., p. 17.

35. "C'est l'endroit ou justement on *pactice*, avec autre chose . . . sans arret, un lieu de négociations . . . " (ibid., pp. 42, 43, and *Au Juste: conversations* [Paris: Christian Bourgeois Éditeur, 1979], p. 82).

36. Lyotard, *Just Gaming*, p. 33.

37. Ibid., p. 41.

38. This characterization of narrative as a common praxis must remain, however, hypothetical and provisional. We are not in a position to tell, from Lyotard's account, to what degree the plot of the narrative functions as directed inertia, the necessary relations which are maintained by the community in order to realize their common end of keeping the story going, or as merely a practico-inert limit of serial activity. What we *are* told, however, is at least consistent with the first possibility, and it is this possibility I would like to explore.

39. Lyotard mentions elsewhere (See "Memorandum sur la légitimité," in *Le Postmoderne explique aux enfants* [Paris: Éditions Galilée, 1986], p. 73) that though young girls, prior to puberty, may hear the narrative, only a man may tell it. There are, as one would expect, limits to reciprocity here.

40. See Habermas, *Communicative Action*, pp. 66–72, where Habermas's critical discussion of myth is informed by Piaget's theory of cognitive development and focused on the inability of a mythically based culture to form a "reflective concept of 'world'." Also, it should be emphasized that my questions here are not rhetorical. I would not want to foreclose the possibility that Habermas is right about the irrationality of a culture based on myth. But such a con-

clusion should not be reached on the basis of their inability to engage in the kind of practices *we* engage in. For the specific reflectivity afforded by such practices may be simply irrelevant to the circumstances of the culture in question. One should be alert, it seems, to the possibility of forms of reflection, negotiation, and reciprocity which may not all be formally mapped onto one another as varieties of some theoretically determined essence of reflection, negotiation and reciprocity. One should be aware, in a way in which Sartre is and Habermas does not seem to be, that such concepts are "individualised universals" which need to be used as notions, not as concepts which would provide us with a univocal theoretical knowledge of their referents. More on this below.

41. See Habermas, *Communicative Action*, pp. 73–74.

42. Sartre, *Critique*, p. 43. Also see Habermas's "What is Universal Pragmatics," pp. 15–20, where he frames his own "rational reconstructions" of the formal-pragmatic rules of speech after the manner of Chomsky's work in linguistics and Piaget's work in cognitive development.

43. Lyotard, *Postmodern*, p. 26.

44. Which, as Habermas says, only needs "a reliable procedure for testing [its] corresponding reconstructive hypotheses" to establish its validity. In playing down the transcendental aspect of his work, Habermas is increasingly drawn toward an overtly empiricistic conception of it. See Habermas, *Communicative Action*, p. 38.

45. I would want to qualify this claim, however, to exclude the thrust of Lyotard's efforts, especially in *Just Gaming* to circumscribe a non–rule-governed understanding of judgement, which seems to point in the direction of just such an idea. See, in particular, the "First Day" of that work, "The Impossible Consensus."

46. I borrow this metaphor from Jacques Derrida's "Signature, Event, Context" (in *Margins of Philosophy*, trans. Alan Bass [Chicago: The University of Chicago Press, 1982], p. 317) where he speaks of every sign as "abandoned to its essential drifting." And though in 'grafting' the metaphor to my own purposes I am not being faithful to its sense as Derrida's uses it, I would argue that there is a complicity between his use and my own. For if any linguistic utterance is set adrift to a fundamental undecidability as to its identity, it is only through such a dialectically open-ended

process of negotiation, fluid enough to deal with the changing exigencies of the context at hand, that a community can cope with their need to determine some semblance of a common significance for their discourse. Perhaps Derrida is himself not so far from such a notion—see the "Afterword" to *Limited Inc* (Jacques Derrida, ed. Gerald Graff [Evanston, Ill.: Northwestern University Press, 1988], p. 116), where he characterizes one sense of "undecidability" as "open[ing] the field of decision or of decidability" and as "call[ing] for decision in the order of ethical-political responsibility."

47. Indeed, it could be argued that Sartre himself is no stranger to the "war on totality" (see Lyotard, *Postmodern*, p. 82) espoused by Lyotard. In *Search for a Method*, he was already condemning what he referred to as the "Scholasticism of the totality" practiced by contemporary Marxists in their rush to totalize every historical phenomenon as univocally defined moments of their own *a priori* concepts. In their hands, as Sartre characterized it, "the heuristic principle—'to search for the whole in its parts'—has become the terrorist practice of 'liquidating the particularity'" (see *Search for a Method*, p. 28). Sartre's emphasis on thought as totalization has never given way to the idea that we could, once and for all, think totality as such. Totalization always involves detotalization, which in the case of thought, involves respecting both the detotalizing as well as the enriching potential of the particular event.

48. Sartre, *Critique*, p. 407.

49. Ibid., p. 381.

50. Ibid., p. 408.

51. Ibid., p. 384.

52. Ibid., pp. 529, 530.

53. Sartre, "On the Idiot of the Family," in *Life/Situations*, p. 113. For a discussion of Sartre's sense of "notion" see above, chapter 7.

54. Ibid.

55. Sartre, *Critique*, p. 56.

56. See Sartre "Notes," p. 137, and above, chapter 5.

57. To this extent, it has affinities to Lyotard's own appropriation of the Kantian understanding of an "idea" as a regulative concept which cannot, however, provide a theoretical knowledge of its object. See, in particular, *Just Gaming*, pp. 46–47 for an exam-

ple of Lyotard's appropriation of Kant's terminology in connection with his understanding of justice. For a more detailed discussion of how Sartre may revise Kant's understanding of a "regulative idea" in connection with the *"totalisation d'enveloppement,"* discussed in the unfinished second volume of the *Critique*, see Julliete Simont's "La problématique de 'l'idée régulatrice' de Kant chez Sartre," in *Sur les écrits posthumes de Sartre* (Brussells: Editions de l'Université de Bruxelles, 1987), pp. 131–53.

Chapter 10

1. Husserl, *Logical Investigations*, p. 88.

2. Ibid., pp. 194–95.

3. See Maurice Merleau-Ponty, *Phenomenology of Perception*, trans. Colin Smith (London: Routledge and Kegan Paul, 1962), pt 2, ch. 3, "The Thing and the Natural World," especially, pp. 330–34.

4. Sartre, *Critique*, p. 35.

5. Ibid.

6. Ibid., p. 152.

7. Ibid., pp. 73, 72.

8. Sartre is quite clear about the historical limitations of his own critical inquiries. In the introduction to the *Critique*, he writes, "If the totalisation produces a moment of critical consciousness as the necessary incarnation of its totalising *praxis*, then obviously this moment can only appear at particular times and places." In particular, Sartre notes that a critique of dialectical reason would be inconceivable before Hegel and Marx had made it possible by elaborating the individualized universals of dialectical thought itself, and before the abuses of dialectical thought by "Stalinist idealism" had made such a critical investigation necessary. "Thus, when we claim that *anyone* can carry out the critical investigation, this does not mean that it could happen at any period. It means anyone *today*." There is a sense of necessity here, but a sense of necessity that unfolds within and in terms of the contingencies of our own historical situations. See Sartre, *Critique*, pp. 49–50, "The Problem of Stalinism."

9. Rorty, "A Reply to Dreyfus and Taylor," p. 39.

10. Hubert Dreyfus, "Holism and Hermeneutics," *Review of Metaphysics* 34 (1980), p. 17.

11. Rorty, "A Reply to Dreyfus and Taylor," p. 44.

12. Rorty, *Philosophy and the Mirror of Nature*, p. 389.

13. Dreyfus, "Holism and Hermeneutics," p. 19.

14. Rorty, "Rorty, Taylor, and Dreyfus: A Discussion," pp. 51–52.

15. Sartre, *Search for a Method*, p. 174.

16. Ibid., p. 83.

17. Sartre, *Critique*, p. 18.

18. Sartre, *Search for a Method*, pp. 169–70.

19. See Ibid., p. 180, where he emphasizes that one comprehend's one's freedom only in and through one's concrete servitude, as a condition of it. See also above, chapter 7.

20. Sartre, *Critique*, p. 803.

21. Feyerabend, *Science in a Free Society*, p. 85.

22. See Sartre, "Notes", p. 137.

23. Lyotard, *The Differend*, p. xi.

24. See, ibid., pp. 9–10, no. 12.

25. See ibid., p. 138, no. 190 and p. 150, no. 217.

26. *Ibid.*, p. 178, no. 253.

27. See Lyotard, *Just Gaming*, p. 17.

28. See in particular, Jürgen Habermas, *Toward a Rational Society*, trans. Jeremy J. Shapiro (Boston: Beacon Press, 1970), ch. 1, where the convergence between communicative rationality and what he describes there as "democratic decision-making" is especially clear.

29. See Michel Contat's characterization of Sartre's politics as a kind of "libertarian socialism" in his interview with Sartre, "Self-Portrait at Seventy" in Sartre, *Life/Situations*, p. 25.

Chapter 11

1. See Sartre, "Kierkegaard: The Singular Universal," p. 161.

2. Ibid., p. 153.

3. Sartre, *Search for a Method*, p. 181.

4. Sartre, "Kierkegaard," p. 155.

5. Ibid., p. 161.

6. Sartre, *Critique*, p. 36.

7. See ibid., p. 20.

8. See above, chapter 8.

9. Hilary Putnam, "Why Reason Can't Be Naturalized," p. 234.

10. Sartre, *Critique*, p. 49.

11. And certainly it is not hard to find such traditions, inasmuch as the idea of knowledge as a historical achievement has only really taken off since Kant's Copernican Revolution made knowledge into a matter of subjective synthesis and Hegel turned this synthesis into an affair of historical spirit.

12. Foucault, *The Order of Things*, p. xxii.

13. Ibid., p. 318.

14. Ibid., pp. 221–36.

15. Ibid., p. 320.

16. Sartre, "Replies to Structuralism," p. 113.

17. Foucault, *The Order of Things*, p. 322.

18. See ibid., pp. 340–43.

19. Dreyfus and Rabinow, *Michel Foucault*, p. 99.

20. Foucault, *Archeology of Knowledge*, p. 203.

21. Ibid., p. 7.

22. See Dreyfus and Rabinow, *Michel Foucault*, pp. 85–90.

23. Foucault, *Archeology of Knowledge*, p. 205.

24. A conclusion Feyerabend seems, at times, to embrace when he characterizes Galileo's arguments in favor of Copernicanism as "propaganda." "One anticipates that arguments will not suffice—an interesting and highly important limitation of rationalism—and Galileo's utterances are indeed arguments in appearance only. For Galileo uses *propaganda*" (*Against Method*, p. 81).

25. See Sartre, *Critique*, p. 31.

26. Rorty, *Philosophy and the Mirror of Nature*, pp. 328–31.

27. Ibid., p. 331.

28. Ibid., p. 328.

29. . . . which should not imply merely mimicking their position, but judging for ourselves, in terms of their historical perspective.

30. Rorty, *Philosophy and the Mirror of Nature*, p. 329.

31. The construction of a strategy able to reinteriorize the dispute as an "adopted heterogeneity" of a common praxis regulated by and regulative for everyone involved.

32. See Immanuel Kant, *Critique of Pure Reason*, A xii, p. 9.

Works Cited

Aristotle. *The Basic Works of Aristotle.* Edited by Richard McKeon. New York: Random House, 1941.

Aron, Raymond. *History and the Dialectic of Violence: An Analysis of Sartre's "Critique de la Raison Dialectique."* Translated by Barry Cooper. Oxford: Basil Blackwell, 1975.

Austin, J.L. *How to do Things with Words.* Cambridge: Harvard University Press, 1962.

Baudrillard, Jean. "Forgetting Foucault." *Humanities in Society* 3 (1982):87–111.

Bernstein, Richard. *Beyond Objectivism and Relativism: Science, Hermeneutics, and Praxis.* Philadelphia: University of Pennsylvania Press, 1983.

————. *Praxis and Action.* Philadelphia: University of Pennsylvania Press, 1971.

Blackburn, Simon. *Spreading the Word: Groundings in the Philosophy of Language.* New York: Oxford University Press, 1984.

Bloom, Allan. *The Closing of the American Mind,* New York: Simon & Schuster, 1987.

Busch, Thomas W. *The Power of Consciousness and the Force of Circumstances in Sartre's Philosophy.* Indianapolis: Indiana University Press, 1990.

Cavallari, Hector Mario. "*Savoir* and *Pouvoir*: Michel Foucault's Theory of Discursive Practice." *Humanities in Society* 3 (1980):55–72.

Chiodi, Pietro. *Sartre and Marxism.* Translated by Kate Soper. Sussex: The Harvester Press, 1976.

Culler, Jonathan. *Framing the Sign.* Norman, OK: University of Oklahoma Press, 1989.

Deleuze, Gilles. "Nomad Thought." In *The New Nietzsche,* edited by David Allison, 142–49. London: MIT Press, 1985.

Deleuze, Gilles and Guattari, Felix. *Anti-Oedipus: Capitalism and Schizophrenia.* Translated by Robert Hurley, Mark Seem, and Helen R. Lane. Minneapolis: University of Minnesota Press, 1983.

Derrida, Jacques. *Limited Inc.* Edited by Gerald Graff. Evanston, Ill: Northwestern University Press, 1988.

_____. "Signature Event Context." in *Margins of Philosophy*, translated by Alan Bass, 307–30. Chicago: The University of Chicago Press, 1982.

_____. "Structure, Sign and Play in the Discourse of the Human Sciences." In *Writing and Difference*, translated by Alan Bass, 278–94. Chicago: The University of Chicago Press, 1978.

Desan, Wilfred. *The Marxism of Jean-Paul Sartre.* New York: Anchor Books, 1966.

Donzelot, Jacques. *The Policing of Families.* Translated by Robert Hurley. New York: Pantheon Books, 1979.

De Saussure, Ferdinand. *Course in General Linguistics.* Translated by Wade Baskin. New York: The Philosophical Library, 1959.

Dreyfus, Hubert L. (with Richard Rorty and Charles Taylor). "A Discussion." *Review of Metaphysics* 34 (1980): 47–55.

Dreyfus, Hubert L. "Holism and Hermeneutics." *Review of Metaphysics* 34 (1980):3–23.

_____. *What Computers Can't Do: The Limits of Artificial Intelligence.* rev. ed. New York: Harper Colophon Books, 1979.

Dreyfus, Hubert L., and Paul Rabinow. *Michel Foucault: Beyond Structuralism and Hermeneutics.* Chicago: The University of Chicago Press, 1983.

Feyerabend, Paul. *Against Method.* London: Verso, 1978.

_____. *Science in a Free Society.* London: Verso, 1982.

Flynn, Thomas R. "An End to Authority: Epistemology and Politics in the Later Sartre." *Man and World* 10 (1977):448–465.

_____. "Praxis and Vision: Elements of a Sartrean Epistemology." *Philosophical Forum* (Boston) 8 (1976):21–43.

_____. *Sartre and Marxist Existentialism.* Chicago: The University of Chicago Press, 1984.

Foucault, Michel. *The Archeology of Knowledge.* Translated by A.M. Sheridan-Smith. London: Tavistock Publications, Ltd., 1979.

———. *The History of Sexuality.* Volume 1, *An Introduction.* Translated by Robert Hurley. New York: Vintage Books, 1980.

———. *The History of Sexuality.* Volume 2, *The Use of Pleasure.* Translated by Robert Hurley. New York: Vintage Books, 1985.

———. *Language, Counter-Memory, Practice: Selected Essays and Interviews.* Edited by Donald Bouchard. Translated by Donald Bouchard and Sherry Simon. Ithaca, New York: Cornell University Press, 1977.

———. *Madness and Civilization: A History of Insanity in the Age of Reason.* Translated by Richard Howard. New York: Vintage Books, 1973.

———. *The Order of Things: An Archeology of the Human Sciences.* New York: Vintage Books, 1973.

———. *Power/Knowledge: Selected Interviews and Other Writings 1972–1977.* Edited by Colin Gordon. Translated by Colin Gordon, Leo Marshall, and Kate Soper. New York: Pantheon Books, 1980.

———. "La Souci de la Vérité." *Magazine Littéraire* 207 (1984):18–24.

Greene, Marjorie. *Sartre.* New Viewpoints: New York, 1973.

Habermas, Jürgen. *Communication and the Evolution of Society.* Translated by Thomas McCarthy. Boston: Beacon Press, 1979.

———. *Knowledge and Human Interests.* Translated by Jeremy Shapiro. Boston: Beacon Press, 1971.

———. *The Philosophical Discourse of Modernity.* Translated by Frederick Lawrence. Boston: Beacon Press, 1987.

———. *The Theory of Communicative Action.* volume 1, *Reason and the Rationalization of Society.* Translated by Thomas McCarthy. Boston: Beacon Press, 1984. *Theorie des kommunikativen Handlens: Band 1, Handlungsrationalitat und gesellschaftliche Rationalisierung.* Frankfurt am Main: Suhrkamp Verlag, 1981.

———. *Toward a Rational Society: Student Protest, Science, and Politics.* Translated by Jeremy J. Shapiro. Boston: Beacon Press, 1970.

Heidegger, Martin. *Being and Time.* Translated by John Macquarrie and Edward Robinson. New York: Harper & Row, 1962.

Husserl, Edmund. *Cartesian Meditations*. Translated by Dorian Cairnes. The Hague: Martinus Nijhoff, 1973.

_____. *Logical Investigations*. Translated by J.N. Findley. New York: The Humanities Press, 1970.

_____. "Philosophy and the Crisis of European Man." In *Phenomenology and the Crisis of Philosophy*. Translated by Quentin Lauer, 149–92. New York: Harper and Row, 1965.

Jakubowski, Franz. *Ideology and Superstructure in Historical Materialism*. Translated by Anne Booth. London: Alison and Busby, 1976.

Kant, Immanuel. *Critique of Pure Reason*. Translated by Norman Kemp Smith. New York: St Martin's Press, 1965.

Kolakowski, Leszek. *Main Currents of Marxism*. Translated by P.S. Falla. Oxford: Oxford University Press, 1978.

Kripke, Saul A. *Wittgenstein: On Rules and Private Language*. Cambridge: Harvard University Press, 1982.

Kuhn, Thomas S. *The Structure of Scientific Revolutions*. Chicago: The University of Chicago Press, 1962.

Lakatos, Imre. "Falsification and the Methodology of Research Programmes." In *Criticism and the Growth of Knowledge*. Edited by Imre Lakatos and Alan Musgrave. Cambridge: Cambridge University Press, 1970.

Le Court, Dominique. *Marxism and Epistemology: Bachelard, Canguilheim, and Foucault*. Translated by Ben Brewster. London: NLB, 1975.

Lyotard, Jean-François. *The Differend*. Translated by Georges Van Den Abbeele. Minneapolis: University of Minnesota Press, 1988.

_____. *The Postmodern Condition: A Report on Knowledge*. Translated by Geoff Bennington and Brian Massumi. Minneapolis: The University of Minnesota Press, 1984.

_____. *Le Postmoderne explique aux enfants*. Paris: Éditions Galilée, 1986.

Lyotard, Jean-François, and Jean-Loup Thebaud. *Just Gaming*. Translated by Samuel Weber. Minneapolis: University of Minnesota Press, 1985. *Au Juste: conversations*. Paris: Christian Bourgois Éditeur, 1979.

Marx, Karl. *Capital.* Volume 1. Translated by Ben Fowkes. New York: Vintage Books, 1977.

———. *Karl Marx: Selected Writings.* Edited by David McLellan. Oxford: Oxford University Press, 1977.

Marx, Karl, and Frederick Engels. *Selected Writings.* New York: International Publishers, 1968.

Merleau-Ponty, Maurice. *Phenomenology of Perception.* Translated by Colin Smith. London: Routledge and Kegan Paul, 1962.

Nietzsche, Friedrich. "On Truth and Lie in an Extra-Moral Sense." In *The Portable Nietzsche.* Edited and translated by Walter Kaufmann. New York: The Viking Press, 1968.

———. *The Will to Power.* Edited by Walter Kaufmann. Translated by Walter Kaufmann and R.J. Hollingdale. New York: Vintage Books, 1968.

Plato. *The Collected Dialogues of Plato.* Edited by Edith Hamilton and Huntington Cairns. Princeton: Princeton University Press, 1961.

Percy, Walker. *The Second Coming.* New York: Pocket Books, 1980.

Putnam, Hilary. "Why Reason Can't Be Naturalized." In *Realism and Reason.* 229–47. Cambridge: Cambridge University Press, 1983.

Rorty, Richard. "A Reply to Dreyfus and Taylor." *Review of Metaphysics* 34 (1980):39–46.

———. "Habermas and Lyotard on Post-Modernity." *Praxis International* 4 (1984):32–44.

———. "In Defense of Eliminative Materialism." *The Review of Metaphysics* 24 (1970).

———. *Philosophy and the Mirror of Nature.* Princeton: Princeton University Press, 1979.

———. "Pragmatism, Relativism, and Irrationalism." *Proceedings and Address of the American Philosophical Association* (August, 1980).

———. "Solidarity or Objectivity." In *Relativism: Interpretation and Confrontation.* Edited by Michael Kransz. 35–50. Notre Dame, Indiana: University of Notre Dame Press, 1989.

Ryle, Gilbert. *The Concept of Mind*. New York: Harper and Row, 1949.

Sartre, Jean-Paul. *Being and Nothingness: An Essay on Phenomenological Ontology*. Translated by Hazel E. Barnes. New York: Philosophical Library, 1956.

_____. "Consciousness of Self and Knowledge of Self." In *Readings in Existential Phenomenology*. Edited by Nathaniel Lawrence and Daniel O'Conner, 113–42. Englewood Cliffs, N.J.: Prentice Hall, 1967.

_____. *Critique of Dialectical Reason*. Translated by Alan Sheridan-Smith. London: NLB, 1976. *Critique de la Raison dialectique*. Paris: Éditions Gallimard, 1960.

_____. *L'Idiot de la famille: Gustave Flaubert de 1821 à 1857*. Paris: Éditions Gallimard, 1971. *The Family Idiot*. Volume 1. Translated by Carol Cosman. Chicago: The University of Chicago Press, 1981.

_____. *Life/Situations*. Translated by Paul Auster and Lydia Davis. New York: Pantheon Books, 1977.

_____. "Kierkegaard: The Singular Universal." In *Between Existentialism and Marxism*. Translated by John Mathews, 141–69. New York: William Morrow and Company, 1976.

_____. "Materialism and Revolution." In *Literary and Philosophical Essays*. Translated by Annette Michelson, 198–256. New York: Collier Books, 1955.

_____ (With Ph. Gavi & P. Victor). *On a raison de se revolter*. Paris: Gallimard, 1974.

_____. "Notes sur les rapports entre le morale et l'histoire." In *Sartre*. Edited by Francis Jeanson, 137–38. Paris: Desclée de Brower, 1966.

_____. *Psychology of the Imagination*. Translated by Bernard Frechtman. U.S.A.: Philosophical Library, 1948.

_____. "Replies to Structuralism." *Telos* 9 (Fall 1971):110–16.

_____. *Saint Genet: Actor and Martyr*. New York: George Braziller Inc., 1963.

_____. *Search for a Method*. Translated by Hazel E. Barnes. New York: Vintage Books, 1963.

Sellars, Wilfred. "Empiricism and the Philosophy of Mind." In *Science, Perception and Reality*. 127–96. New York: The Humanities Press, 1963.

Shiner, Larry. "Reading Foucault: Anti-Method and the Genealogy of Power/Knowledge." *History and Theory* 21 (1982):382–98.

Simont, Juliette. "La problématique de 'l'idée régulatrice' de Kant chez Sartre." In *Sur les écrits posthumes de Sartre*. 131–53. Brussels: Editions de l'Université de Bruxelles, 1987.

Stone, Robert, and Elizabeth Bowman. "Dialectical Ethics: A First Look at Sartre's Unpublished 1964 Rome Lecture Notes." *Social Text* 13/14 (Winter/Spring 1986)195–215.

Taylor, Charles. "Foucault on Freedom and Truth." *Political Theory* 12 (1984):152–83.

Wittgenstein, Ludwig. *Philosophical Investigations*. Translated by G.E.M. Anscombe. New York: The Macmillan Company, 1953.

Index

Active passivity, 80, 87, 220n.25
Alienation, 63, 76–78, 81, 83, 88,
  113–114, 143–144, 172, 181, 185,
  216n.23, 220n.25
Alterity, 79, 84–85, 88, 93, 139–
  141, 219nn.19, 23, 222n.45
Anthropology, 21, 112–115, 117–
  118, 125, 178, 179, 195–197
Argument, 149, 151, 153, 155,
  157–160
Aristotle, 47, 105, 125–126
Austin, J. L., 150
Authority, 40, 43, 66, 81–85, 87,
  88–89, 91–92, 143–144, 200–202;
  epistemic, 75, 99–100, 102, 104,
  168
Autonomy, 54, 66, 71–72, 77, 79–
  80, 108, 219n.23

Baudrillard, Jean, 213n.52
Belief, 81–82, 84–85, 89, 92, 143,
  222n.44
Bentham, Jeremy, 40
Bloom, Allan, xi–xiii
Bowman, Elizabeth, 76, 220n.23

Chiodi, Pietro, 216n.23
Chomsky, Noam, 234n.42
Communicative action, 148–149,
  151, 159
Comprehension, 112–117, 119,
  125, 132, 134, 136–139, 141, 164–
  165, 168, 177–178, 179–184, 199;
  and practice/praxis, 58–60, 62,
  120–122, 172–173, 187, 192, 197;
  theory laden character of, 114,

188–189; transhistoricity of, 187–
  190, 192, 198
Consciousness, 9, 19, 21–23, 25,
  55, 58, 86
Consensus, 128, 148, 152–156,
  157–158
Contingency, xiii, 8, 10, 11, 69–70,
  71, 73, 79, 93, 97, 111, 135, 138,
  167–168, 171, 187, 236n.8
Counter-finality, 63–64, 66, 70, 71,
  81, 83, 141, 172, 216n.23, 219n.23
Critique, xiii, 10, 89, 92, 93, 168,
  173, 185, 197, 203–204, 236n.8

DeSaussure, Ferdinand, 61
Deleuze, Gilles, 49–50
Democracy, 85, 89, 108, 185
Derrida, Jacques, 35, 234–235n.46
Desan, Wilfred, 206n.12
Descartes, René, xiv, 22, 193
Dialectic, 7–10, 18, 111, 120; external, 4–8, 15, 111, 121, 123, 160;
  as universal law, 14, 21, 178
Dialectical reason, 7–8, 21–22, 24,
  121, 129, 130, 132, 133, 136, 139,
  147–148, 160, 161, 166, 167, 181,
  190, 192, 203–204, 206n.12; and
  empiricism, 10, 12, 14; and the
  human sciences, 18, 27, 97, 108,
  198; and non-theoretical foundationalism, 93, 112, 120, 122,
  125, 131, 171–173; and practice/
  praxis, 121–123, 135, 145, 184;
  transhistoricity of, 199, 202, universality of, 27, 28, 97, 147
Differend, 182–183

249